Praying

GOD'S WAY

TALKING WITH THE FATHER AND WALKING TOGETHER

GOD'S WAY

TALKING WITH THE FATHER AND WALKING TOGETHER

RICK SHEPHERD

AMG Publishers™

Following God

PRAYING GOD'S WAY

ISBN: 0-89957-312-6

Editing and layout by Rick Steele
Cover illustration by David Barber
Cover design by Daryl Phillips at ImageWright

Printed in Canada
08 07 06 05 04 03 –T– 6 5 4 3 2 1

This work is dedicated to

T. W. Hunt

discipler, mentor, and pray-er who began teaching me about the Mind of Christ and prayer in 1976. He prayed with me and for me in the adventures of beginning to understand biblical prayer, biblical ministry, and a Christlike walk. He and his wife Laverne prayed with us and for us as Linda Gail and I experienced the adventures of meeting and marriage (then, budgets and a baby carriage). They continue to encourage and challenge us in Christ-centered praying and living.

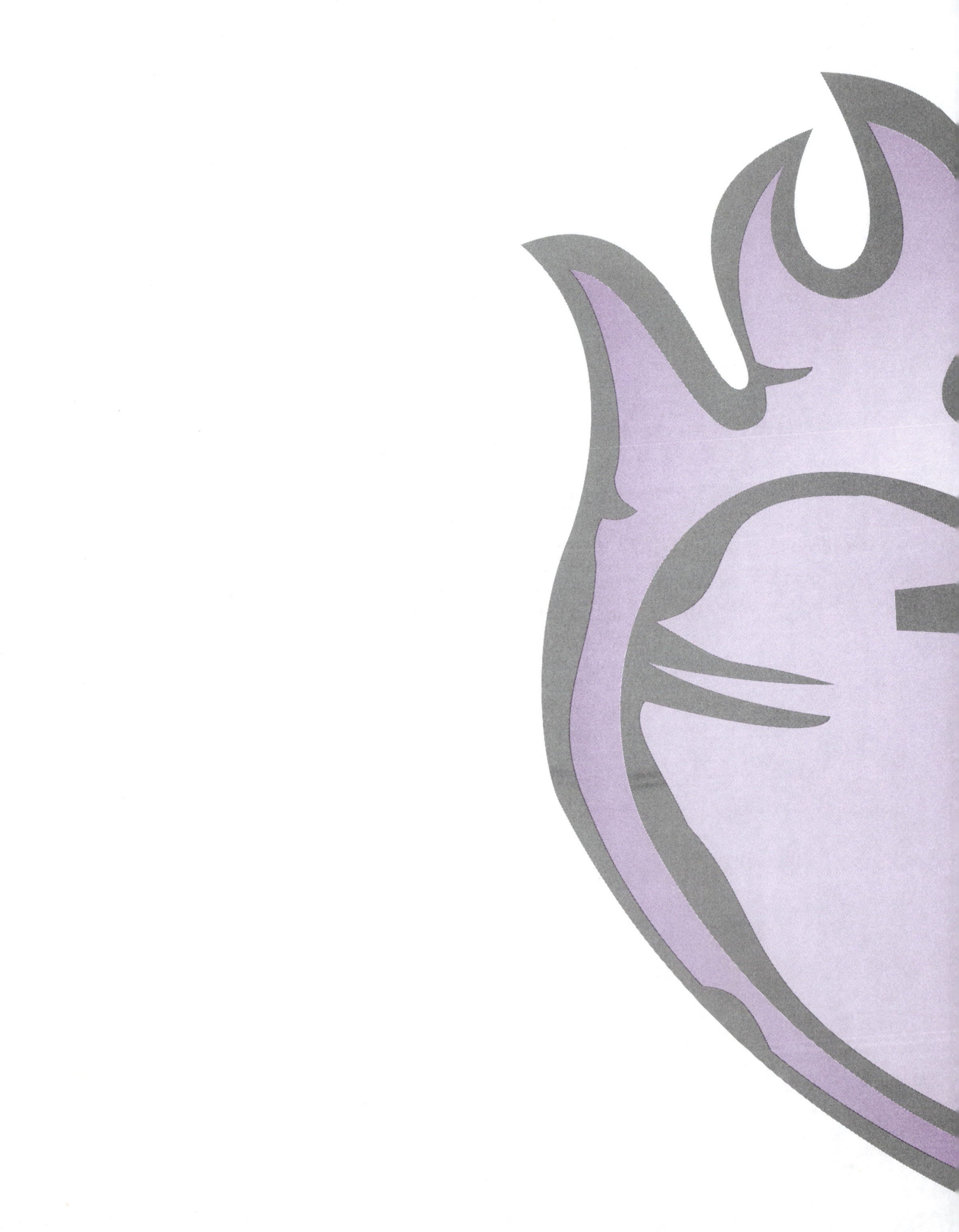

Acknowledgments

I am most grateful to the Lord Jesus for His work and His ways in my life—for the people He has put in my life, for the places He has sent me, and for His purposes at work in my life. I am very thankful to my wife Linda Gail for her prayers, encouragement, proofreading (and more prayers and proofreading), and patience in the process. I am grateful and indebted to John Franklin for the use of his excellent research on corporate prayer. This was most helpful in preparing Lesson 11 on "Praying Together." I am grateful to a host of pastors, staff, and lay people in numerous congregations for their insights, encouragement, and prayer support in the task of completing this work. I hasten to add that this book could not have been done without the vision and skill of the folks at AMG Publishers. Special thanks to Rick Steele, Trevor Overcash, Dale Anderson, Warren Baker, and Dan Penwell for their encouragement and their desire to see the Body of Christ equipped for every good work!

Rick Shepherd

About the Author

Richard L. Shepherd has been engaged in some form of ministry for over twenty-five years, focusing on areas of teaching, discipleship, and prayer. He has served in churches in Alabama, Florida, Texas, and Tennessee and now serves as Director of Prayer and Spiritual Awakening with the Florida Baptist Convention. For nearly seventeen years (1983–2000), Rick served as an associate pastor at Woodland Park Baptist Church in Chattanooga, Tennessee. The Lord's ministry has taken him to several countries, including Haiti, Romania, Ukraine, Moldova, Italy, Israel, England, and Greece, where he has been involved in training pastors, church leaders, and congregations. Rick has also lectured on college and seminary campuses. He graduated with honors from the University of Mobile and holds a Master of Divinity and a Ph.D. from Southwestern Baptist Theological Seminary in Fort Worth, Texas. He and his wife Linda Gail have four children and make their home in Jacksonville, Florida.

About the Following God Series

Three authors and fellow ministers, Wayne Barber, Eddie Rasnake, and Rick Shepherd, teamed up in 1998 to write a character-based Bible study for AMG Publishers. Their collaboration developed into the title, *Life Principles from the Old Testament.* Since 1998 these same authors and AMG Publishers have produced five more character-based studies—each consisting of twelve lessons geared around a five-day study of a particular Bible personality. More studies of this type are in the works. In 2001, AMG Publishers launched a different Following God category called the Following God™ Discipleship Series. The titles introduced in the Discipleship Series are among the first Following God™ studies to be published in a topically-based format (rather than Bible character-based). However, the interactive study format that readers have come to love remains constant with each new Following God™ release. As new titles and categories are being planned, our focus remains the same: to provide excellent Bible study materials that point people to God's Word in ways that allow them to apply truths to their own lives. More information on this groundbreaking series can be found on the following web page:

www.amgpublishers.com

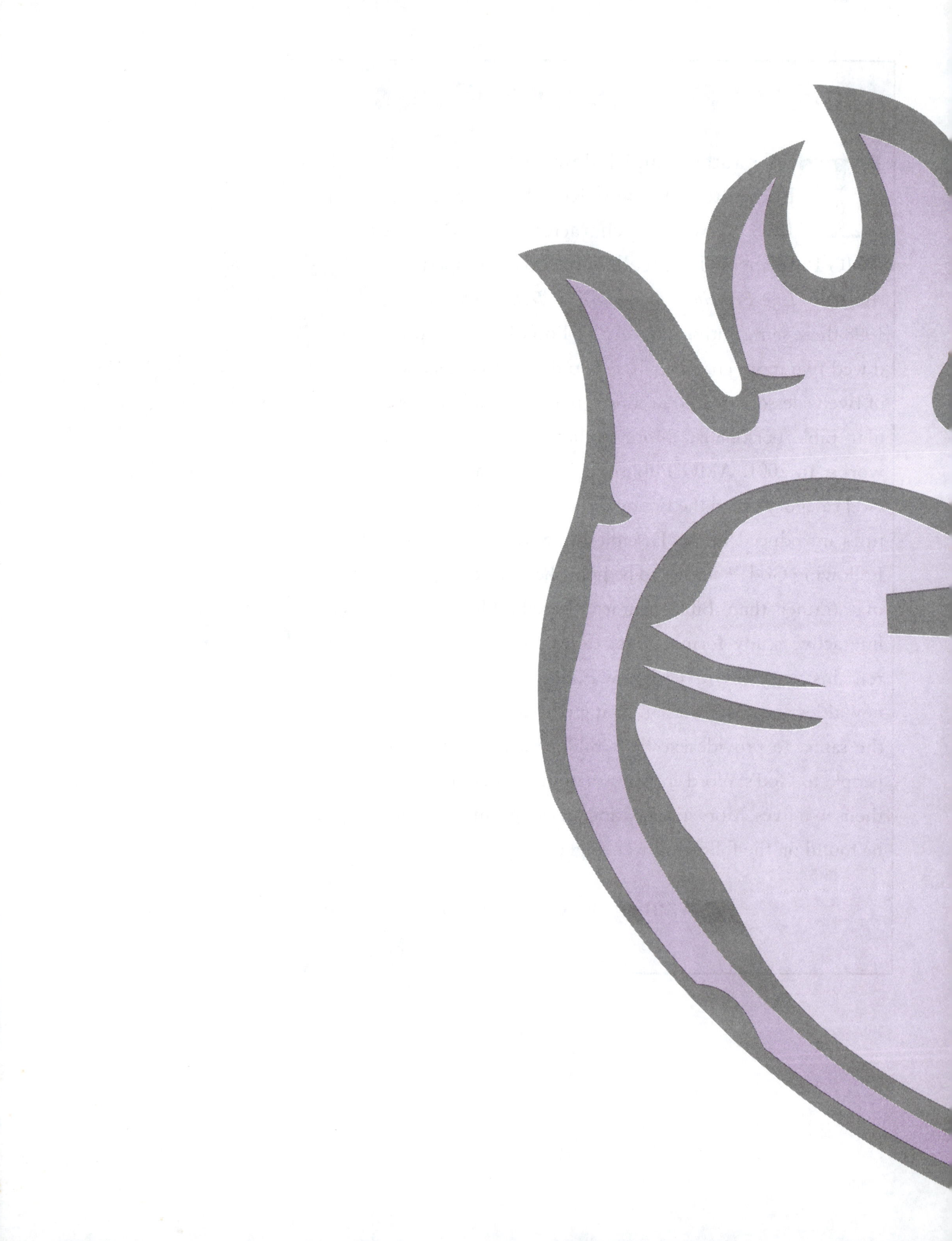

Preface

What does it mean to pray God's way? Is prayer just a cosmic emergency switch—"Pull in case of a really big emergency"? Is it just something to make us feel better when we are down? Is it a method or formula to get our way with "a little help" from heaven or a way to twist God's arm when He is reluctant to grant us our "first, second, or third wish"? **No.** Prayer is a living, real two-way communication with the God of Heaven, the all-powerful Creator who is our loving, heavenly Father.

Scripture is clear about how we are to talk with God, showing us what prayer is and what it is not. Prayer is not about rituals and formulas for coming to God. It is not about getting our way, twisting God's arm, or coming up with enough points on our side to get God to agree with our wishes. Prayer is a relationship with God, but not with just any god; it is with God the Father, the Father of our Lord and Master, Jesus Christ. Prayer is part of following a Person, the Lord Jesus, by the power and wisdom of His Holy Spirit. Rituals and formulas?—Never! Relationship and following?—Always! How do we enter into that relationship, and how do we follow? That is what we will see in *Praying God's Way.*

Think of this study as a journey. In any journey we must make sure we have clear directions to our destination, adequate supplies, and a reliable guide. We have that in the Bible and in the presence of the Holy Spirit in our lives. We have twelve stops or lessons on this journey. They are described as follows:

1) For all of us the journey begins when we first call on the name of the Lord for salvation. We then discover who He is as Lord and Savior. **2)** When we come to Him, we begin to know, love, and follow Him as our Father. **3)** As we do, we realize the necessity of a humble heart in walking with Him and praying to Him. **4)** Following God also means seeing more about our sin and His forgiveness and cleansing on a daily basis. **5)** We begin to see the value and necessity of the Word of God for praying God's way. As He teaches us to abide in His Word and ask in His name, He shows us how His Word and prayer touch every area of life. He teaches us to hear His Word and ask in line with that Word—His promises and His principles. **6)** His Word leads us to honor and adore Him with the honor that is due Him. We give Him praise and thanks for being our Father and for calling us to His Son.

7) As we continue the journey, we begin to see that praying God's way is meant to be as incense offered in the Temple, and we are now His Temple, continually offering the sweet aroma of God-centered, Spirit-directed prayer to our joy and His. **8)** As our prayers are offered up as incense, He begins showing us all about asking—coming to Him with our needs, personal and relational, so we can become all He intends. **9)** We also face opposition—our own flesh and the temptations that are particularly "tasty" to us, the world system with its doubts and wrong opinions about God and His ways, along with the devil's darts, those pointed, poisoned accusations, distractions, and deceptions. **10)** The more we pray in line with His Word, the more we "catch" His burden for others and learn to pray His way for believers and for those who are lost. **11)** We soon (or should soon) find that others face the same challenges and needs that we face. As we understand that God made us to be a family, a body, an army—all groups that must learn to live and work together—we will see the value of praying together. **12)** All in all, He is leading us to Christlikeness. Seeing Jesus pray and teach us to pray can only bring us closer to the goal He has for us, conformity to the image of Christ. With this conformity, He is bringing us closer to our destiny as kings and priests, trained in prayer to reign with Him everywhere in His Kingdom—a destiny big enough for eternity and a destiny worth giving our lives to. Welcome to the journey!

Hopefully, praying God's way will prove to be just the thing you need to get you further along in your journey. These truths have certainly helped me along the way, and I trust God to make them *"the finest of wheat"* and *"honey from the rock"* to satisfy and strengthen you for your journey of following God (Psalm 81:16).

Following Him,

Richard L. Shepherd

RICHARD L. SHEPHERD

Table of Contents

1

CALLING ON THE NAME OF THE LORD
THE START OF TRUE PRAYER

If we are to understand true prayer—**praying God's way**—then we must see how people prayed in Scripture. What are the requirements for praying God's way? Is there a certain formula or certain arrangement of words we must repeat? Must we follow a carefully prescribed ritual? What do we find in the Bible? The Bible is the source of answers and the place we will find ordinary people praying God's way and seeing Him answer His way.

In the Scriptures, we find that prayer is not about formulas and rituals, but about faith and relationship—a **living-faith relationship** with God. First, we were meant to walk in a **living faith**, trusting God in all the details of life, all life long. A **living** faith is meant to be real and alive every day, touching all the aspects of life, affecting heart, mind, body, and soul. But a living faith does not mean simply having "faith" or adhering to "a particular faith" or religious persuasion. Biblical faith is always linked to a Person and to a personal relationship. That is the second angle of a living-faith relationship. This living-faith relationship is a **faith relationship**—that means we are meant to **relate** to God with a personal trust in Him. Life is meant to be a walk with Him, a walk learning from Him and following Him by faith, calling on Him day by day.

How do we know if we are walking with Him, following Him by faith? One of the ways is seen in our prayer lives. Are we

PRAYING GOD'S WAY

Prayer is not about formulas and rituals, but about faith and relationship, a relationship with God the Father. In that relationship, are we calling on Him daily, walking and talking with Him, listening and learning from Him. Are we depending on Him moment by moment? That is what He created us for in the beginning, and that is what He recreated us for in Christ.

praying? Are we calling on the name of the Lord daily, walking and talking with Him, listening to His Word, and learning from Him? Are we depending on Him moment by moment? That is what He created us for in the beginning, and that is what He recreated us for in Christ.

We will see these truths more clearly as we journey through the pages of Scripture. We will discover more of what it means to live a life of praying God's way and seeing Him answer His way. Calling on the name of the Lord is an adventure—the ultimate adventure in following God. Let's get started.

Calling on the Name of the Lord

DAY ONE

Right from the Start

If we are going to understand true prayer, we must see it right from the beginning. Where do we find the first exercise of prayer mentioned in the Bible? Genesis is the book of beginnings. We know that the Lord talked to Adam and Eve in the Garden of Eden (Genesis 2—3). In Genesis 4, we see Cain and Abel interacting with the Lord—Abel truly worshiping the Lord and the Lord dealing with Cain over his failure to worship properly. It appears that Abel knew what it meant to call on the name of the Lord and Cain did not. After this event, where in Scripture do we see people calling on the name of the Lord? What does it mean to experience calling on the Lord's name? It is the start of understanding **praying God's way.**

📖 To get a clear picture of what is going on and where prayer fits in, read Genesis 4. Record the main events in that chapter.

____

____

____

____

____

____

____

____

Adam and Eve gave birth to two sons, Cain and Abel. Cain was a farmer, and Abel raised livestock. Both men brought an offering to the Lord. The Lord saw Abel and his offering as acceptable, but *"He had no regard"* for Cain and his offering. Both Cain and his offering were unacceptable. This angered Cain, and God questioned him about his anger. If he would simply do the right thing, he would find the Lord responsive to him, but he chose instead to hold on to his anger and murder his brother Abel. As a result, the Lord cursed Cain's ground, the place of all his labors as a farmer. Cain left that place and walked away *"from the presence of the LORD."* He chose not to follow the Lord or to seek Him in worship. In the land of Nod, he raised his family, and we read of his son Enoch and of the city Cain built named after this son. Other generations followed. Note that there is no mention of God in what occurs in the line of Cain. We see a secular, godless lineage concerned only with business and pleasure.

Notice the line of Cain, especially Lamech. What details do you see about Lamech in Genesis 4:19–24?

____

____

____

____

____

Lamech was not only in the lineage of Cain physically but was also of the same spiritual nature. As an example of his rebellion, he disregarded God's original intention of one wife for one husband and married two wives. Then we see his brazen heart more fully. He murdered a man for wounding him and a boy for striking him and boasted that he would continue to avenge himself toward any who offended him. The Hebrew word for "killed" is *harag,* which means to "slaughter," the same word used when Cain murdered Abel. Lamech was a man of cruelty and violence and boasted of it before all who would listen. The downward spiral of sin continued through this godless line.

Now look at Genesis 4:25. What was significant about the birth of Seth?

____

____

____

Eve saw Seth as a son given in place of Abel whom Cain had murdered. Seth was more than just another child or a replacement for Abel. For Eve, Seth was a son who would hopefully carry on with the heart of Abel. When Eve spoke of *"another offspring in place of Abel"* she literally said *"another seed."* In Genesis 3:15, God had promised that a "seed" would be born to the woman, a seed that would be wounded by the serpent, but who would also crush the serpent's head. This is a prophecy of the coming of **the Seed,** the Lord Jesus who would come and crush sin and evil and bring eternal life through His death and resurrection. Eve did not understand exactly what God meant in the prophecy of the Seed, but she evidently recognized that Cain had acted with the nature of the serpent in murdering Abel (see 1 John 3:12), and by faith she declared that in Seth there was the potential for a godly seed to carry on and fulfill the promise God had given.

Genesis 4:26 reveals a new day in the history of mankind up to that point. (Notice any contrast with Genesis 4:19–24.) What do you find there?

____

____

____

Seth had a son whom he named Enosh, meaning "weak or frail" pointing to the mortality of man. It was an admission of the weakness and need of man. Where could man turn in his weakness and frailty? Was the answer in the kind of society Cain and his descendants were building? Verse 26 goes on to reveal what happened in the days of Seth and Enosh. *"Then men began to call upon the name of the LORD."* Some Hebrew scholars translate this, "then men began to be called by the name of the LORD," meaning they began to

Word Study

THE SOCIETY OF CAIN

When Cain *"went out from the presence of the LORD,"* he also left any worship of the Lord or any acknowledgement of the Lord in his daily life. The name of his son, *Enoch,* means "dedication," "commencement," or "initiation," pointing to Cain's own efforts at starting over. Cain thus named a city after himself, "Enoch," Cain's self-initiated society. When we look at the names of the children born in Cain's line, we also discover a self-seeking, self-initiated society. Lamech's two wives reveal a focus on outward beauty alone and not on a heart seeking God. *Adah* means "adorned," or "ornament," and *Zillah* means "shady" or "tinkling" as in the tinkling of jewelry. The sister of Tubal-cain was named Naamah, meaning "lovely" or "pleasant." What is noteworthy in Genesis 4:16–24 is not only what is stated, but what is not stated; there is no mention of the Lord or the things of the Lord. All is built on what man can do unaided by God, a worldly, secular society independent of God. There is no calling on the name of the Lord here; rather we see a society going in *"the way of Cain"* (Jude 11).

follow the Lord and His ways and thus were labeled or called followers of the Lord. That is a possible translation. Others translate this verse *"then men began to proclaim the name of the LORD."* That, too, is a conceivable translation. The key thought here is this: if one is called **by** the name of the Lord, it is because that person has first called **upon** the name of the Lord; he or she has begun to follow and obey the Lord. That also means he or she will be characterized by telling others about the Lord, proclaiming who He is and what His will is. Those were the marks of those who began following the Lord in the days of Seth and Enosh.

Word Study "CALL UPON THE LORD"

"Call upon" in the Old Testament is a translation of the Hebrew word *qara*, meaning, "to cry out" or "call aloud." It refers to **a specific cry** to **a specific person** with the expectation of **a specific answer**. This is not a random cry for help—"Anybody out there?"—but a focused calling on the LORD.

PRAY As we begin this look at praying God's way, there is a basic question each of us must ask: Am I in the line of those that call on the name of the Lord, or am I living a life independent of the Lord like Cain, a life full of self-will, self-seeking and self-glory? Pause and talk to the Lord about where you are in your daily walk.

____

____

____

____

____

____

____

____

____

____

What does it really mean to *"call upon the name of the* LORD"? To what example can we look? Abraham is the father of the faithful and shows us what it means to walk in faith calling on the name of the Lord. We will walk with Abraham in Day Two.

Calling on the Name of the Lord

DAY TWO

A LOOK AT ABRAHAM CALLING ON THE NAME OF THE LORD

What does it really mean to *"call upon the name of the* LORD"? There are three key words here that we must understand: **call**, **name**, and **LORD**. To "call" is from the Hebrew word *qara*, meaning "to cry out or call aloud." It refers to **a specific cry** to **a specific person** with the expectation of **a specific answer**. This is not a random cry for help—"anybody out there?"—but a focused calling on the Lord.

The **"name** of the LORD" is not just a label or identification tag. The "name" of the LORD refers to all He is, His character, His person, who He is and what He can do. Specifically, the title **"the LORD"** (spelled with all capital letters) refers to the Hebrew word *YHWH,* often rendered *"Yahweh"* or *"Jehovah,"* which refers to the self-existent nature of God. He is the God men began to call upon in Genesis 4:26 and, as we will see in today's study, the God upon whom Abraham called. Abraham and others encountered God and discovered that to call on His name means to connect with all that He is. We must discover the same today. (For further insight into the various Hebrew and Greek words related to prayer, see the charts at the end of this lesson.)

Word Study

THE NAME OF THE LORD

The Name of the Lord refers to all that He is, His character, His person, who He is and what He can do. Specifically, the title **"the Lord"** (spelled with all capital letters) refers to the Hebrew word *YHWH,* often rendered *"Yahweh"* or *"Jehovah." YHWH* is rooted in the Hebrew word *havah,* meaning "to become" and may be connected to the Hebrew word *hayah,* meaning "to be" or "to become." *Hayah* is translated "I AM" in the encounter between God and Moses when God explained His name as, "I AM WHO I AM" (Exodus 3:14). This explanation referred to God's self-existent nature as God and Lord. The Septuagint (Greek translation of the Old Testament) focuses on the same truth, stating, "I AM He Who is" (*egō eími ho on*). He is God, the creator, sustainer, and foundation of all that exists. He needs nothing and can provide all that man needs. He is the God men began to call upon in Genesis 4:26 and the God we must call on today. To call on His name means to connect with all that He is.

📖 Having read the phrase *"call upon the name of the Lord"* in Genesis 4:26, we find it again in Genesis 12:8. Read Genesis 12:1–9 to see the full context. Who is involved in these events?

____

____

____

____

Based on the call and command of God, Abram (later named Abraham by God) left Ur of the Chaldees and traveled to Canaan with his wife Sarai and his nephew Lot. God appeared to Abram at the oak of Moreh and promised him He would give the land of Canaan to Abram's descendants. Abram traveled from there to the place between Bethel and Ai and from there to the Negev (the South region of Canaan).

📖 What do you find in Genesis 12:8? What is the significance of an altar? What connection is there between the altar and calling on the name of the Lord?

____

____

____

____

____

____

When Abram came to the place between Bethel and Ai, he built an altar. An altar was a place of sacrifice, of death, of giving. It was a place to truly acknowledge one's weakness and sin, to openly recognize the Lord as God, and to unselfishly surrender to Him, giving Him the honor, praise, and worship He deserves. With an altar of sacrifice and a heart sincerely calling, Abram expressed the desire to follow the Lord, walking dependent on Him day by day.

With an altar of sacrifice and a heart sincerely calling, Abram expressed the desire to follow the Lord, walking dependent on Him day by day.

📖 What did Abram do after he called on the name of the Lord, according to Genesis 12:9?

____

____

____

After calling on the name of the Lord, Abram journeyed on to the Negev or south region of Canaan. In the context, it is possible that when he called on the name of the Lord, he was seeking the Lord about exactly where to settle down. Verse 9 is in direct connection to verse 8. After calling on the Lord, *then* Abram took the next step of the journey in his new homeland.

APPLY How about you? Where are you in your spiritual journey? Are you calling on the Lord seeking Him daily? Is there an "altar" in your heart, signifying your surrender to the Lord and to His will and His ways? Stop and evaluate where you are in the journey. Ask the Lord to reveal the truth about your heart condition. Perhaps you need some "altar" time as well as some "call" time with the Lord before you take any other steps.

____

____

____

____

____

____

📖 A few years later (Genesis 15), we find Abram in prayer. After Abram successfully rescued Lot and his family from the five kings, he was blessed by Melchizedek, a priest of God Most High (Genesis 14). After these events, the Lord came to Abram in a vision. What did He tell Abram according to Genesis 15:1?

____

____

____

____

____

____

The Lord spoke words of assurance and comfort. He assured Abram there was no need to fear, because God Himself would be Abram's shield of protection and would reward him greatly. Some translate that verse, pointing to God Himself as Abram's reward. God promised Abram that as God He would provide for him and protect him.

📖 How did Abram respond in verses 2–3?

____

____

____

____

Abram was concerned about who would inherit what God would give him, and he voiced that concern in open, honest prayer. God had promised a son, and no son had come. Abram offered his own solution—his servant Eliezer could be made the heir, an acceptable custom in that day. We too sometimes offer our own solutions to the Lord as we pray. How did God respond?

📖 What did God say in answer in verses 4–5?

____

____

____

God said Eliezer would not be the heir. Abram would have his own son. Then the Lord took Abram outside and showed him the thousands of stars in the night sky and promised that his descendants would be too many to count. God the Creator had created all that Abram could see. He was also able to give Abram a son, even many descendants. When we come to the Lord in prayer, concerned over some question or burden or heartache, God will sometimes show us some evidence of His power or wisdom. As we pray, we need to be watchful for those God-moments.

How did Abram respond, and what did God do according to Genesis 15:6?

____

____

____

____

____

Abram believed in the LORD (Yahweh) and His ability to do what He promised. That is the essence of true faith. Hebrews 11:6 says, *"But without faith it is impossible to please Him, for he who comes to God must believe that He is, and that He is a rewarder of those who diligently seek Him"* (NKJV). Abram believed that God is the true God and that He is a giver or a rewarder, able and ready to give what He promises. Abram placed faith in the Lord, and the Lord credited Abram's account with His own righteousness—by grace as a gift through faith. Romans 4 speaks of this righteousness by faith as the heart of the relationship between God and Abraham and the heart of our relationship with God.

This faith relationship is vital to praying God's way. How can we be sure we are walking in that faith relationship? We will explore that in Day Three.

Did You Know?

ABRAHAM, ISAAC, AND JACOB

Not only did Abraham call on the Lord in his early days in Canaan, but we find him back at the altar of Bethel, calling on the name of the Lord after he returned from Egypt (Genesis 13:1). Years later, when Isaac was still young, Abraham made a covenant with Abimelech at Beersheba, and there *"he called on the name of the LORD, the Everlasting God"* (21:33). Isaac, too, called on the name of the Lord at the altar in Beersheba (26:25). We see Jacob praying, seeking the Lord several times in his life as well (28:18–22; 32:9–12; 43:14; 48:15–16).

WHERE DO WE START CALLING ON THE NAME OF THE LORD?

Calling on the Name of the Lord

DAY THREE

We have seen examples of how men and women in the Old Testament began following the Lord and living a life of calling on the name of the Lord. What do we find in the New Testament? How or where do we start calling on the name of the Lord since Jesus came? It is vitally important in this first lesson to make sure you understand where you are in your relationship with God and that you know what the Scriptures say.

We have seen in Genesis and in Romans that Abraham entered into a faith relationship with God, trusting His promises and believing in His person. How do we do that? In writing to the Romans, Paul went into great detail about the salvation God brought through Jesus Christ—the salvation that is absolutely necessary for a right relationship with God. In chapters 1—3, he spoke about the sin problem all men have—the barrier that must be dealt with.

📖 What do you see in Romans 3:21–26?

____

____

____

____

____

All—no exceptions—have sinned against God, offended Him and become candidates for the wrath of God, but it does not have to remain that way. One can actually become a child of God experiencing the forgiveness of God and knowing the very presence of His Spirit within. A person can be made right—declared righteous before God *"through faith in Jesus Christ."* Jesus died on the cross for our sins and rose from the dead, showing that His death did indeed pay for that sin and bring about our justification (see Romans 4:25). Being justified (counted right) before God is a gift paid for by the death of Christ, a death in which He redeemed us or purchased us out of our slavery to sin and its death penalty. By Christ's death, God satisfied His justice in dealing with sin, and He made the way open to be *"the justifier of the one who has faith in Jesus"* (3:26).

Word Study

JESUS IS JEHOVAH

In the Old Testament the word *YHWH* is translated Jehovah or Yahweh in its literal rendering, but is most often translated LORD (spelled with all capital letters) in our English versions. The Greek translation of the Old Testament (the Septaugint) uses the Greek word *kúrios* ("Lord") when it translates *YHWH. Kúrios,* from its root word *kuria,* translated "Lord" or "Master," literally means "having power or authority." *Kúrios* is used of an owner of anything, a master over many servants, or of a king or emperor. Jesus referred to Himself as Lord (John 13:13), and the disciple Thomas declared when he saw the resurrected Jesus, *"My Lord and my God"* (John 20:28). Paul spoke often of the Lord Jesus Christ (1 Corinthians 1:3; 8:6; 12:3; Philippians 1:2). *Elohim* and *Adon* or *Adonai,* two other names for God in the Old Testament, are sometimes translated with *kúrios* as in the quotes from the Old Testament in Matthew 22:44 and 1 Peter 1:25. (See also Psalm 34:8 with 1 Peter 2:3.) Jesus is *YHWH, Elohim,* and *Adonai,* the sovereign Lord.

📖 How does one express this faith in Jesus once he or she knows this truth? In Romans 10, Paul began speaking of his great desire and prayer for the salvation of the Jews who had not trusted in Jesus Christ for their salvation. How are they to express faith in Christ? Read Romans 10:1–10 and record your insights.

____

____

____

____

____

The heart is the focus of Romans 10. An external righteousness based on works of the Law will never gain one right standing before God, because no one can fulfill the Law perfectly. The way into right standing with God is through the heart. The mouth confesses what the heart truly believes, and a confession that agrees with what God says brings the salvation God alone can bring.

📖 What is essential according to Romans 10:8–10?

____

____

____

____

When one confesses (agrees with God) and expresses with the mouth Jesus as Lord and believes in the heart that God has raised Jesus from the dead, that one shall be saved. This is more than mental assent or speaking some exact words. It is genuine faith in the ability of God to do what He has promised. When one believes from the heart and confesses with the mouth that Jesus is Lord and that His death and resurrection actually secured salvation, God credits Christ's perfect righteousness to his account—the result is receiving the Lord's righteousness and His salvation. That person then begins a walk of following Jesus as Lord—obeying His Word and trusting His ways. This is a walk of knowing His continual forgiveness for sin and the power of His life for right living.

📖 What do you find in Romans 10:11–13? How does all this relate to calling on the name of the Lord?

____

____

____

____

____

____

____

____

____

____

The Lord is willing to save anyone who will place his or her faith in Christ for salvation. That one *"WILL NOT BE DISAPPOINTED"* or literally, "will not be put to shame." God will act according to His promise and save the one who calls on Him, trusting Him to be the God He has revealed Himself to be. Just as Abraham was not disappointed, neither will the one who calls on the Lord. Whether Jew or Greek (Gentile), the Lord is *"abounding in riches for* **all who call upon Him**" (emphasis added). Paul sums up all he has said with a quote from Joel 2:32, *"WHOEVER WILL CALL UPON THE NAME OF THE LORD WILL BE SAVED."* That is **how one starts** life as a Christian—that is **how one lives** life as a Christian.

"WHOEVER WILL CALL UPON THE NAME OF THE LORD WILL BE SAVED" (Romans 10:13). That is how one starts life as a Christian; that is how one lives life as a Christian.

What about you? Have you called upon the name of the Lord from the heart, trusting Him as your Lord and Savior? If you have, you now know His forgiveness and the presence of His Spirit in your life. If you have other questions, you may want to read **"How to Follow God,"** a supplemental section found at the end of this book after Lesson 12, or you may want to talk to a pastor or other leader in your church.

Just as we saw God at work in the lives of men in the days of Enosh when men began to call on the name of the Lord, so today, anyone who will call in that same way will be saved—will begin a personal relationship with the true God. We know more of God's revelation through Jesus Christ today, but the essence of the relationship is the same—we begin a life of calling on the Lord, depending on Him for salvation as well as following Him day by day. How can we grow in knowing and calling on the Lord? We will see that more clearly in Days Four and Five.

Calling on the Name of the Lord

DAY FOUR

A LIFE OF CALLING ON THE NAME OF THE LORD

The Christian life is more than a one time "calling on the name of the Lord." Yes, that is how we enter into salvation and we never have to call on Him again for that salvation—it is settled—but that does not mean we never call on Him anymore. As a matter of fact, calling on Him for salvation is the start of a life of calling on God in daily prayer. Let's look at that in Scripture.

When the church started on the Day of Pentecost, it started with people calling on the name of the Lord. Read Peter's sermon in Acts 2:14–41, noting verse 21. Summarize what you discover there.

____

____

____

Did You Know?

THE TEMPLE COMPLEX AND SOLOMON'S PORCH

The Temple complex was a massive area constructed by Herod to accommodate all the Jews who came to Jerusalem for the Feast Days such as Passover, Pentecost, the Day of Atonement, and the Feast of Tabernacles. Herod built massive retaining walls and a courtyard measuring over 900 by 900 feet surrounding the Temple. This area could hold some 250,000–plus people during these occasions. Roof-covered columns surrounded this platform, and the area on the east side was known as Solomon's Porch (called in Acts 3:11 *"the so-called portico of Solomon"* [NASB], or *"Solomon's Colonnade"* [NIV]). It could have easily held the growing numbers of the early Church (over 20,000 believers).

Pentecost was a Jewish feast day, and Jews from many countries were in Jerusalem. The hour was around 9:00 A.M. when most of them would have been at the Temple for one of the two daily prayer times coinciding with the offering of incense in the Temple (9:00 A.M. and 3:00 P.M.). The Holy Spirit descended on the band of 120 disciples, and they received the Spirit into their lives just as Jesus had promised (John 14:17). A crowd gathered when they heard the noise that sounded like a mighty wind and then heard in their native languages the disciples proclaiming the mighty deeds of God. Peter stood and began to relate what all this meant to those gathered (most likely at the Temple area, probably at Solomon's Porch). It was the beginning of the fulfillment of the prophecy of Joel about the coming of the Spirit and the inauguration of the last days. In that prophecy, the Lord had promised through Joel, and now through the apostle Peter, *"EVERYONE WHO CALLS ON THE NAME OF THE LORD SHALL BE SAVED."* Peter applied that promise to that day and beyond and *"about three thousand souls"* called on the Lord in repentance and faith.

How did these new believers live out their new faith? What do you discover in Acts 2:42, 46–47?

____

____

____

____

These three thousand-plus believers were *"continually devoting themselves"* to the apostles' teaching (using the Old Testament and adding the truths we now have in the New Testament), to fellowship with other believers in encouraging one another and learning together, and to the breaking of bread (probably a reference to eating together, often in observance of the Lord's Supper). In addition to these three things the believers were also devoting themselves to prayer (literally "the prayers"), which is most likely a reference to the daily prayer times at the Temple (9:00 A.M. and 3:00 P.M.). Since the

Temple area was the only area that would hold the large numbers of believers coming to faith in Christ, this served as the ideal place for gathering as a group. Acts 2:46 points to these daily meetings in the Temple area as well as the daily meetings from house to house in smaller groups for meals and for fellowship and prayer. These first Christians started with a lifestyle of daily calling on the name of the Lord personally and with other believers.

Out of her infancy in Jerusalem, God's universal body of believers began to grow rapidly in the form of local church congregations throughout the Roman Empire. One of these early churches was located in the city of Corinth in southern Greece.

🕮 What marked believers in this city? Read 1 Corinthians 1:1–3, noting especially verse 2. What do you find about calling on the name of the Lord?

____

____

____

Paul, an apostle of Jesus Christ, spoke with the authority of Jesus Christ in writing to the Corinthians (around A.D. 56). He addressed them as the church of God at Corinth, as those who were sanctified or made holy (cleansed and set apart) in Christ Jesus and were therefore "saints" or holy ones by calling. He then added one other group of people besides the believers in Corinth: he addressed *"all who in every place call* (literally, "are calling") *upon the name of our Lord Jesus Christ, their Lord and ours."* Paul saw himself as part of the whole family of God, the whole body of Christ, and the one characteristic that he focused on, the one "family" trait he highlighted, was calling on the name of the Lord. He also made it clear that the Lord upon whom they all called was none other than Jesus Christ. Jesus is Lord of all who call on Him. Jesus is the same Lord upon whom men called in the days of Enosh and Abraham and Isaac and Jacob. Jesus Christ is the Lord upon whom we call today.

Word Study
"CALL ON"

"Call on" in 2 Timothy 2:22 is a translation of the Greek word *epikaléōmai,* the middle voice of *epikaléō. Epikaléō* means "to call on someone as a helper or as one's ally." The middle voice refers to calling on the Lord for help for oneself or on one's own behalf. It was used of Stephen's call to the Lord when he was being stoned (Acts 7:59) and in the Septuagint (Greek Old Testament) of Samuel calling on the Lord to deal with the sin of the people (1 Samuel 12:17–18). It is also found in the invitation to call upon the Lord for salvation in Romans 10:12–14.

Calling on the Lord is a predominant mark of a believer. This was certainly true of the first Christians. Around A.D. 67, Paul wrote a letter to Timothy, who was then a pastor in Ephesus. Part of the counsel he gave Timothy highlights this matter of calling on the Lord.

🕮 Read 2 Timothy 2:22 and write your insights.

____

____

____

Paul exhorted Timothy to flee youthful lusts, the desires that would lead to wickedness and uncleanness addressed in verses 19–21. In the context of chapter two, that included not only sexual lusts but also the intense desire to be argumentative with false teachers or with any who opposed Timothy's ministry. Instead, Timothy should *"pursue righteousness, faith, love, and peace,"* those traits that build up believers in their walk rather than tear them down. The best way to pursue such ideals is through keeping company with other faithful believers. How can faithful believers be identified? They *"call on the Lord from a pure heart."* This verse could be translated, "those who are continually calling on the Lord from a pure (a cleansed, unsoiled, or unstained) heart." **Continual calling** on the Lord is what Paul expected of Christians, and he personally exhorted Timothy to make it his practice to do so and to join with other like-hearted believers.

Is your personal life marked by daily calling on the Lord? Do you have times of prayer with other believers, starting with your husband or wife and your children and extending to other believers at work, school, or church? That is God's desire and call to you.

Calling on the Name of the Lord

DAY FIVE

FOR ME TO PRAY GOD'S WAY

We have seen that calling on the Lord is the mark of those who know Him, who have experienced His salvation. Calling on the Lord is the daily practice of a true believer. It is part of talking and walking with Him, listening and learning from Him, and following and obeying Him. As with any relationship we learn how to communicate more deeply and intimately as the relationship grows. The same is true in our relationship with the Lord. At first, calling is that simple cry for salvation. Then, as we grow, we call on Him in greater detail and with more consistency. How can we know the fullness of a life of calling on the name of the Lord—the fullness of a life of true prayer, of **praying God's way**? We will begin to see that in today's Scripture adventure and then examine this question in greater detail in the lessons to come.

📖 There are several examples of calling on the Lord in the Scriptures and there are several exhortations and encouragements to seek the Lord in prayer. One of these is found in Psalm 105. Read verses 1–4 and list all the aspects of calling on the Lord.

____

____

____

____

____

____

____

Calling upon the name of the Lord includes giving thanks to Him, singing to Him, praising His wonders. Boasting or glorying in His holy name is all part of calling on Him. To call upon the name of the Lord also involves seeking Him and His strength. Recall that the Hebrew word translated "call" is *qara,* meaning a specific cry to a specific person expecting a specific response. We can call on Him, expecting Him to give us strength. Calling on Him also means seeking His face, a person-to-person meeting. When anyone looks at another's face, that encounter involves seeing their eyes (the way they see things), hearing their words (what their will is), and being able to speak to them with the understanding that they can hear. It also means having open, honest communication between two persons, no hiding the face in shame or turning away in anger. Verse 4 calls us to *"seek His face continually,"* another exhortation to continual calling.

📖 What do you discover about the Lord and His relationship with His people in verses 5–14?

____

____

____

____

The Lord is marked by many wonders (wonderful acts) on behalf of His people. His words reveal incredible brilliance and wisdom. When He gives a judgment on a matter, it is true in every detail. The descendants of Abraham and Jacob are called to remember these characteristics of the Lord and to honor Him as God. He is ever faithful to His covenant with Abraham, Isaac, and Jacob, confirming His gift of the land of Canaan even when His chosen people were few in number and strangers in the promised land. He protected them in all their journeys in and around Canaan. This is the Lord they called upon and the Lord we are urged to call upon.

Perhaps all faithful men and women have faced death or some grave danger through various circumstances in one form or another. Often the Lord delivers us from these hardships. Psalm 116 contains just such a testimony. This psalm is a very personal testimony about calling on the Lord. We do not know who wrote this psalm, but we know the author was one who called on the name of the Lord in a variety of circumstances, even when facing death. Look at the three categories and the verses listed in each box and write what you discover.

WHAT THE PSALMIST FACED OR SAID OR REQUESTED	HOW GOD ACTED, RESPONDED OR ANSWERED	HOW THE PSALMIST RESPONDED TO GOD'S ACTIONS
verse 1 prays	**verses 1–2** hears	**verses 1–2** will call upon Him as long as I live
verses 3–4 pain, death, hell trouble sorrow prays	**verse 5** gracious merciful	**verse 5** praise
verse 6 brought low	**verses 6–7** preserves & saves deals bountifully	**verse 7** rest
verse 8 death, tears falling	**verse 8** delivered	**verse 9** walk before the Lord
verses 10–11 afflicted hurt angry	**verses 12 & 16** gives all His benefits	**verses 13–14 & 17–19** I am your servant pray, pay vows thanksgiving

Praise

The psalmist believed in the Lord and regularly called on Him. The more of life he faced, the more he called on the Lord and the more he found God answering in His grace and compassion. The Lord continually heard his voice and inclined His ear to listen, therefore the psalmist called on the Lord even more. Whatever he faced—distress, sorrow, death's door, tears, stumbling, various pressures and afflictions, betrayal, or bonds—the Lord answered and rescued. God dealt bountifully with this believer and gave him many benefits. For all that, the psalmist was grateful and expressed his thanks to the Lord, surrendering afresh to walk in obedience, praise, and worship.

There are times when we do not understand all the ways of God, but that does not necessarily mean He is not listening or that we are out of His will.

There are times when we do not understand all the ways of God, but that does not necessarily mean He is not listening or that we are out of His will. The New Testament provides us a picture of this and another example of calling on the Lord in the life of Stephen.

📖 Read Acts 6:7–15 and 7:1–60, noting especially verses 59 and 60. (This passage covers many verses, but it will help you to see the full picture) What insights do you see about Stephen's calling on the name of the Lord?

____

____

____

____

____

Stephen was a man who walked in obedience to Jesus as his Lord. He was very wise and knowledgeable of Scripture and longed to share with others the message of life in Christ and what it meant to know Him and follow Him. Some opposed Stephen and his teachings and falsely accused him before the Jewish authorities. At his trial, Stephen gave a very forceful presentation of the gospel, showing how God was working by His Spirit to bring people to faith in Christ. The leaders hated the message and Stephen the messenger. Therefore, they rushed to stone him to death. As they did, Stephen revealed his heart more fully than ever. He was a man who called on the Lord in all of life, and this point in life was no different. As they stoned him, *"he called upon the Lord,"* yielding his spirit to the Lord and expressing his forgiveness of his executioners. His prayer was very similar to the words of Jesus on the cross—*"Father, forgive them,"* and *"Father, into Thy hands I commit My spirit."* (Luke 23:34, 46) We see here that at least two characteristics marked Stephen's life—**1)** the control and character of the Spirit of Christ and **2)** a lifestyle of calling on the Lord.

APPLY Thinking of how Stephen or the psalmist in Psalm 116 faced the various difficulties and calamities of life, what applications do you see in your life?

____

____

____

____

____

Do you need to make any changes in your view of God or in your response to His actions in your life?

In your walk with the Lord, are you calling on Him consistently, or does your prayer life need something?

Lord, teach me to pray, to be able to testify to others what it means to call upon the name of the Lord all my days.

Talk to the Lord about these things. Surrender today to a new walk of calling on Him. Ask Him to give you His wisdom as you walk through these lessons on **praying God's way.**

Lord, I thank you for Your work in my life. I thank You that You first called me to Yourself—to repentance and faith. I'm so grateful You gave me the grace to come to You and to call on You for forgiveness and salvation. Too many times since then, I have tried to handle things in my own wisdom and strength rather than calling on You. Forgive me. May I recognize each pressure, each need, each challenge as an opportunity to call on You, trusting You to lead me each step of the way, each day of the journey. I praise You that You are able to handle whatever comes my way, just as You did with Your people throughout Scripture. Teach me to pray, to be able to testify to others what it means to call upon the name of the Lord all my days. In Jesus' name, Amen

Write your own prayer or journal entry in the space provided.

HEBREW WORDS FOR PRAYER IN THE OLD TESTAMENT WITH *STRONG'S CONCORDANCE* NUMBERS

HEBREW WORD	MEANING	SCRIPTURE
Anna (577)	An interjection of beseeching or entreating, sometimes translated "please," "earnestly pray," or "O."	Jonah 4:2
Bea (Aramaic) (1156)	To ask, seek, request, inquire, make petition. *Bea* also carries the idea of boiling up.	Daniel 6:11
Baqash (1245)	To seek, search out, beseech, request. By implication, the word pictures intensity in striving for the request.	2 Samuel 12:16 Ezra 8:23
Zaaq (2199)	To cry, to call out, or to cry with a loud voice. *Zaaq* is used of a cry of deep sorrow, fear, complaint, seeking help and deliverance from an enemy or from harsh servitude. It is also found in one calling out because of danger in battle or distress at sea.	1 Samuel 12:10; 15:11; Psalm 22:5; 107:13, 19; 142:5; Isaiah 30:19; Jeremiah 11:11; Lamentations 3:8; Hosea 7:14; Joel 1:14
Chalah (2470b)	To entreat or seek the favor of someone, to appease. It is literally, "to be smooth" and often is found with the Hebrew words translated "the face" with the idea of smoothing the face or countenance of one, that is, to appease the anger or wrath and gain favor by humble entreaty. (Possibly related to the Arabic word meaning to be acceptable or sweet, thus the idea of making the face of someone peaceful or friendly). Daniel 9:13 is literally ". . . we have not softened the face of the LORD our God."	Exodus 32:11; 1 Kings 13:6; 2 Kings 13:4; 2 Chronicles 33:12; Jeremiah 26:19; Daniel 9:13; Zechariah 7:2; 8:21, 22; Malachi 1:9
Chanan (2603a)	To ask for or beseech favor, grace, or mercy from a person or from God.	Deuteronomy 3:23; 2 Kings 1:13; 2 Chronicles 6:37; Esther 8:3; Psalm 30:8
Mishalah (4862)	*Mishalah* is a request or a petition, reflecting the desires of one's heart (Psalm 37:4). It is rooted in *shaal* (7592), "to ask, inquire, seek favor."	Psalm 20:5; 37:4
Na (4994)	*Na* is a particle translated as an interjection of entreaty, "I pray now" or "I beseech."	Numbers 12:12
Anah (6030a)	*Anah* means "to answer," "to hear," or "to respond" and is used of one crying out for God to answer.	1 Kings 18:26, 37; Psalm 4:1; 13:3; 20:1, 6, 9; 34:4; 38:15; 55:2; 60:5; 69:13, 16, 17; 86:1; 118:21; 119:145; 120:1; 143:7
'Athar or *'Atar* (6279)	From a root meaning to make abundant and applied to abundance of smoke as with incense. *'Athar* pictures burning incense, meaning to make fervent prayer or entreaty, to pray with intensity, crying to God with a deep sense of need	Genesis 25:21; Exodus 8:8, 28–30; Judges 13:8; 2 Samuel 21:14; 24:25; 1 Chronicles 5:20; 2 Chronicles 33:13, 19; Job 22:27; 33:26
Paga (6293)	To meet or encounter, make contact, or approach, in order to intercede for another. It carries the idea of approaching God on behalf of another.	Isaiah 53:12; Jeremiah 7:16; 27:18; 36:25

HEBREW WORD	MEANING	SCRIPTURE
Palal and *Tephillah* (6419) and (8605)	The range of this word includes "to judge or decide, to act as a mediator, to pray, intercede on behalf of someone, make supplication." People called on God to act as judge or mediator or to intervene and answer. *Palal* is used 84 times in the Old Testament. *Tephillah*, the most common word for "prayer" (used 76 times), is rooted in *palal* and means intercession or supplication. It is used as a title of many psalms. In addition to the Scriptures listed to the right, *palal* is found in these verses: Isaiah 16:12; 37:15, 21; 44:17; 45:20; 56:7; Jeremiah 7:16; 11:14; 14:11; 29:7, 12; 32:16; 37:3; 42:2, 4, 20; Daniel 9:4, 20; Jonah 2:1; 4:2	Genesis 20:7, 17; Numbers 11:2; 21:7; Deuteronomy 9:20, 26; 1 Samuel 1:10, 12, 26, 27; 2:1; 7:5; 8:6; 12:19, 23; 2 Samuel 7:27; 1 Kings 8:28, 30, 33, 35, 42, 44, 48, 54; 2 Kings 4:33; 6:17, 18; 19:15, 20; 20:2; 2 Chronicles 6:24; 7:1, 14; 30:18; 32:20; 33:13; Ezra 10:1; Nehemiah 1:4, 6; 2:4; 4:9; Psalm 5:2; 32:6 plus many others
Tsela (Aramaic) (6739)	"To pray." This word is in Aramaic. Aramaic is a Semitic language closely related to Hebrew. Before the Christian era, Aramaic had become the language of the Jews in Palestine.	Ezra 6:10; Daniel 6:10
Tsaaq and *Tseaqah* (6817) and (6818)	*Tsaaq* is the verb "to cry out or call." *Tseaqah* is the noun meaning "an outcry or call."	Exodus 3:7, 9; 8:12; 14:10, 15; 15:25; 17:4; 22:23, 27; Numbers 12:13; 20:16; Deuteronomy 26:7
Qara (7121)	To call upon. To cry out or call aloud. It refers to a specific cry to a specific person with the expectation of a specific response and answer. This is usually not a random cry, but a focused calling.	Genesis 4:26; 12:8; 21:33; 26:25; 1 Kings 8:43; 18:24; Psalm 34:6; 81:7; 116:17; 145:18; Isaiah 55:6; Joel 2:32; Zephaniah 3:9
Qashab (7181)	To prick up as in pricking up or sharpening the ears (pictured in a watchful animal). To listen carefully, give heed, or pay close attention.	2 Chronicles 6:40; 7:15; Nehemiah 1:6, 11; Psalm 17:1; 55:2; 61:1; 66:19; 86:6; 130:2; 142:6
Shaal and *Shelah* (7592) and (7596)	*Shaal* is the verb meaning, "to ask, to inquire, to seek favor" and shelah is the noun referring to what is requested. *Shelah* is used in 1 Samuel 1:27 of Hannah's request for a son.	Joshua 9:14; 1 Samuel 23:2; 30:8; 2 Samuel 2:1; 5:19; 1 Kings 3:10; Psalm 21:4; 27:4; 122:6; Isaiah 7:11
Shava (7768 [Verb Root]) *Shua* (7769), *Sheva* (7773), and *Shavah* (7775)	*Shava* means to cry out for help, and the nouns derived from that refer to the cry for help from one in distress.	1 Samuel 5:12; Psalm 5:2; 18:6, 41; 22:24; 28:2; 30:2; 31:22; 34:15; 39:12; 40:1 72:12; 88:13; 102:1; 119:147; 145:19
Siyach (7878)	"To ponder, meditate, to repeat a matter in one's mind, to talk with oneself, to pray." It may sometimes be translated "complain" as in Psalm 77:3	Psalm 55:17; 64:1; 77:3, 6, 12; 119:15, 23, 27, 48, 78, 148
Techinnah and *Tachanun* (8467) and (8469)	*Techinnah* (used 25 times) and *Tahanun* (18 times), both nouns rooted in the verb *chanan* (2603a), mean "supplication" or more particularly, "supplication for favor or mercy." *Tahanun* means "supplication" but with greater intensity.	(8467) 1 Kings 8:30, 38; 2 Chronicles 6:29, 35, 39; Psalm 6:9; 55:1; 119:170; Jeremiah 36:7; (8469) Jeremiah 3:21; 30:9; Daniel 9:3, 17, 18, 23; Zechariah 12:10

GREEK WORDS FOR PRAYER IN THE NEW TESTAMENT WITH *STRONG'S CONCORDANCE* NUMBERS

GREEK WORD	MEANING	SCRIPTURE
aitéō (154)	*Aitéō* means "to ask," usually of someone lesser requesting something from a superior (man to God—Matthew 7:7; child to father—Matthew 7:9–10; citizen to king—Acts 12:20; beggar to people—Acts 3:2–15)	John 14:14; Ephesians 3:20; Philippians 4:6; Colossians 1:9; James 1:5–6; 4:2–3; 1 John 3:22; 5:14-15
aítēma (155)	Rooted in *aitéō, aítēma* refers to a "petition" or "request."	1 John 5:15
déomai (1189)	*Déomai* means "to desire or long for" and carries the idea of being in want for oneself or to be in need. It is rooted in the word *déō,* meaning "to be deprived of or in need."	Matthew 9:38; Luke 5:12; 10:2; 22:32; Acts 4:31; 10:2; Romans 1:10 1 Thessalonians 3:10
déēsis (1162)	*Déēsis*, which is rooted in *déomai,* refers to a want or need and is used of "supplication" to God, emphasizing the strong sense of need.	Luke 1:13; 2:37; Ephesians 6:18; Philippians 1:4; 4:6
énteuxis (1783)	*Énteuxis* means "intercession." It is rooted in the idea of encountering someone or meeting with someone and making a request. It comes from the verb *entugchánō* (see below). *Énteuxis* was often used of coming before a king and usually refers to a request before a superior. In the Scriptures, it refers to intercession to God on behalf of someone else.	1 Timothy 2:1; 4:5
entugchánō (1793)	*Entugchánō* means, "to make intercession." Its fuller meaning is "to fall in with a person or to meet with a person, to come with free access on behalf of another or to interrupt someone in speaking for the purpose of making a request for another." It means to make intercession for someone or to entreat on behalf of another.	Romans 8:27, 34; 11:2; Hebrews 7:25
epikaléōmai (1941)	*Epikaléōmai* is the middle voice of *epikaléō*. *Epikaléō* means "to call on someone as a helper or as one's ally." The middle voice refers to calling on the Lord for help for oneself or on one's own behalf. Examples include Stephen's call to the Lord (Acts 7:59) and Samuel calling on the Lord (1 Samuel 12:17–18 [Septuagint {Greek OT}]).	Acts 7:59; Romans 10:12–14; 2 Timothy 2:22 1 Samuel 12:17–18 (Septuagint [Greek Old Testament])
erōtáō (2065)	*Erōtáō* means "to ask," used especially of a person speaking to an equal. It is used of Jesus talking to His Father. (*Aitéō* [see above] is never used of Jesus praying to His Father.)	Luke 14:32; John 14:16; 16:26; 17:9, 15, 20 Philippians 4:3
euchháristos (2170) and *eucharistéō* (2168)	*Euchháristos* is made up of two words—*eu* (well) and *charízomai* (to give)—and means to be thankful, as does *eucharistía*. The verb *eucharistéō* means to give thanks. These words are found numerous times.	Romans 1:8; 1 Corinthians 10:30; 2 Corinthians 1:11; 9:11; Philippians 4:6; 1 Timothy 2:1; 4:4
eúchomai and *euchḗ* (2172) and (2171)	*Eúchomai* means "to pray expressing one's desire or wish." The noun *euchḗ* refers to a vow, wish, or prayer.	Acts 26:29; 2 Corinthians 13:7, 9; James 5:15; 3 John 2
hiketēría (2428)	*Hiketēría* is translated "supplication," referring to a humble, earnest request. It was used in ancient times of a "suppliant" (*hikétēs*) carrying an olive branch.	Hebrews 5:7
parakaléō (3870)	*Parakaléō* means "to call alongside to help" and is used of prayer in Matthew 26:53. *Parakaléō* is a stronger appeal or request than *aitéō* (see above).	Matthew 26:53 Mark 5:17–18
proseúchomai (4336) and *proseuchḗ* (4335)	*Proseúchomai* (used 86 times) means "to make a request toward someone" and always refers to one's request to God. *Proseuchḗ* (*prós*—"toward" plus *euchḗ*—"request") is the word for prayer in general (used 36 times) and is found in Matthew 21:22; Luke 6:12; Acts 16:13, 16; Ephesians 6:18; Philippians 4:6; 1 Timothy 2:1; 5:5, and others	Matthew 5:44; 6:5, 6, 7, 9; Luke 6:12; Romans 8:26; Ephesians 6:18; Philippians 1:9; 1 Thessalonians 5:17; James 5:17; Jude 20

Notes

Notes

KNOWING AND LOVING THE FATHER
THE HEART OF TRUE PRAYER

We have begun to see what praying God's way involves. It involves calling upon the name of the Lord, first, in confession of sin, crying out for His salvation, and then second, in a daily cry of dependence. That daily cry reveals a heart surrendered to God, one that desires to follow Him. But prayer is more than that. Prayer is a **relationship** with God the Father. Prayer is not about rituals and formulas. It is about a relationship of knowing, loving, and following God our Father and Jesus our Lord by the power and wisdom of His Holy Spirit. How can we know His heart more intimately, more truly, more deeply? In this lesson, we continue the journey of praying God's way as we look at who God is as a Father and what it means to know and love **our** "Abba! Father!"

Prayer is not about rituals and formulas. It is about a relationship of knowing, loving, and following God our Father and Jesus our Lord by the power and wisdom of His Holy Spirit.

Two verses of Scripture focus our attention on knowing and loving the Father. John 17:3 says, *"And this is eternal life, that they may know Thee, the only true God, and Jesus Christ whom Thou hast sent."* This is more than **knowing about** God—mere facts—it is knowing Him in **personal experience.** We also read Jesus' words in Mark 12:30, *"AND YOU SHALL LOVE THE LORD YOUR GOD WITH ALL YOUR HEART, AND WITH ALL YOUR SOUL, AND WITH ALL YOUR MIND, AND WITH ALL YOUR STRENGTH."* The more we know and love the Father, the more we will call on Him in truth. The more we call on Him in truth, the more we will know and love Him and lead others to know and love Him.

One of the greatest revelations of Scripture is that God is a loving, holy Father. He has a Father's heart. He wants His children to come to Him, talk to Him and listen to Him. While God is the Almighty, the Sovereign Lord, Ruler over heaven and earth, He makes it clear in Scripture that He wants us to come to Him not only because He is our God, but also because He is our Father. He wants us to come with the heart of a trusting, loving child, since He is always working in our lives as a loving Father. God the Father is at the heart of true prayer. We must look at our "Abba Father" in the revelation He has given us in His Word. There we will meet Him and grow in our understanding and love of Him. There we will begin to grow and mature as sons and daughters who are learning to pray God's way.

Knowing and Loving the Father

DAY ONE

Jesus Reveals the Father

It is very important that we understand the concept of God as our Father if we are to know **how** to pray to Him. God the Father and His greatly loved Son, our Lord Jesus, are one in heart, mind, essence, and purpose. They are both mysteriously and equally God. They think and act alike. Therefore, the Father sent His Son to show us what the Father is like, to reveal His love and eternal purposes, and to accomplish all that was necessary to save us and bring us to Himself as His children. What can we learn about the Father from the Lord Jesus and His revelation in Scripture?

What do you discover about Jesus and the Father in John 1:1–4, 14, 18?

____

____

____

____

____

____

____

____

Word Study

EXPLAINING THE FATHER

John 1:18 says Jesus *"has explained"* the Father to us. The word "explained" is the Greek word *exēgéomai,* meaning "to bring out or to declare thoroughly" (*The Complete Word Study Dictionary New Testament,* ©1992 AMG Publishers, p. 604). Jesus brought out or recounted the truth about the Father, revealing His nature, His work, and His will. He told His listeners in John 10:30, *"I and the Father are One,"* meaning one in essence. This means He can show us what the Father is like since He alone is one with God. Having the Father's same nature, Jesus is able to explain Him to man.

Jesus is The Word who has always existed. He is God and the Creator of all; in Him is life. Jesus, the Word, became flesh and "dwelt" or lived among men. The word "dwelt" literally means "tabernacled" like the Tabernacle in the wilderness during Old Testament times. As the Tabernacle in the wilderness housed the glory of God, so Jesus revealed the glory of the Father. As the *"only begotten from the Father,"* He revealed to man what the Father is like, showing His grace and truth as never before seen.

John 1:18 points out that no man has seen the full person, nature, and essence of God at any time, but Jesus has revealed Him so we can know Him. Jesus has a close, intimate relationship with His Father, never hindered by the limitations of sin. Because of that, all He reveals is pure and true, never diluted or deceptive. We can count on what He says. If we are to know the Father and to experience the fullness of praying God's way, we must continually look carefully at what Jesus did and what He said about the Father.

📖 Look at each of these Scriptures and record what Jesus reveals about the Father.

Matthew 5:45

____

____

____

Matthew 5:48

____

____

____

Matthew 6:26–32 (note verses 26 and 32)

____

____

____

Luke 6:35–36

____

____

____

The Father is very gracious and giving, showing love to all, giving sun and rain to the evil and the good, the righteous and the unrighteous. Furthermore, the Scriptures show us that *"your heavenly Father is perfect,"* meaning He is complete in every way, loving us perfectly and able to guide us and provide for us whatever is needed. He feeds the birds of the air and knows we need food and clothing. The Father, who is also called the Most High, is even *"kind to ungrateful and evil men,"* showing Himself merciful time after time. What an encouragement to pray and discover these truths in your own daily experience!

📖 Jesus spoke of the Father and His work in many ways. Read the verses listed below and record your insights about the Father and His ways.

Matthew 10:29–31 with Luke 12:6–7

____

____

____

____

Matthew 10:16–20

____

____

____

____

Word Study

A PERFECT FATHER

The Greek word translated "perfect" in Matthew 5:48 is *téleios* meaning fully mature or complete. It is rooted in *teléō*, "complete," which is from *télos*, "to reach the goal or purpose." *Télos* was used of a ripe seed, meaning a seed in its fullest form. *Téleios* was used of sacrifices or offerings without any deficiency, spotless in every detail. *Téleios* is also used of the gifts of the Father, which are "good" and "perfect" (James 1:17), meaning they satisfy the need at hand. The Father, ***your*** heavenly Father, is *Téleios*, the One who is the fullness of life, absolutely perfect in every way, having no deficiency in any way, and meeting every need in the best way.

Matthew 16:13–17

____

____

____

The Father's care is in the smallest details. If He watches over the movements of a sparrow, never forgetting the smallest detail, and knows the number of hairs on one's head, how much more does He know about the smallest details of His children! This is particularly true as we tell others the message of Jesus and His great love. When we face opposition, the Spirit of our Father guides us in what to say when we need to say it. He is the one who reveals spiritual truth to our hearts as He did to Simon Peter, and He is the one who guides us in sharing that truth with others.

Did You Know?

THE FIFTH SPARROW

Jesus illustrated the care of the Father for His children, pointing to His care of sparrows. Two were sold in the market for a "cent" (a Roman *assarion*, the smallest Roman coin, made of copper and worth about 1/16 of a denarius, a day's wage). Luke 12:6 says five sparrows were sold for two cents so that the fifth sparrow was thrown in for free. The **fifth sparrow** was considered of no value to the seller, but had the constant attention of the Father—*"not one of them is forgotten"* at any time *"before God."* Jesus instructed His disciples that as they told others about Him and His message, God would care for them in great detail—a great lesson to learn and remember (see Matthew 10:24–42 and Luke 12:1–12).

📖 What kind of relationship does the Father want with us? Read John 4:21–24. (You may want to read John 4:1–42 to see the full context.) What does Jesus reveal to the woman at the well?

____

____

____

____

____

____

____

Jesus revealed that the Father is interested in true worship and that true worship does not depend on the location of a person (Mount Gerizim or Jerusalem) but the place of one's heart—wherever that person may be. The Father is seeking those who will worship Him in spirit and truth, open and honest before Him, fully depending on Him. The Father is not interested in rituals and religious formulas, but in an honest relationship from the heart.

📖 Jesus revealed the Father so that we could know the Father personally. Read John 14:1–10 and record your insights about knowing the Father.

____

____

____

____

____

KNOWING AND LOVING GOD

Jesus said, *"And this is eternal life, that they may know Thee, the only true God, and Jesus Christ whom Thou hast sent"* (John 17:3). Jesus also stated, *"AND YOU SHALL LOVE THE LORD YOUR GOD WITH ALL YOUR HEART, AND WITH ALL YOUR SOUL, AND WITH ALL YOUR MIND, AND WITH ALL YOUR STRENGTH"* (Mark 12:30).

The night before Jesus went to the cross, He spoke to His disciples of the eternal home they would have with Him and the Father, promising that He would take them there. They did not know **how** this could happen—they did not understand the way Jesus would do this. But then Jesus assured them that because they knew Him, they already knew the way. He told them that He was **the way** *to* the Father; there is no other way. No one could ever come to the Father except through Jesus. He is **the truth** *about* the Father, and He is the one who reveals **the life** *of* the Father. Because the disciples had seen and known Jesus, they had seen the Father. Philip requested some further revelation. Jesus plainly told him that seeing Him is seeing the Father. *"Do you believe that I am in the Father, and the Father is in Me?"* Then, Jesus reminded them that the words He spoke did not come by His own initiative, but were evidence of the Father abiding in Him and doing His works.

Do you know the Father through Jesus? That is the only way to know His eternal life and have a living faith relationship with the Father. Such a relationship is essential for praying God's way. The more we know of the Father, the easier it will be to talk to Him and to understand His Word to us.

What more can we see about the Father, so we can know and love Him more fully and pray more confidently? We will see more of how the Father works in Day Two.

Knowing and Loving the Father

DAY TWO

The Father Is Working

The Father was continually working in and through the Lord Jesus—through His works and His words. Many did not know or believe the Father or Jesus, so they did not understand Him or His ways. If we are to understand God's ways in prayer, we must understand how He works, what He wants done or not done, and how prayer fits into that.

In John 5:17, Jesus said, *"My Father is working until now, and I Myself am working."* He said that after He healed a lame man. Read John 5:1–17. Summarize what you find there and record your insights about the statement Jesus made in verse 17?

___

___

___

Look at John 12:44–50 and compare that passage with the other passages we have reviewed. What do you find about the work of the Father, the work of the Son, and the response of men and women?

Jesus came to Jerusalem for a feast (probably Passover) and, while there, saw a man who had been lame for thirty-eight years. Jesus asked this man if he wanted to get well, and the man responded that no one could help him when the opportunity was there. The people believed an angel stirred the waters *"at certain seasons"* and whoever stepped in first was made well. No one had ever helped the man, and he indicated by his response that he wanted to be well. Jesus simply commanded him to take up his pallet and walk, and the man did so. However, there was one little "problem." This was the Sabbath day, and the man was not supposed to carry anything on the Sabbath. Furthermore, when the Jewish leaders found out that Jesus had healed on the Sabbath, they complained that He had broken the Sabbath "law." Jesus gave His reason for doing what He did. He saw the Father working and wanting to heal this man, and so Christ joined the Father and healed him. This incident is just one instance of the Father working through Jesus.

📖 What do you find about the Father's working as evidenced in John 8:26–29?

___

___

___

In the midst of many who did not believe the words or works of Jesus, Christ made it clear that the Father had sent Him and spoke to Him. The words Jesus heard from the Father, He spoke to the world. All that Jesus did, He did by the Father's initiative—speaking what the Father taught Him, living in the presence of the Father moment by moment, in constant communication with the Father, and doing the works the Father gave Him to do. While on earth, Jesus was always pleasing the Father in what He said and did.

How and where did Jesus get His instructions from the Father? We get some clues in two passages of Scripture. Read Isaiah 50:4, a prophecy about the Messiah. Then, read Mark 1:35–38 and record your insights from these two passages.

____

____

____

____

____

____

Doctrine

THE FATHER RESURRECTED JESUS

Scripture is clear in several places that one of the works of the Father was raising Jesus from the dead. We find in Romans 6:4 that *"Christ was raised from the dead through the glory of the Father,"* and Acts 2:24 says, *"God raised Him up again."* Romans 10:9 declares, *"that if you confess with your mouth Jesus as Lord, and believe in your heart that God raised Him from the dead, you shall be saved."* (See also Acts 2:32; 3:15, 26; 4:10; 5:30; 10:40; 13:30, 33–34, 37; 17:31; Romans 4:24; 8:11; 10:9; 1 Corinthians 6:14; 15:15; 2 Corinthians 4:14; Galatians 1:1; Ephesians 1:20; Colossians 2:12; 1 Thessalonians 1:10; Hebrews 13:20; 1 Peter 1:21.)

Isaiah spoke of how the Messiah would be taught and become a learned or discipled man. Morning by morning, the Father woke Jesus and spoke to Him. Jesus listened as a disciple and learned what to say to those He met. The Father taught Him so that He knew what to say—*"how to sustain the weary one with a word"*—as well as what works to do. We find an example of this in Mark 1:35–38. Jesus was in Capernaum and went out early in the morning *"while it was still dark"* to *"a lonely place"* to pray. There the Father taught Him and gave Him directions for the day. When the disciples found Jesus, they told Him of more people in Capernaum who wanted to see Him, but Jesus said they must go to other towns nearby. Why did Christ say that? Evidently, this is the direction the Father gave Him in prayer.

What work does the Father continue to do today? Read John 6:35–51 and record your insights about the Father's will and work.

____

____

____

____

____

Jesus made it very clear that He was the Bread of Life sent from the Father in heaven and anyone who would come to Him, believing in Him would find his or her spiritual hunger and thirst satisfied by Him. Jesus promised, *"the one who comes to Me I will certainly not cast out."* That is the will of the Father, and He is ever working, drawing people to Jesus. When anyone comes to Jesus believing in Him, that one is assured of eternal life and the promise of resurrection. The Father is continually at work, speaking to the hearts of men and women, and those who hear, learn, and come to Jesus find life forever. We do not understand all that goes on in this work of the Father, but we know that He is at work and that we too can join Him doing what He shows us day in and day out as we seek Him in prayer and in His Word.

What is the primary work He wants us to do according to John 6:28–29?

____

____

____

____

____

At the heart of the Father's work is faith—He wants us to believe Jesus, all He did and all He said. That means continually listening carefully to His Word, so we can **know** His will. It means following His Spirit day by day, so we actually **do** His will. We continually seek Him in His Word and in prayer, trusting Him to guide us so we join Him where He is working. We continually listen and learn from Him, so that we grow in faith doing His will.

What assurance do we have of the Father's work in our lives? Read Romans 8:14–16 and Galatians 4:4–7 and record what you find.

____

____

____

____

____

____

____

Each child of God receives the Spirit of God into his life at the point of calling on the Lord to save him. Galatians 4:5 says, *"God has sent forth the Spirit of His Son into our hearts."* Romans 8:15 says we have *"received the Spirit of adoption as sons"* and by that Spirit we cry out *"Abba! Father!"*—"Daddy, Papa"—a very personal, warm cry of a child for his loving father. This is a cry of assurance and joy, not of alarm or fear. The Spirit assures us that we are children of God and leads us as His children. He guides us in *"putting to death the* [sinful] *deeds of the body"* and empowers us to do righteous deeds, the *"good works which God prepared beforehand"* for us to carry out (see Ephesians 1:5 and 2:8–10). He also assures us of our future as heirs of God. (In Day Five, we will see more about how the Spirit helps us in prayer.)

We can hear the Father's voice. He may speak through a passage of Scripture, a song, a testimony from a fellow believer, or through that still, small voice in the heart. When the Father speaks, what He says **always agrees** with Scripture. That's one of the reasons the Father commands us to walk in the truth (2 John 4). The devil tries to counterfeit truth with his thought darts (Ephesians 6:16). The more we know the true Word of God, the sooner we recognize the counterfeit and respond to the truth.

The Father wants to continually talk to you, teach you, and take you further in your walk with Him, and He wants you to talk to Him in prayer, all day, about all of life. Stop for a moment; talk and listen.

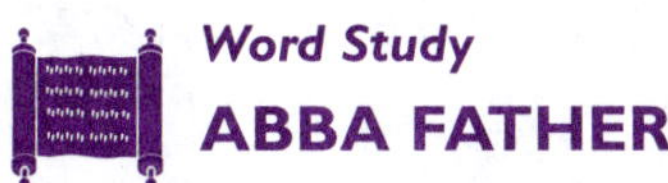

Word Study

ABBA FATHER

"Abba! Father!" cries the child of God in Romans 8:15. Why? Because he or she has *"received the Spirit of adoption"* guaranteeing the eternal relationship with **God the Father** through the work of **His Son the Lord Jesus** applied by the **Holy Spirit of God** (Romans 8:1–17). "Abba" is rooted in the Hebrew "*Ab*" and comes through the Chaldean "*Abba,*" meaning "father." In the Greek translation of the Old Testament (the Septaugint), *Abba* is translated with the Greek word *pater,* which we translate "father." *Pater* is rooted in the word *pa,* which literally means "one who nourishes, protects, and sustains." ***Ab***, ***Abba***, and ***pater*** all carry the idea of source or originator, one who gives and sustains life, who nourishes, provides and protects so as to bring to maturity and fullness of life. That is who God is as our "Abba! Father!"—the one to whom we can come in prayer to express our love and trust, to call upon for any need, any care, or to simply talk to as we seek to follow Him with a whole heart.

Knowing and Loving the Father

DAY THREE

THE FATHER AT WORK IN OUR LIVES

What is our heavenly Father doing in our lives? What is His work once we place our faith in His Son? There are many ways in which He works as He brings us to maturity, to the fullness of the image of Christ. As we see His ways and what He is doing, we will also gain insights into how we can grow in our prayer lives—how we can more fully walk praying God's way.

Read Ephesians 1:3–14 and record what you find about the Father's work in our lives. According to verses 15–21, what did Paul do in light of this work?

____

____

____

____

____

____

____

Did You Know?

ROMAN ADOPTION LAWS

Roman adoption laws in Paul's day guaranteed the stance of an adopted child. To guarantee the legality of a Roman adoption, seven witnesses were required to be present to validate the adoption. Furthermore, Roman law provided that an adopted child could not be disinherited, while a natural born son could be banished from the family with nothing. How much more secure is each child of God who has the guarantee of the witness of the Spirit of God in his heart and life now and the promise of His presence for all eternity.

The Father has chosen to bless us *"with every spiritual blessing in the heavenly places in Christ."* That includes being chosen in Christ to be holy and blameless in His sight—no guilt or shame when we stand before Him because we stand in Christ. He adopted us as sons, guaranteeing our place and our inheritance in His family. By His blood, He redeemed us or purchased us out of slavery to sin and self and forgave us all our trespasses (every time we have stepped over the line). He gave us the Holy Spirit as a seal of His salvation and a pledge (like an engagement ring) of our inheritance (the guarantee that there is still yet more to come). In light of all this, we can know He welcomes us when we come to Him in prayer even as Paul Himself prayed in verses 15–21 (note Paul's confidence in verse 15, *"for this reason. . . "*).

"See how great a love the Father has bestowed upon us, that we should be called children of God; and such we are. . . ."

I John 3:1a

What other work do you find the Father doing in 1 Thessalonians 3:11–13?

____

____

____

____

____

In writing to the believers, Paul prayed for an opportunity to come back to Thessalonica, looking to the Father to *"direct our way to you."* Paul was confident that the Father is the one who guides and guards our paths (like the Shepherd of Psalm 23). Paul prayed for the Thessalonians to grow in love for one another and for all men, and he prayed that when the Lord Jesus returns they would stand unaccused (*"unblamable"*) before the Father because they had walked in love, obedient to Him.

🕮 What do you find in 2 Thessalonians 2:16–17 and 1 John 3:1–3? What should be our response?

____

____

____

____

____

The Father has loved us who are Christians and in that love has given us *"eternal comfort and good hope by grace."* The Father has given us a confident expectation about His love and about our life that will forever be spent with Him. In light of that, Paul prayed for the believers in Thessalonica to be comforted and strengthened in the present as they walked in good works and spoke good words. First John adds a declaration of the awe and wonder over the Father's love in actually making us His children and preparing an eternity that is indescribable. Christ is coming for us one day, and we will be united with our Father who loves us so much. Then we will be like Him, made in the image of our Father and His Son, the Lord Jesus. Because of that confident expectation of being like Him then, we should be walking in purity now—in thought, attitude, word, and deed. The more we seek Him, praying God's way, the more we will grow in that likeness and purity.

🕮 There is another necessary work the Father does, and it greatly affects all aspects of our walk, including our prayer life. What do you see in Hebrews 12:1–13, especially verses 5–11?

____

____

____

____

The Father loves us enough to save us and redeem us no matter where we are, but He loves us too much to leave us there.

As we run the faith-race set before us, we must focus on Jesus. There will be hardships, difficult days, spiritual struggles, mental battles, and times when we want to quit. We must focus on Jesus and follow faithfully. While we do this, we must remember that some of the battles we face come with the child training through which the Father is taking us. He loves us enough to save us and redeem us no matter where we are, but He loves us too much to leave us there. He wants to grow us up into fully mature sons, and so He disciplines, reproves, even scourges us. As we submit to Him, we grow in Him. We share more of His holiness; we are made more into the image of Christ; and we enjoy more of the *"peaceful fruit of righteousness."* As we face those days of discipline, we can grow in knowing our Father through prayer and seeking Him in His Word. He will instruct us and guide us. We simply must pray and look to Him.

🕮 What the Father takes us through has a purpose and reveals His great care. What truth do you discover in 2 Corinthians 1:3–5?

____

____

____

____

God the Father continually loves us through all the details of life. He is the *"Father of mercies and God of all comfort"* and as such knows how to comfort us, whatever the affliction. The Greek word translated "affliction" is *thlípsis*, which pictures something crushing, pressing, squeezing. It means pressure enough to break us. In the midst of that pressure, God shows mercy and gives His unique comfort, comfort in abundance. As a result we are better able to comfort others in their pressures. These pressures teach us to pray and they show us the value of prayer. (We will see Paul's admonition in 2 Corinthians 1 for believers to pray together in Lesson 11.)

Are you facing pressures or one of those discipline days? Are you aware of how much the Father loves you? Have you been discouraged from praying because your circumstances seem too overwhelming? Every need is a call to prayer. Every worry is like an alarm clock waking us up to pray. Every emptiness we face is a call to seek our Father, longing for His fullness for that need. Pause now and talk to the Father. There is no better time than **now**.

Knowing and Loving the Father

DAY FOUR

PRAYING TO OUR FATHER

One of the first things Jesus taught His disciples concerned prayer to the Father. They had seen a lot of praying in their lives—at the local synagogue every Sabbath, probably at home most days, certainly in Jerusalem at the Temple, especially on Feast days when the crowds were large and the religious leaders made themselves known. What did Jesus say about prayer?

What was Jesus' first counsel concerning prayer in Matthew 6:5? What did He want His disciples to avoid according to Matthew 6:7?

____

____

____

____

____

When Jesus first addressed prayer, He condemned "professional" prayer, prayer prayed by religious men to be seen and heard by other men. Our English translations of the Bible state that Christ called these pretentious leaders "hypocrites," translated from the Greek word *hupokritēs* and used by Christ figuratively to describe actors on a stage. In other words, these men were not genuine and sincere in their orations. These men *"loved to stand and pray"*; they enjoyed praying—as long as it was in the crowded synagogue or on a busy street corner where others could see them. They **wanted to be seen** by others, they **were seen** by others, and that was their full reward. Don't be like them, Jesus said. Neither are we to be like the "Gentiles" (the people who do not know the Father) who use *"meaningless repetition"* in an effort to be heard by their god. The Greek word used here is *battalogéō*, made up of two words *battos,* "stammerer" and *logéō,* "to speak." The word itself sounds like babble—"batta, batta, batta." Jesus said that using many words, or repeated words, or chants, or rote memory,

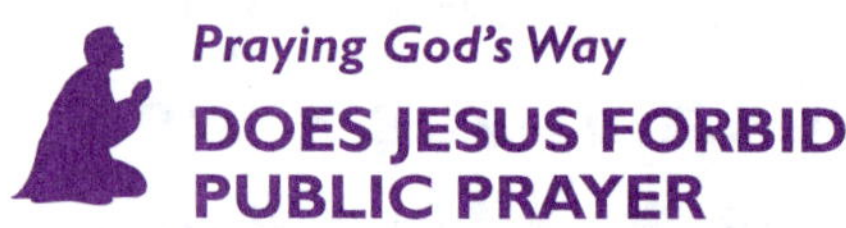

Praying God's Way

DOES JESUS FORBID PUBLIC PRAYER

No, He just forbids "showy" prayer. There are several instances in Scripture of men praying in public to the glory of God—Solomon at the dedication of the Temple (1 Kings 8); Ezra preparing to journey to Israel (Ezra 8:21–23); Nehemiah rebuilding the walls of Jerusalem (Nehemiah 4:9; 8–9); and the saints in Acts in numerous prayer meetings (Acts 1:14, 24–25, 4:24–31). Jesus Himself prayed out loud at times in the presence of His disciples (Matthew 11:25–26).

or anything like that is useless, meaningless, and empty. Don't pray that way.

How is your praying? Is any "show-off" praying going on? What about cold, empty repetition? We can easily fall into this at mealtime prayers, bedtime prayers, public offering prayers, opening and closing prayers at church gatherings, etc. God wants real prayer from a warm heart, praying that thinks about what is being said, that really talks to God as our Father. Pause now and offer a simple, heartfelt prayer to your Father.

🕮 How did Jesus want His disciples to approach prayer? Read Matthew 6:6 and record your insights.

____

____

____

____

First of all, Jesus wanted His disciples to find a place of quiet concentration, a private place. For them in that day, houses had an inner room, a storeroom with a door that could be closed. It was a place where a person could concentrate and talk to his heavenly Father. It would never be a showplace. Jesus focused on the very personal nature of prayer—*"pray to* **your** *Father who is in secret."* Talking to Him is a one-on-one conversation, with *"your* **Father**,*"* one of the closest relationships. The Father also sees in secret. He knows the heart and whether one is talking to Him or to the general public. From that place the Father can hear you clearly, and He will answer.

🕮 Jesus gave His disciples an assurance about their Father in Matthew 6:8. What do you find there?

____

____

____

____

Jesus continually pointed to the personal relationship the Father has with His children—*"***your** *Father."* You belong to Him, and He knows you. Not only does He know each of His children, He also knows *"what you need before you ask Him."* Here is the amazing providence of God; He knows what you need, not only before you ask, but even before you know you have a need. Even before the need exists, He is aware and able to meet the need. We can rest in that assurance as we come to Him in prayer.

Jesus gave His disciples a pattern for prayer in Matthew 6:9–13. We will begin looking at that in Lesson Five, **"Honoring Our Father."** For now we need to look at one other word from Jesus about praying to the Father.

In Matthew 7:1–6, Jesus gave a word about relationships—do not criticize others, but first make sure your own viewpoint is right so that you can honestly help a brother. In trying to help people, you will find some who are not of the same nature as you, not part of the family of God, and not teachable. These are the dogs and hogs, which would not accept a word of correction

ELIJAH'S PRAYER MEETING

Elijah's Prayer Meeting on Mount Carmel had some of everything. The prophets of Baal tried everything to "show-off" to their god, even cutting themselves. They used empty, meaningless repetition over and over again—for about six hours. Then Elijah prayed like he was talking to his Father. He prayed from the heart, to the point, and it took about a minute—then the fire of God fell, revealing the Lord God as the true and living God. The people responded in worship of the true God (1 Kings 18:20–40).

"Pray to your Father who is in secret, and your Father who sees in secret will repay you."

Matthew 6:6b

or exhortation if you gave it. How do we know when to try and help and when not to try? **We must pray**. That is the context of Matthew 7:7–8.

Jesus' purpose in coming to earth was to honor the Father by doing His will, especially seeking and saving the lost. He was sent for that, so the hearts of men and women and their relationships with one another were always on His heart. He knew no man could easily navigate the rivers of relationships without the Father's power and wisdom. So He called His followers to pray.

📖 What are His commands and exhortations in Matthew 7:7–8, and how do you see those verses impacting relationships with others (noting what has been said in 7:1–6)?

____

____

____

____

____

____

____

If we are to live as the Father wants, with a loving heart toward Him and others, we must depend on Him. We show our dependence through prayer. When we have a personal need, Jesus said to keep on asking, seeking, and knocking. When we have a relationship need, the same is true—ask, seek, knock. There is an increased desire with each of these, first asking, then seeking, then knocking. Some needs are met quickly. Some relationships are made right in short order. Others take time, even agonizing periods of lengthy time in prayer. The promise is that those who follow His instruction will receive and find and see doors opened. He makes sure we understand this is not just for some spiritually elite group. Verse 8 says *"**everyone** who asks receives"* (emphasis added), a strong encouragement for any of His followers. If we ask, we will see needs met and relationships mended and strengthened.

Whether dealing with relationships or simply seeking the Father for a personal need, we can ask, seek, and knock with a confidence in our Father. He understands. He cares. He answers.

📖 Looking at Matthew 7:9–11, what encouragement does Jesus give to further emphasize the impact of prayer God's way?

____

____

____

____

Jesus considers a day in the life of an ordinary family. If a son asks his father for a loaf of bread (a small flat baked cake), the father would not give him a stone (like one of the many stones around the Sea of Galilee, the same size, shape, and color of baked bread). The father would not trick his son with that, nor would he give the boy a snake if the boy asked for a fish. Jesus acknowledged the sinfulness of all men, the source of all relationship breakdowns—*"you being evil"*—but He also pointed to the basic instincts of a father, one who knows how to meet the basic needs of his child. Jesus exclaims, *"How much more shall your Father who is in heaven,"* the Father who is perfect in every way, give exactly what is needed to the child who simply asks.

Whether dealing with relationships or simply seeking the Father for a personal need, we can ask, seek, and knock with a confidence in our Father. He understands! He cares! He answers!

Are you trying to meet your own needs apart from the Father? Are you trying to "fix" some broken-down relationships without seeking the Father in prayer? Consider what we have seen today and spend some time in prayer.

Knowing and Loving the Father

DAY FIVE

FOR ME TO PRAY GOD'S WAY

Calling on the name of the Lord is the start of prayer. Knowing and loving the Father is the heart of prayer. As you think back over what you have seen about your relationship with the Father, it is important to ask yourself: *How well do I know God as my Father? If I know Him, am I loving Him with a whole heart and calling on Him as my Father each day. Am I looking to Him to direct my life, my daily decisions, and all my relationships?* As long as we remember that each day is a walk with the Father, we can start the day confident that He already knows what we need and is waiting to interact with us about it. When we recall the immeasurable love of the Father, we can face both the delightful days and the discipline days. Today, we want to make some applications that can help us grow in learning to **pray God's way.**

Pray God's way!

God created us and recreated us in Christ to **know Him and love Him**. Knowing and loving God is at the heart of true prayer. How do we obey and fulfill the greatest commandment to love God with all our hearts, minds, souls, and strength?

📖 Read Mark 12:28–30 thinking about what it means to love God and how loving God should look in your life. Write your insights about the meaning of each and then record how you are doing.

____

____

____

____

____

____

____

What does it mean to love God with all your …

… Heart?—

How are you doing? Check where you are…

Not doing well ◄ 1 2 3 4 5 ► Doing well

… Soul?—

Not doing well ◄ 1 2 3 4 5 ► Doing well

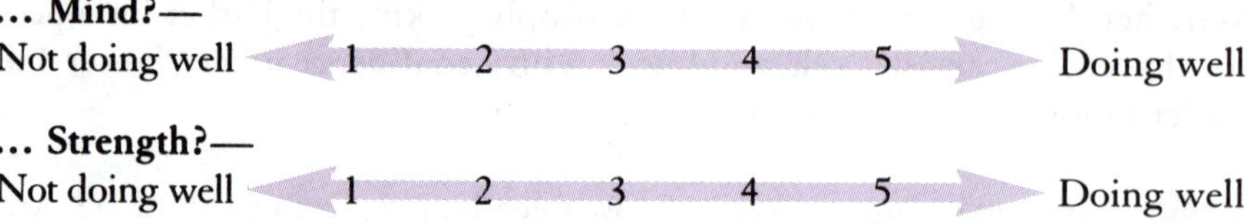

God created us and recreated us in Christ to know Him and love Him.

To love God with all one's **heart** points to one's **DEVOTION** in life, one's passion for Him and His will, for His ways and His desires. If a person loves God with all his or her heart, it will be revealed in the way that person uses time, including time spent with God in His Word and in prayer. It will show up in the way he or she seeks to follow God's heart desires. To love God with all one's **soul** has to do with one's **DIRECTION** in life—one's choices, where one is headed in life, where one's attention is centered and choices are focused. If one's devotion is toward God, one's life direction will follow.

To love God with all one's **mind** focuses on the various **DIMENSIONS** and **DETAILS** of life, the various areas one thinks about. That includes one's life work, but not just his or her occupation. The mind that loves God thinks a lot about one's life assignment from God, the plans and **details** of life viewed **from God's perspective**—What occupies your mind? What do you read? Listen to? Look at? What do you think about often? How do you think and act toward the people God places in your life. To love God with all one's **strength** looks at one's **DAILY USE of TIME** and **ENERGY**—how one carries out the devotion of the heart, the direction of one's choices, and the details of life. Ask yourself . . . *How do I use my time? To what do I devote most of my energies? What activities consume my strength?* The answers to those questions will answer what or whom you love with all your strength, and they reveal the real focus of your heart, your soul, and your mind.

If you know God as your Father, that means you personally know Jesus as your Lord and Savior and the Holy Spirit as your constant companion, encourager, and guide. It is vitally important to know what part the Spirit plays in helping us **know the Father** and **pray to the Father.** It is vital to see how that applies to our daily lives.

📖 Read Romans 8:26–28 and write your insights, recalling what we have already seen in Romans 8:14–16.

____

____

____

____

Not only does the Spirit assure us that we are children of God, He also guides us in righteous living, that is, in the good works He wants us doing (see Ephesians 2:10). He also helps us in prayer. One of the most extensive works of the Spirit is in prayer. Paul states, *"the Spirit also helps our weakness."* What weakness? He goes on to tell us, *"for we do* **not know how to pray** *as we should."* It is vital to know that **the Holy Spirit** is always our Helper and **we** are always weak and ignorant in prayer. The Greek word translated "helps" in verse 26 paints a very encouraging picture. It is the word *sunantilambánomai*, a long Greek word with incredible encouragement in prayer. It could literally be rendered—"together facing one another he takes hold of"—It was used of two men picking up a log and moving it, something one man alone could not do. Anyone alone would need help, but together, facing one another, two men could take hold of the log and move it. That is what the Holy Spirit does for us in prayer.

We cannot handle all the burdens we face. We do not know how to pray when we face them. We need **help**. The Holy Spirit knows how to help **and** how to pray. Paul goes on to say, *"but the Spirit Himself intercedes for us."* He intercedes for us in ways we cannot understand. Like the Lord Jesus who also intercedes for us (Romans 8:34; Hebrews 7:24–26), the Spirit is showing His care. We can be sure that His intercession is effective, because the Father who continually searches every heart *"knows what the mind of the Spirit is."* He is working all things together in line with His will, His purposes, and the Spirit's insightful intercession. Furthermore, the Spirit is interceding *"for the saints according to the will of God"*—in line with the plans and purposes of God. Here we see yet another way in which God is caring for His children in every detail throughout our journey with Him. We can pray with confidence **in Him,** admitting our weakness at the same time.

INTERCEDES

Romans 8:26 tells us, *"the Spirit Himself intercedes for us."* The word translated "intercedes" is *huperentugchánō*, which is made up of two words, *huper* which gives the idea of "for" or "on behalf of" and *entugchánō*, which means "to make intercession." Its fuller meaning is "to fall in with a person or to turn to or meet with a person, to come with free access on behalf of another or to interrupt someone in speaking for the purpose of making a request for another." It means to make intercession for someone or to entreat on behalf of another, pictured especially in *huperentugchánō*. Romans 8:27 speaks of this intercession using *entugchánō* as does Romans 8:34, which encourages us with the fact that Jesus Himself intercedes for us at the right hand of God the Father.

As you spend time in prayer, you will grow in your knowledge of and love for the Father. There are many areas that can be corrected or changed to help you in your praying. Look at the list below and check the things that are sometimes a hindrance to you **in prayer** or **in setting aside time** to pray.

❐ Not sure what to say/pray ❐ Too sleepy in the morning

❐ Too tired at night ❐ Sleeping too late

❐ Going to bed too late ❐ Battling bad thoughts when I try to pray

❐ No Bible time scheduled ❐ No prayer time scheduled

❐ Too much TV ❐ I fall asleep praying

❐ Too many outside activities ❐ Too much listening to Music

❐ Feeling guilty all the time ❐ My mind easily wanders

❐ Too involved in sports . . . hobbies . . .

❐ Too involved in my job ❐ I don't strongly sense the need to pray

❐ I have everything I need. Why pray?

❐ I'm just too busy

What's your biggest hindrance? ______________________________
The best thing to do is take at least one step, trusting the Holy Spirit to help you in prayer. What is one thing (or even two things) you could do differently this week?

____

____

____

____

____

Doctrine
HEART SEARCHER

Romans 8:27 speaks about *"He who searches the hearts,"* referring to God the Father. The word for "search" is *ereunáō,* which means to search, explore, or track, indicating the detail with which God searches. The LORD told Samuel as he was looking for God's choice for king, *"Do not look at his appearance or at the height of his stature, . . . for God sees not as man sees, for man looks at the outward appearance, but the LORD looks at the heart"* (1 Samuel 16:7). David told his son Solomon, *"Know the God of your father, and serve Him with a whole heart and a willing mind; for the LORD searches all hearts, and understands every intent of the thoughts"* (1 Chronicles 28:9). Solomon declared in his prayer in 1 Kings 8:39, *"For Thou alone dost know the hearts of all the sons of men."* Jesus told the Pharisees, *"God knows your hearts"* (Luke 16:15). When seeking God about Judas' replacement, Peter prayed, *"Thou, Lord, who knowest the hearts of all men, show which one . . . Thou hast chosen."* (Acts 1:24) Finally, Jesus declared in Revelation 2:23, *"I am He who searches the minds and hearts"* (ereunáō). (See also Psalm 139.)

Everyone needs a PLACE for prayer, a TIME for prayer, and a BIBLICAL PATTERN to follow in prayer.

Here are some suggestions based on what Jesus taught His disciples.

Set aside a **PLACE** where you can meet with God, a place where you can be undistracted and focus on talking and listening to your Father.

BEST PLACE ______________________

Set aside a **TIME** when you can pray, a time when you will be alert and uninterrupted. Make sure it is enough time.

BEST TIME ______________________

Follow a **BIBLICAL PATTERN** in time with the Lord. There is no set way to spend time with the Father, but there are some basic elements that should be in your prayer time. Remember, this is a relationship of following Him, and that requires some form and some flexibility. Here are some thoughts for your pattern. Follow the pattern of **the Lord's Prayer** in Matthew 6:9–13. (We will see more about this pattern in the upcoming Lessons.) There are **Five Basics in Prayer** based on principles drawn from the Lord's Prayer that may be of help. Read through these as a possible guideline for time with the Father.

WORSHIP—Love and worship go together. If we love the Lord, we will surrender to Him and His will. Surrender to the Lord each day; spend time in praise and thanksgiving; die to self, deal with any unconfessed sin, and yield to the control of His Spirit.

WORD—Spend time in His Word. There God shows us His will. Purpose to obey what He says and pray for yourself, your family, and others using the Word of God.

WITNESS—Pray about your witness today to your family, your neighbors, your work or school associates, and any "divine appointments" God gives you.

WORK—Pray about your work (the job God has given you along with finances and provision) as well as your work in the Body of Christ, the ministry area in which God has placed you.

WAR—Submit to God, **reckoning** yourself dead to sin and self, **counting** yourself dead to the world, and **resisting** the devil.

We have seen a lot in this lesson about knowing, loving, and praying to the Father. Let's close our time with prayer.

Lord, I thank You for being a Father, for being my Father who loves me so much. I gladly admit I need You to counsel and guide me. I need Your provisions. I need You! Thank You for the work You do in guiding my way, in disciplining and training me, in continually working in my life showing me how to treat my brothers and sisters in the family of God. Thank You for stretching me, even when I don't feel like being stretched, for revealing my weaknesses when I would rather not think of those, and for reminding me of your unconditional, unchanging love for me. Thank You for Your purposes in my life—they are so much better than anything I could have thought of on my own. Thank You, Father, for drawing me to Your Son, calling me to turn to Him, and bringing me into the family of God. I praise and bless You for Your goodness and kindness to me, for answering so many prayers, and for being patient with me in my prayerlessness. I love You. May I be more consistent in loving You and in joining You in Your eternal work, rather than trying to get You to join me in the temporary plans I may want. May I honor You and Your Son and bring You the glory You deserve by my walk and my talk. In Jesus' name, Amen.

Record a journal entry or write your own prayer in the space provided.

Notes

3

THE NECESSITY OF HUMILITY

OVERCOMING PRIDE AND WALKING IN THE FEAR OF THE LORD

We start the Christian life calling on the name of the Lord, realizing our desperate need for forgiveness and for freedom from the penalty and power of our sin. We enter into a life of calling on Him, discovering how much we are loved by Him as our Father and how many ways He is at work bringing us to full maturity as sons and daughters. The work He is doing focuses on training us to depend on Him, to walk by faith, trusting Him. As we walk with Him, we discover there is some opposition, a war is going on—with the world and its anti-God ways, with the devil and his deceptions, and even with ourselves, our "flesh" and its self-centered, self-pleasing, self-exalting focus. The taproot of each of these enemies is fed by the river of pride, exalting "I," "me," "my," and "mine." God never bows to pride. He hates it in all its manifestations and fights it wherever it shows up, especially in His children. If we are to pray God's way, we must understand the problem of pride and the necessity of humility.

If we are to pray God's way, we must understand the problem of pride and the necessity of humility.

Pride comes in many forms, all of which stop true prayer. Focusing on ourselves rather than God stops effective prayer. Focusing on others—whether downgrading them (in bitterness or envy) or exalting them (seeking man's approval)—short-circuits effective prayer. Focusing on circumstances rather than on the Lord over circumstances detours our prayers away from heaven back to the circumstances. Looking only at our requests instead of the God who answers requests, not only fails to find answers for those requests, but can also overwhelm us, even cause us to stop praying. Two common elements in each of these failures in prayer are the absence of true humility and the presence of self-centered pride.

How can we overcome the problems of pride and walk in the humility to which God calls us? **Prayer God's way** will always be marked by humility, admitting needs, acknowledging that we cannot meet the needs, and agreeing that God alone can answer and meet the needs, in the right way and the right time. Let's see how we can walk in humility and overcome prayer-killing pride.

DAY ONE

"HEAVEN, WE HAVE A PROBLEM!"

The Apollo 13 mission to the moon made famous one simple sentence, "Houston, we have a problem." The mission was in danger, but even more, the lives of those men were in jeopardy. Because of a mechanical failure, they could not complete their mission to the moon and almost did not make it back home again. As Christians, we might proclaim, "Heaven, we have a problem." We have a problem completing our mission, especially when it comes to effective prayer. One of the first things we must ask is, "Why do so few people pray the way God wants, even in churches, even on Sundays?" Humbly admitting our needs, seeking to quickly get things right in confession of sin, making things right with others, and giving heartfelt praise and thanksgiving all seem to be rare in many Christians' lives. I have seen this lack of humility in my own life at times. What is the problem? Scripture shines its searchlight, and we see it: **the problem of pride**. Pride has to be dealt with, if we are to truly pray God's way. What can we learn about pride as it relates to our study on prayer?

Pride divides and destroys relationships. Jesus understood that and told a parable to demonstrate the danger of pride. In teaching this, He also revealed some things about the problem of pride in prayer.

📖 Read Luke 18:9–14. What is the focus of the Pharisee according to verses 11–12?

____

____

____

____

Did You Know?

TIMES TO PRAY

Most likely the Pharisee and the tax-gatherer went up to the Temple to pray at one of the two daily times for prayer there. People gathered for prayer at 9:00 A.M. and 3:00 P.M., the times of the morning and evening sacrifices, which included the offering of incense, a picture of offering up prayer to the Lord.

A Pharisee went to the Temple to pray. His focus however was more on himself than on God. He stood thinking of himself, thankful for himself, comparing himself with others, exalting himself over others, giving himself points for all his meticulous goodness—fasting twice a week (Monday and Thursday) and paying tithes of *"all that I get,"* not just money, but even things like *"mint and rue and every kind of garden herb"* (see Luke 11:42). The only fast that was required under the Law was the annual Day of Atonement. All these other fasts observed by the Pharisees were added for their own vainglory. Pride likes to add up points and compare, so it can exalt self and think of and thank self.

What was the Pharisee's standard of measurement?

____

____

The Pharisee compared himself with others, but note, not just any "others." He chose those who were *"swindlers, unjust, adulterers,"* or men like *"this tax-gatherer"* standing near him. His standard was not the perfect and holy Lord God of Israel, who cannot lie, who can never break a covenant, nor steal, nor be deceptive. His standard was society's dregs; an easy standard to beat. Pride likes to compare itself so that it gets a hands-down victory.

📖 Look at Luke 18:9? What characteristics are given describing the Pharisee and those like him?

____

____

____

____

Jesus knew in His heart that those around Him were trusting in themselves and their works—righteousness based on their own man-made standards. The word translated *"trusted"* literally means "standing in a fully-persuaded stance." They had absolutely convinced themselves that they were righteous—they met the standard and more. Their self-righteousness came out of their pride and arrogance—that puffed up sense of importance and near perfection. As a result they continually *"viewed others with contempt,"* valuing others and showing kindness and care.

📖 Look at verse 13. Where was the tax-gatherer focused? What did the tax-gatherer say about himself in that verse? What else do you see about this man?

____

____

____

____

____

____

Even though the tax-gatherer would not lift his eyes to heaven, his focus was there. He was looking to God, and in the light of what he knew, the tax-gatherer saw himself as *"the sinner,"* greatly in need of the mercy and forgiveness of God. Even his place at the Temple speaks of his heart condition; he was *"standing some distance away,"* within the Temple area but probably on the outskirts of the court of Israel, where the Jewish men would be. There he stood, beating his breast—a sign of his grief and sorrow over the sinfulness of his heart. In that condition, he prayed for God to be merciful and to forgive him.

📖 What did Jesus say about each of these two men in verse 14?

____

____

____

Word Study

BE MERCIFUL

In the prayer of the tax-gatherer, *"God, be merciful to me, the sinner!"* the phrase *"be merciful"* is a translation of the Greek word *hiláskomai,* meaning "to be propitiated, to be shown kindness, mercy, and grace in the full payment and forgiveness of sins." In Hebrews 2:17, we see Christ Himself as the High Priest offering the sacrifice *"to make propitiation for the sins of the people."* He offered Himself as the sacrifice according to I John 2:2. The word propitiation means, "to satisfy," which refers to satisfying the just demands of God against sin. By His death, Jesus satisfied God's justice and provided forgiveness. (See also Romans 3:25; I John 4:10.) The tax-gatherer was pleading with God, acknowledging his sinful, undeserving state. He knew that God alone could forgive and cleanse and change him. That is what he cried out for.

Jesus forcefully declared that the tax-gatherer went to his home "justified," declared righteous, in the right, by God Himself, but the Pharisee went home the same way he came to the Temple, unrighteous in the sight of God.

What was at the heart of Jesus' evaluation? How do you see that in His response to the heart of each man?

____

____

____

____

"GOD IS OPPOSED TO THE PROUD, BUT GIVES GRACE TO THE HUMBLE."

I Peter 5:5c

At the heart of Jesus' evaluation was the heart of each man—one man's heart was full of pride, and the other willingly humbled himself before God. To Jesus, the essential element was **humility** before God. The tax-gatherer humbled himself before God, honestly admitting who he was, where he was wrong, and why he needed the forgiveness of God. His sin had offended the Righteous One of Israel, and God alone could forgive him. Seeking forgiveness was this man's focus. As a result of humbling himself, God graciously forgave and accepted him, exalting him to a place of fellowship with Himself, of right standing before Him. Pride, on the other hand, merits God's judgment. God is opposed to the proud (see 1 Peter 5:5).

APPLY The problem of pride will shut down your prayer life as quick as anything, Not only that, you may find yourself in a battle with God. Why? Because He knows pride is based in lies and He stands for the truth. He will deal with His proud children to bring them back to humility and fellowship. Where are you right now? You can be a recipient of grace now if you will walk in humility. Your prayer life will take on a whole new life.

The Necessity of Humility

DAY TWO

MOVING FROM PRIDE TO HUMILITY

Jesus presented a very clear picture of pride versus humility in the parable of the Pharisee and the tax-gatherer, pointing us to the problem of pride as well as the honor of humility. It is important that we see the fuller picture painted in Scripture so that we can move beyond the problem of pride to the true prayer that flows from a humble heart. We will see this transition from pride to humility today in the pages of the Old Testament, a picture that reveals not only the path of pride but also the reality of prayer that occurs when God has dealt with that pride. Let me introduce you to a man who struggled greatly with the problem of pride and the perils that often go along with it. This man was the ancient king, Nebuchadnezzar.

Read Daniel chapter 4:1–37 to get the full picture of what is going on. Then answer the questions below concerning this passage of Scripture.

Who does Nebuchadnezzar exalt in Daniel 4:2? What does he recognize about this God in verse 3?

____

____

Nebuchadnezzar, king of the Babylonian Empire, exalts the Most High God, declaring His signs and wonders. Nebuchadnezzar recognizes that God's signs and wonders are indeed great and mighty. Unlike earthly kingdoms and empires, the kingdom of the Most High God lasts forever, and His reign goes beyond one or two generations to include all generations.

What led Nebuchadnezzar to glorify God in such endearing fashion? He didn't come to this conclusion overnight but became painfully aware of God's power and majesty through a series of missteps and their dire consequences. Summarize what you find about Nebuchadnezzar and the events surrounding him in Daniel 4:4–33.

In Daniel 4, Nebuchadnezzar relates in retrospect the unfortunate events that prevented him from governing the Babylonian Empire for a period of seven years. As the king admits in this chapter, it was his own pride that got in the way of his relationship with God and brought his reign to an unceremonious seven-year hiatus. However, after this period of seven years, Nebuchadnezzar repented of his pride and arrogance and was restored to his kingdom.

As Nebuchadnezzar relates, everything had been going well for him prior to his misfortunes—he was *"at ease"* in his house *"and flourishing in* [his] *palace."* One day, God gave him a dream, a vision of a great tree prospering with abundant leaves and fruit, filled with the birds of the air and giving shade to the beasts of the field. This was a picture of Nebuchadnezzar and his influence in the world, something of which he was very proud. In this vision, the Most High God issues a decree to cut the tree but leave the roots. Daniel interpreted the dream as such—Nebuchadnezzar would be cut down from his throne and roam in the fields like a beast for seven years. Yet God's judgment upon Nebuchadnezzar was not enacted for another twelve months. During these months, Nebuchadnezzar had apparently dismissed Daniel's interpretation of the vision. On one particular occasion, he began to extol the greatnesses of his kingdom, his palace, his ability, his power, and majesty. Suddenly, a voice came out of heaven, and Nebuchadnezzar was whisked away from his lofty position and placed in the fields—to live like an animal until his hair grew like eagle's feathers and his nails like long bird claws.

📖 List the specific sins that were the fruit of Nebuchadnezzar's proud heart according to Daniel 4:27? What do you hear coming from Nebuchadnezzar's heart in verses 28–30?

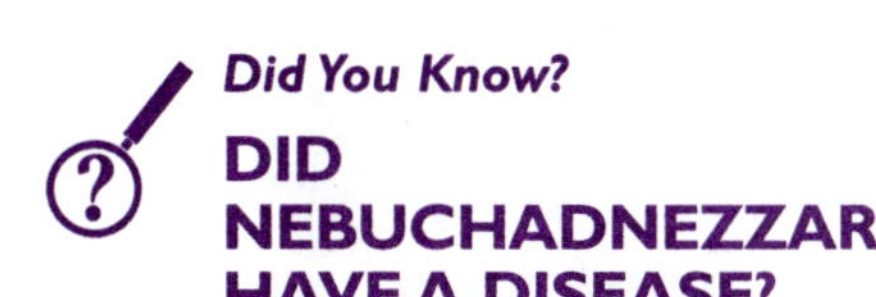

Did You Know?

DID NEBUCHADNEZZAR HAVE A DISEASE?

Some see in the description of the conditions under which Nebuchadnezzar lived for seven years as the symptoms of a disease known as *boanthropy*, a type of monomania. The person thinks of himself as an ox and acts in that manner, including eating grass and drinking rainwater. Historical records that allude to this incident include the writings of Berossus, a Babylonian priest around the third century B.C., Abydenus, a writer in the second century B.C., and Josephus, the Jewish historian of the first century A.D. We are not sure what his illness was, only that God used it to get his attention and that Nebuchadnezzar responded rightly. God honored him and restored him to full health and service.

Nebuchadnezzar was proud, and in that pride he committed acts of unrighteousness. It appears, from what Daniel advised in verse 27, that Nebuchadnezzar was ruthless in his rule, showing no mercy to the poor. It is likely that he practiced certain injustices and maintained a heavy hand, making sure he got what he wanted when he wanted it—marks of a man filled with pride. He was certainly marked by self-will and self-glory. Such a focus on self is seen in his pompous statements: *"I myself have built"* . . . *"my power"* . . . *"my majesty"*—clear marks of unchecked pride.

Look at God's decree in verses 31–33 and the results in verses 34–35. What occurred in Nebuchadnezzar's heart according to Daniel 4:34–35?

____

____

____

____

____

Nebuchadnezzar lifted his *"eyes toward heaven"* and recognized that the Most High is indeed ruler over the world. Evidently, Nebuchadnezzar had turned from his sins, as we see in his testimony from this chapter that he now desired to follow the true God. He blesses God in this chapter, giving Him praise and honor as the eternal ruler over an everlasting kingdom. The king saw himself as a mere man under this sovereign Lord. The Most High does as He pleases on the earth, and there is no one who can stop Him from accomplishing His purposes.

Read verse 36 and record what occurred in Nebuchadnezzar's relationships with others?

____

____

____

When the king's reason returned to him, his *"majesty and splendor were restored"* to him. His counselors and nobles recognized his healing and began seeking his counsel and leadership. He was reestablished as king and highly honored, being given *"surpassing greatness."* Where once he was ignored as a madman, now he was given a majestic welcome.

Are you giving praise, honor, and thanksgiving to your heavenly Father, or are you stifled by your pride and focused more on yourself?

📖 What insights do you glean from Daniel 4:37?

____

____

____

____

Now that Nebuchadnezzar has been restored to his position of power and majesty, he no longer focuses on himself. He focuses his attention and his praise on the Most High God—*"I . . . praise, exalt, and honor the King of heaven."* Daniel reasoned earlier that the purpose of the tragic events in the king's life was so that Nebuchadnezzar would *"recognize that it is Heaven that rules"* (4:26). The king now chose to exalt the King of heaven, the Most High God.

He praises God that *"all His works are true and His ways just,"* something he had failed to do before his seven-year exile. Now, Nebuchadnezzar recognizes God's righteous reign and doubtless begins to rule that way as well. In his statement, *"He is able to humble those who walk in pride,"* Nebuchadnezzar gives testimony to what God had done in his own life. Pride in himself turned to humility before the Most High God. Self-rule had became surrender to God. Nebuchadnezzar's mind was focused on God after the Lord dealt with his pride, and his heart expressed the humble praise that filled it. Now, the palace halls were full of honor, glory, and thanksgiving to the Lord.

Does true prayer mark your life? Are you giving praise, honor, and thanksgiving to your heavenly Father, or are you stifled by your pride and focused more on yourself? Humility recognizes God, honors Him, and thanks Him for His good works, for His many gifts, even for the simple things of everyday life. Pause now and spend some time in prayer, in thanks, and in praise to your Father.

The Necessity of Humility

DAY THREE

God's Response to Humility

We have already seen how God heard the tax-gatherer who humbled himself in prayer but would not hear the proud Pharisee. If pride shuts down our prayer lives and humility opens the heart of God to hear, it is vital that we understand the difference and know how to avoid pride and embrace humility. We must realize that it is an honor to be heard by God—the Majestic and Almighty Lord of heaven and earth, the God who rules over all, who needs nothing and gives everything. He is ready to hear us pray, if we will pray His way, in tune with His heart.

In one of the more familiar verses of Scripture, God addresses the issue of humility and prayer. Let's go back in history and see what God said. In 960 B.C., Solomon finished the Temple, the place of prayer and the place God chose to dwell with His people Israel. After Solomon dedicated the Temple, the Lord came to Solomon at night and spoke to him, giving him both warnings and promises.

"If My people who are called by My name will humble themselves and pray and seek My face, and turn from their wicked ways, then I will hear from heaven, and will forgive their sin and heal their land."

2 Chronicles 7:14 (NKJV)

Read what God said in 2 Chronicles 7:11–14. What does God command in verse 14 concerning those times when He must deal severely with His people? (Note what comes first.)

____

____

____

____

____

When God sends no rain or commands a plague of locusts or a pestilence (or any other judgment or crisis), if the people will first humble themselves, He promises to be open to hear their prayer. The implication is that if one or all comes with a proud heart, a blame-somebody-else heart, or an unsurrendered heart, then God will not listen. People must **first humble** themselves and **then pray** and seek His face and turn from their wicked ways.

Each of those conditions is significant—humility **admits** its need while prayer **voices** the need. Seeking God's face means calling on Him to turn back. The fact that we are seeking His face assumes that He has turned His face from us in judgment rather than shining His face upon us in blessing. This is why we as God's people must turn from the wickedness that has brought disciplinary judgment. We must repent—change our minds, hearts, and opinions from wickedness to righteousness and totally agree with God about our sin—and even agree that God was just in sending the judgments in the first place.

It is important to see how this process of seeking God was carried out in the lives of the people of God. One of the most graphic displays of both pride and humility is seen in a series of events in the life of Hezekiah. In 701 B.C., Sennacherib, the proud king of Assyria, invaded Judah and conquered several cities including Lachish, south of Jerusalem. He then sent his field commander (Rabshakeh was an officer's title) and a band of soldiers to Jerusalem to deliver a threatening message to the people of Judah and to humiliate King Hezekiah.

Did You Know?

SENNACHERIB'S THREAT

The Assyrian army was no idle threat to King Hezekiah and to the citizens of Judah. History shows that Assyria conquered many cities and kingdoms in the tenth, ninth, and eighth centuries B.C. Tiglath-pilesar III (2 Kings 15:29; 16:7–10), also known as Pul (2 Kings 15:19; 1 Chronicles 5:26), ruled Assyria from 745 to 727 B.C. and collected tribute from several cities and regions, including Samaria in northern Israel (2 Kings 15:19–20). Judah's King Ahaz, the father of Hezekiah, paid tribute to Tiglath-pilesar III (2 Chronicles 28:19–21). In 732 B.C., Assyria conquered Damascus, Syria (2 Kings 15:30). Shalmaneser V continued a war-like rule from 727 to 722, besieging and overrunning Samaria in 722 B.C., taking captives into the area of the Euphrates and into Media (2 Kings 17:6). Under Sargon II (722–705) and his successors, the Assyrian empire reached its greatest extent. Sennacherib came to power in 705 and defeated many, including the Babylonians. In 701, he conquered several cities of Judah, including Lachish (2 Kings 18:13–14). Hezekiah paid tribute to him. When Sennacherib threatened Jerusalem, the Lord dealt a deathblow to his troops, and the defeated king returned home. He was slain by his sons in 681 B.C.

Read Isaiah 36 and 37:1–4. What was Hezekiah's response to the threats of Assyria? How did Isaiah respond (37:5–7)?

____

____

____

____

____

After hearing of the many proud threats by the Assyrian officials and of how Assyria had conquered so many other cities and nations, Hezekiah tore his clothes in an expression of grief and humility and went to the house of the Lord, the Temple, to seek the Lord. Then he sent his officials to the prophet Isaiah, asking him to pray and seek the Lord, admitting his own weakness and desiring that the Lord would respond to the Assyrians. The Lord spoke through Isaiah, *"Do not be afraid,"* and promised that Sennacherib would be defeated.

Meanwhile, Rabshakeh and his entourage returned to King Sennacherib to report on Judah's refusal to surrender to foreign control. The Assyrian king promptly sent messengers back to Hezekiah with a curtly-worded letter (37:8–13). This letter apparently was Sennacherib's final warning to Hezekiah not to depend on Jehovah for deliverance but to comply with the demand for total surrender. What did Hezekiah do when he received the letter according to Isaiah 37:14? What do you see about Hezekiah in his prayer in verses 15–20?

____

____

____

____

____

Hezekiah's first response was to take the letter to the Temple and spread it out before the Lord. He began praying to the Lord, acknowledging Him as Lord, as the only God over all the kingdoms of the earth. As creator of heaven and earth, He is owner of heaven and earth. Hezekiah asked God to hear and see all that Sennacherib had said and done. The king agreed that the Assyrians had indeed conquered many nations and burned their gods—but those gods were lifeless idols, and Israel's God was the true and living God. He prayed that God would deliver Jerusalem and thus reveal Himself as God, *"that all the kingdoms of the earth may know that Thou alone, LORD, art God."*

Did You Know?

THE ANGEL OF THE LORD

The Angel of the LORD spoken of in Isaiah 37:36 refers to God Himself, a pre-incarnate manifestation of the Lord Jesus. He is also spoken of as appearing in the burning bush in Exodus 3:2–6 as well as in Genesis 16:7; 21:17; 22:11, 15; 18:1—19:1; 32:24–30 Exodus 14:19; 23:20–23; Numbers 20:16; 22:22; Deuteronomy 33:16; Joshua 5:14; 6:2; Judges 2:1–5; 6:11–14; 13; I Chronicles 21:15–30; Isaiah 63:9 and other verses.

📖 How did the Lord respond to Hezekiah as recorded in Isaiah 37:21? (The word of the Lord is found in verses 22–35.) What specific promise do you see in verses 33–35, and what action did the Lord take in verse 36?

____

____

____

____

____

____

____

God honored and rescued Hezekiah and the people of Jerusalem. Why did God do this? Isaiah 37:21 says, **"because you have prayed to Me."** God promised that the king of Assyria would not so much as shoot an arrow in Jerusalem nor build a siege mound against it. Sennacherib would return to his own land. God Himself promised to defend Jerusalem for His own sake and the sake of His promises to David. Isaiah 37:36 tells us that *"the Angel of the Lord"* (God Himself), struck 185,000 troops in the Assyrian camp. Sennacherib went home a defeated king and was slain there by his two sons in the temple of the god Nisroch.

"If My people who are called by My name will humble themselves and pray and seek My face, and turn from their wicked ways, then I will hear from heaven, and will forgive their sin and heal their land."

2 Chronicles 7:14 (NKJV)

Hezekiah recognized his need and recognized that God alone could meet the need. This sober recognition is one of the clearest marks of humility. Humility is also one of the traits of one who walks in the fear of the Lord.

Proverbs 22:4 links **humility** and **the fear of the Lord,** noting the reward of *"riches, honor, and life."* Such an indelible link was certainly true in the life of Hezekiah (see 2 Chronicles 32:26–33). What other truths can we learn about walking in the fear of the Lord? What does God say?

📖 Look at these verses on the fear of the Lord and note **what marks** one who walks this way.

Exodus 20:20

____

____

____

Proverbs 1:7

____

____

____

Proverbs 3:7

____

____

____

Proverbs 8:13

____

____

Proverbs 9:10

____

____

____

"The fear of the Lord is the instruction for wisdom, and before honor comes humility."

Proverbs 15:33

One who walks in the fear of the Lord lays a foundation for understanding life and walking in wisdom. The fear of the Lord is the first thing one should learn; it is the *"beginning of knowledge,"* giving one an openness to learn and grow in wisdom. One who fears the Lord has a teachable, humble heart to receive instruction. Without a humble heart, one can easily become a fool, whether "educated" or not. The foolish man thinks he already knows all he needs to know. The wise man's education begins in knowing *"the Holy One,"* who is the source of all wisdom and insight. One walking in the fear of the Lord hates evil and all that goes with it—pride, arrogance, an evil lifestyle, and a perverted, twisted mouth usually marked by lies and deceit. Like the children of Israel who saw God at Mount Sinai, we too can see God for who He is and recognize our humanity and frailty, as well as our accountability to Him. Knowing our weaknesses is a deterrent to sin and an encouragement to a humble, obedient walk.

What is God's response or reward to one who walks in the fear of the Lord? Look at these verses on the fear of the Lord and record what you discover?

Psalm 33:18

____

____

____

Psalm 34:7, 9

____

____

____

Psalm 103:11, 13

____

____

____

Extra Mile

THE FEAR OF THE LORD

Read these other verses on the fear of the Lord and see what applications God has for your life—Genesis 22:12; Exodus 18:21; Leviticus 25:17; Deuteronomy 4:10; 5:29; 6:2, 13, 24; 10:12, 20; 13:4; 17:19; 31:12–13; I Samuel 12:24; I Kings 8:43; 2 Chronicles 19:6–10, Psalm 19:9; 25:14; 67:7; 111:5, 10; 119:38; 147:11; Proverbs 10:27; 15:16; 16:6; 19:23; 23:17; 24:21; 29:25; Ecclesiastes 3:14; 8:12; 12:13; Matthew 10:28; Acts 9:31; 2 Corinthians 5:11; 7:1; Ephesians 5:21; I Peter 1:17; 2:17; Revelation 14:7; 19:5.

Psalm 145:17–21

____

____

____

Proverbs 14:26–27

____

____

____

Extra Mile

PSALM 25

Read Psalm 25 and look at the focus of David, especially in verses 1–3. What confidence does David have for those who are humble, who walk in the fear of the Lord?

The Lord is ever watchful over those who follow Him, who desire to walk in humble obedience. He rescues them in times of trouble (sometimes taking them **through** the difficulty rather than removing them **from** it). He continually shows His lovingkindness, mercy, and compassion like a father to a loving child. He is near to them, hears their cry and saves them. Those who walk in the fear of the Lord grow in their confidence in Him and His ways, knowing His will is always best and His character always trustworthy. Following God brings life and rescues from death. Those who fear the Lord experience Him as a fountain of life.

Stop and think about what we have seen today—God's response to humility. Are you battling with some area of pride? Where there is sin, are you contrite and bowing before the Lord in repentance? Ask God to show you any area where you should confess and turn from sin, calling on Him with a humble heart. Ask Him to reveal any point of pride as you humble yourself before Him.

How can we walk in humility and in the fear of the Lord? How does God bring us to that stance? We will see in Day Four.

The Necessity of Humility

DAY FOUR

God's Recipe for Humility

What is God's "recipe" for humility? How does He help us turn around and face our pride so that we can face Him with a humble heart? Recall that we are not alone in this endeavor. God sent His Son to give His life **for us** so He could place His life **in us**—by His Spirit. The Holy Spirit has been sent to work in us and bring us to Christlikeness—to walk as Christ walked, to actually empower us to do what we could never do apart from Him. The Holy Spirit takes the things of Jesus and teaches them to us, showing us who He is in ever-greater depths. He guides us in walking in the fear of the Lord, which is the foundation for a walk of humility. How can we cooperate with Him? How can we follow God's recipe for humility?

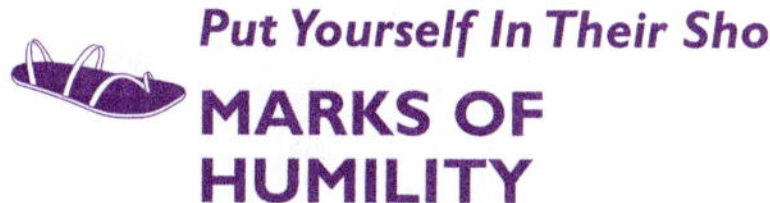

Put Yourself In Their Shoes

MARKS OF HUMILITY

- admits one's need
- admits one cannot meet the need
- acknowledges God can meet the need
- asks God to meet the need
- always trusts God with the way in which He decides to meet the need, including His timing

A Definition First. The basic word for humility in the Old Testament is *anah* (Hebrew), which means to be bowed down. In the New Testament, the Greek word *tapeinos* means "low-lying." To make oneself humble means, "to make low." The word translated pride or proud in the Old Testament often can literally be translated "lifted up" (Deuteronomy 8:14) or "high" (used in one incident in Hezekiah's life in 2 Chronicles 32:25). The contrast to pride, then, is bowing down or making oneself low. To walk in humility is to take our proper place, not exalting ourselves, but honoring God in His place as God.

📖 We have seen in our look at Nebuchadnezzar (Day Two) that God often must get our attention to show us any area of pride. Look at James 4:6 and note what God does when He sees pride in His children.

____

____

____

____

James tells us, *"God is opposed to the proud."* Does that mean He simply does not like attitudes and actions of pride, or is there more involved here? There is a distinct word picture in this statement by James. The word "*opposed*" is a translation of the Greek word *antitássō*, which means "to stand against" or "to place oneself against." God places Himself against the proud person. *Antitássō* is used of setting an army in battle array to fight against a foe. God fights against us when we are proud. Pride is a lie, and He who is the Truth always stands against lies, especially in His children.

What is the pattern God follows in dealing with pride or in training us to watch out for pride? First Corinthians 10:11 tells us the incidents in the Old Testament were written for our instruction. God gave us pictures to explain His character and His ways and to guide us in right living. One of those pictures is the wilderness experience in Moses' day.

📖 Read Deuteronomy 8:1–6. What did God focus on, especially in verses 2 and 3? What reason did God give for His actions?

____

____

____

____

____

____

____

God purposely led the children of Israel into the wilderness, into places without food or water so that they would discover Him as their provider—giving manna in a supernatural way and providing water in a desert land. During the forty years, God led them in paths of need to humble them and to test them at those points of need to see clearly what was in their hearts. Would they trust Him and obey what He said or grumble about His way and try to go their own way? He wanted them to see and reverence Him as a faithful Father. He wanted them to know firsthand that whatever He said always led to the fullness of life. Bread alone could never fully satisfy, because man is more than a physical creation. Human beings are meant to live a life full of the life of God—relating to Him in all things, depending on Him in every circumstance, being governed by Him and His Word in every relationship and experiencing Him day by day.

📖 Now look at Deuteronomy 8:7–20, especially verses 11, 14, and 17. About what does the Lord warn the children of Israel in the wilderness?

____

____

____

Humility looks like weakness but is really strength. Pride looks like strength but is really weakness.

God tells His people in this passage that He would soon bring them to the bountiful land and the blessings He had promised them. Though God wanted Israel to experience the blessings of this promised land, He did not want them to become complacent and to take these blessings for granted. He commanded them, "beware," or to be on guard, never forget who the Lord is or what He has said. Once they experienced the abundance the Lord had promised, once they had *"eaten and* [were] *satisfied,"* they would move one step closer to arrogance. He cautions them not to allow their hearts to become proud (literally, *"your heart becomes lifted up"*), self-exalted, as though their skills, their wisdom, or their abilities had reaped for them bountiful dividends. God brought them out of Egyptian slavery into promised land satisfaction. They were instructed to never forget that.

Note that the danger of which the Lord warns them—the danger of forgetting *"the LORD your God"* and all that He has done. Forgetting God was indeed a danger in their day. Today, we face a similar danger. When we presume to think we can live the Christian life or pray in our own power and wisdom, we are filled with pride and are forgetting that it is God upon whom we must depend. To admit, "I can't, but He can" is to walk in humility, taking our proper place of trusting Him, resting in the power of His Spirit and His wisdom from above. That is the essence of taking the low place of humility and releasing Him to honor and exalt us in His way and His timing, and thus honor Jesus Christ for His work in us and through us.

PAUL'S HUMILITY TRAINING

The apostle Paul prayed three times to have his thorn in the flesh removed. God answered, "No," and Paul saw it as part of his training in humility. He said he could now boast in his weaknesses since they were avenues through which to experience the grace and power of Christ (2 Corinthians 12:1–10).

Here is a vital truth—God tests us to train us, not to draw us into sin—that is what the devil does. God wants to draw us into a new level of humility, of knowing Him, seeing His power and wisdom in a new dimension. He wants to move us to a new level of faith, of trust in Him. He wants us to walk in humble dependence manifested in prayer and obedience to His Word. The alternative is a proud self-will that always leads to sin and disobedience. Understand this: every sin is rooted in pride. Every sin is the result of believing a lie. When Satan fell, his first step was pride. When Satan tempts, the sharp point of his thought darts are filled with the poison of pride, prompting us to exclaim, "**I** deserve that" . . . "**I** need this" . . . "**I** want this." . . . "**I** must have that." Every righteous work, on the other hand, is rooted in humility that obediently follows our Father. It is a result of obedience to the truth. Humility is weakness that can know the strength of God. Pride is man's self-reliance that will ultimately be revealed in its weakness.

Let's sum up what we have seen. We have seen a definition of humility. We need to add to that a definition of a humbling situation: an event over which we have little or no control. In such an event, we are brought into a lower position instead of a higher position; we have less power and authority rather than more power and authority. God brings us into a pressure point—a humbling circumstance, a perplexing situation, a difficult relationship. In this tenuous situation, we face a test—we have a choice, either **(A)** humbly look to Him trusting His Word and His ways (His nature and character) or **(B)** proudly look to our own devices, the wisdom and plans of men, the opinions of the world and our own proud selves independent of God. If we choose **"A,"** we pass the test. That is God's will. How do we do that? We humbly call on Him in prayer. We carefully listen to His Word.

What do you see about the danger of pride and the place of humble prayer in your life? Remember this, we are never far from a proud heart, nor do we have to travel far to come to a humble heart. It is as close as our hearts bowing before the Lord and our lips confessing the sin of pride to Him. Where are you now? Talk to the Lord; listen to His convicting Word, and humble yourself before Him.

We only saw one half of James 4:6, *"GOD IS OPPOSED TO THE PROUD."* What about the other half of the verse that says, *"BUT* [God] *GIVES GRACE TO THE HUMBLE"*? In Day Five, we will see how that works out and how humility can be real in our praying and in our daily walk.

The Necessity of Humility

DAY FIVE

FOR ME TO PRAY GOD'S WAY

"Thus says the Lord, "Heaven is My throne, and the earth is My footstool. . . . For my hand made all these things, thus all these things came into being," declares the Lord. But to this one I will look, to him who is humble and contrite of spirit and who trembles at My word."

Isaiah 66:1a, 2

We have seen a proud Pharisee and a humble tax-gatherer. We have seen proud king Nebuchadnezzar and humble king Nebuchadnezzar as well as humble Hezekiah. We have seen that a proud heart is never far away, easily accessed by a wrong choice, and that a humble heart is also nearby if we are willing to bow. What can we do to walk and pray in humility? Of course, Scripture shows us. Let's begin first with a visit with Isaiah. Isaiah wrote of the heart in which God delights in Isaiah 57:15. A friend once asked me if I knew of the two thrones of God. That was his way of describing this verse from Isaiah.

📖 Read Isaiah 57:15 and record your insights. What do you learn about God and about humility?

____

____

____

____

____

____

____

____

____

The Lord is *"the High and Exalted One, Who lives forever,"* He is not only above all creation; He is the ruler over time and eternity. He is holy in who He is and all He does. Where He dwells is called *"a high and holy place."* His throne in heaven is characterized by sovereign power and absolute purity. He also delights to dwell *"with the contrite and lowly of spirit."* The one who humbles himself or herself before Him, acknowledging any sin, admitting any needs, aware of many weaknesses, and surrendering to His holy reign, will find Him listening with full attention (See Isaiah 66:1–2). Where God dwells He brings life; He revives or makes alive. That is His promise to the humble heart. The context of Isaiah 57 is God's rebuke to Israel for the nation's foolish idolatry, and His promise is one of great hope. For the one who humbles himself with a contrite and repentant heart, God promises revival—new life. What a promise, what an honor, especially to anyone who has walked in pride and selfishness! The God who lives with incorruptible, indestructible life can give His kind of life to the humble heart.

Word Study

REVIVE

The Hebrew word for "revive" in Isaiah 57:15 is *chayah,* which means "to live, to make alive, to restore to life." It refers to God's life-giving power and grace. Where sin has broken fellowship, God is willing to restore, to breathe new life into that relationship, if a person will first humble himself before the Lord.

James 4:6 says, *"BUT* [God] *GIVES GRACE TO THE HUMBLE."* Grace is God's enabling power made real in each situation. We have heard people speak of "dying grace" for the day of death. He also gives "difficulty grace" for each trial and "living grace" for all the paths of daily life (even things like traffic headaches, money problems, and raising kids!). How do we access that grace? James 4:7 contains the word "therefore," which links us to how we can walk in humility and access the grace of God.

Read James 4:6–7, asking God to open your eyes and your heart to all He is saying. Summarize the main thoughts in those verses.

____

____

____

____

____

____

____

In light of the fact that God resists or opposes the proud and gives His grace to the humble, He commands therefore that we submit to Him. The word "submit" is a translation of the Greek word *hupotássō,* which pictures one placing himself under someone else, arranging life under the command and direction of another. It was used as a military term, picturing one ranking under another or the act of placing oneself under the leadership of another. It is also used of submitting to governing authorities or to one's master. When we yield to God, we are then open to receive His grace in abundance.

"He leads the humble in justice, and He teaches the humble His way. . . . Who is the man who fears the Lord? He will instruct him in the way he should choose."

Psalm 25:9, 12

With that submission to God, we resist the devil. "Resist" is a translation of the Greek word *anthístēmi*, meaning to place oneself against, to stand against or oppose. Our submission to God is at the same time a resistance to the devil. What is the devil's place in this matter of pride versus humility? Pride marked Satan's character from the first. One of the Old Testament descriptions of Satan is found in Isaiah 14:12–15 in the five proud "I will" statements ending with *"I will make myself like the Most High."* For that statement, he was judged and sentenced to be *"thrust down,"* and he will one day be fully judged. Today, Satan tempts with deceptive, proud thoughts. We must resist him, stand against him. When we do, God promises that Satan will flee and that we can walk in the grace that comes from submitting to our Lord Jesus.

What or whom do you bow to as Lord? To what are you submitting each day? What or who is the primary guide in your life? What determines how you spend your time and money and energies? Look at the various "lords" listed below and see if you recognize any in your life.

- ❐ financial considerations
- ❐ my bank account
- ❐ the economy
- ❐ the weather
- ❐ my boss at work
- ❐ sports—I love sports!
- ❐ pleasure, ease
- ❐ anything fun!!!
- ❐ food
- ❐ travel
- ❐ things, "stuff"
- ❐ sex
- ❐ my friends
- ❐ my family
- ❐ God and His Word—"Jesus is Lord!"
- ❐ my favorite hobby
- ❐ academics, books
- ❐ music
- ❐ TV, entertainment, movies, media
- ❐ my job

Other ____.

What should accompany our submission according to James 4:8–10? What do you see about **prayer God's way?** [You may want to look at the context of this passage, especially James 4:3–4, to get the full picture.]

____

____

____

____

____

____

God wants us to draw near to Him and promises He will draw near to us. When we draw near to God, we will recognize sin and find His cleansing. We will see where we have been double-minded, seeking the world or our selfish desires while supposedly praying and seeking His will. He sees through that hypocrisy and resists us in our efforts. He does not give what we ask; He sees our proud, adulterous hearts and opposes us in our pride. We need to yield to Him, genuinely mourning over our sin, our proud laughter, and our surface joy. How? We must humble ourselves in the presence of God, coming before Him in prayer, bowing to Jesus as Lord and yielding to His will, seeking Him and His Word. When we do, He will lift us up, and we will experience His grace. We will know true joy and answers to prayer—prayer His way.

"Draw near to God and He will draw near to you."
James 4:8

Lord, I know I have walked in pride too many times. I thank You for forgiving me and restoring my heart to fellowship with You. I think too highly of my self and my opinion on too many occasions. Forgive me. I am grateful You do not give up on me. You discipline and teach and train me to understand Your will and Your ways and Your opinion which is always Truth and always for the best. May I learn to recognize the subtle seeds of pride, the vain, empty avenues I sometimes want to travel, and the foolish choices that always lead to sorrow for me, for those closest to me, and for

You. May I learn more each day what it means to walk in the fear of the Lord, knowing that I am ultimately accountable to You for every thought, word, attitude, and deed. *"So teach [me] to number [my] days that [I] may present to Thee a heart of wisdom,"* wisdom that recognizes and honors You as God and that walks in genuine humility and dependence on You. Thank You for Your work in my life. In Jesus' Name, Amen (Psalm 90:12).

In light of all we have seen about pride and humility, write your own prayer to the Lord or make a journal entry.

Notes

4

FORGIVEN AND CLEAN

PRAYING WITH A HEART THAT KNOWS THE FORGIVENESS AND CLEANSING OF CHRIST

What does it mean to know you are forgiven? Think about it. Have you experienced the forgiveness and cleansing of sin offered by God? If so, have you grasped the truth of forgiveness through Jesus Christ's death on the cross? How does the reality that you have been forgiven affect your praying? Can a person pray effectively without the forgiveness of God? Jesus told us to pray, *"forgive us our debts."* What about forgiving others' sins, especially the sins of those *"who have trespassed against us,"* who have offended or hurt us in some way? These questions and others must be answered if we are to know the fullness of what it means to live a life of **praying God's way.**

Jesus considered this issue of forgiveness one of the most important issues in His ministry. It was one of the most vigorously contested issues in the minds of many of Christ's opponents—"Can this man forgive sin?" they often asked. Jesus was very clear about His ability and authority to forgive. We need to understand Christ's authority and power to forgive and live in the truth of that divine power every day.

As we come to know by personal experience this marvelous and merciful forgiveness of Jesus Christ, we will pray in the confidence of an open heaven where the open heart of God is ready to listen and respond.

As we come to know by personal experience this marvelous and merciful forgiveness of Jesus Christ, we will pray in the confidence of an open heaven where the open heart of God is ready to listen and respond. If we do not understand what the Scriptures say about this matter of forgiveness and cleansing, we will battle with doubts or believe the deceptive lies of Satan that we cannot be forgiven or that we are not really welcomed before our Father's throne. We will tend to think of God's heart and God's heaven as closed to any cry we make. The Lord Jesus came to make the way open for us, and He calls us today by His Spirit and by His written Word to come boldly to His throne of grace to find help in time of need. Let us honor His sacrifice, believing and rejoicing in His resurrection, by coming often with the confidence of a beloved, forgiven child to an open-armed Abba Father!

Forgiven and Clean

DAY ONE

GOD COMES—GOD CALLS

First things first—we must understand how God sees sin if we are to know the necessity and gift of forgiveness. When we look at how God first dealt with sin, we discover some wonderful truths for daily life. Adam and Eve did not fully understand the impact of sin on them or on the entire creation. Neither did they understand the heart of God toward that sin and toward them, the first two sinners. To see God's heart is to recognize the awfulness of sin and the holiness and love of our Father. In seeing sin the way God sees it, we can learn to treat sin as He does and walk in the forgiveness and holiness God desires.

📖 What boundaries did God give Adam in Genesis 2:16–17?

____

____

____

____

What would be the consequences of any disobedience?

____

____

____

____

God clearly instructed Adam that he had free access to all of the Garden of Eden, all its land and fruit, except the fruit of one tree, the Tree of the Knowledge of Good and Evil. The boundary line was clear, and to cross that line, to eat of that tree would mean certain death.

📖 Read Genesis 3:8–9. What was God's response to the sin of Adam and Eve?

____

____

____

____

____

What added truths do you discover about the consequences of that sin in Genesis 3:7–19? Summarize what you find.

____

____

____

____

God came walking in the garden apparently to meet with Adam and Eve. This appears to have been a normal pattern for those first days. This time Adam and Eve were hiding from the Lord, and the Lord responded by calling out, "Where are you?" This was not a geographical inquiry. It was a relational question. God already knew where they were hiding. He already knew about the sin, and the attempted cover up—sin's consequences had already begun their deadly work of destroying relationships. God wanted Adam to admit where he was in his heart. After questioning them and hearing the "blame-game," God told them the further consequences of sin, for the serpent, for the woman, and for the man—pain in bearing children, toil in daily provision, and one day, death completed. (Their bodies began the death and decaying process the moment they first sinned.) With that word of judgment, there was also a promise of a "seed" to come, one who would be bruised by the serpent but who would crush the serpent and all evil with it. That was a prophecy of the coming of the Lord Jesus, the Messiah. In the Garden of Eden, God came, and God called, and God gave hope.

"The LORD God called . . . , Where are you? . . . Have you eaten from the tree? . . . What is this you have done?"

Genesis 3:9, 11, 13

Think about the coverings of animal skins God gave to the man and the woman in Genesis 3:21. What significance did these animal skin coverings hold? What message would these coverings send to Adam and Eve?

____

____

____

____

____

The animal skins given to Adam and Eve meant that certain animals had to die, perhaps sheep. Those skins provided a protective covering, but more than that, they were reminders of the costliness of sin—death. They were reminders both of the holiness of God in dealing with their sin and of the love of God in being gracious to them. He could have executed them on the spot. Instead, He gave a promise of the "seed" to come, took care of their immediate need for covering, and with that showed His heart of forgiveness.

In the garden, God came, and God called, and God gave hope.

God placed Adam and Eve outside the Garden of Eden. There, this couple began to raise a family. We read of the first two sons of Adam and Eve, Cain and Abel, and their offerings to God. God continued to deal with the issue of sin. He had to deal with Cain over his failure to offer the proper offering, but Cain refused to heed God's call. He failed to guard himself against the enslavement of sin. That led him to killing his brother Abel, another sin that God dealt with promptly. God continued to deal with the sin of mankind, eventually judging all the earth except Noah and his family. He brought Noah and his family through the flood and started the human race all over again. The historical record shows God continually putting boundaries in place to keep men and women from destroying themselves in their sin.

For instance, many centuries after the universal flood, God **came** to Abram and **called** him to follow. In that call, God called Him to a life of dealing with sin and surrender as we saw in Lesson 1. As God came to Abram and called him, so He **came** to Moses and **called** him. Exodus 3 reports the incident of Moses in the desert of Midian, where God revealed Himself in a burning bush. There God called Moses first to treat that place and that encounter as holy, to honor the presence of the Lord, then to obey Him in leading the children of Israel out of Egypt. Why was this encounter so significant? What did God want to do among the children of Israel? What does this have to do with us knowing the forgiveness of God, and what does it have to do with prayer? We will see in Day Two.

Forgiven and Clean

DAY TWO

GOD'S CALL—TO WALK AND TALK WITH HIM

In every encounter God has with people, He continues to direct them to a righteous walk, to lead His people in a walk of holiness. This direction and guidance is brought out most graphically in the revelation given to Moses and the children of Israel at Mount Sinai. After bringing them there, God showed Moses the pattern of the Tabernacle, which gave them the pattern for worship, for dealing with sin, and for a righteous walk with the Lord. A look at that pattern will help us in understanding God's view of sin. We will also see what should be our response to the sin He reveals in our lives. It will help us know more fully what it means to walk and talk with God, to **pray God's way.**

"Let the wicked forsake his way, and the unrighteous man his thoughts; and let him return to the LORD, and He will have compassion on him; and to our God, for He will abundantly pardon."

Isaiah 55:7

Look at Leviticus 9:1–7. What offerings were essential for Aaron the high priest to offer, according to verse 7?

____

____

____

What does this tell you about God's view of sin?

____

____

____

____

Moses mentioned several different offerings to be offered at the Tabernacle, but the two mentioned most often and the ones emphasized in verse 7 were the sin offering and the burnt offering. The emphasis found throughout the precepts governing Tabernacle worship was upon mankind's need to deal with sin, to offer a sacrifice to make "atonement" for sin. The Hebrew word *kaphar* (translated "atonement") literally means "covering," pointing to the fact that in those sacrifices would be a covering for the sin of the people. The blood of the sin offering would cover or hide the sin of the people and alleviate the judgment of God on them. This opened the way for the people to fellowship with God and experience His presence in their midst—*"that the glory of the Lord may appear to you"* (9:7).

Word Study

ATONEMENT

The Hebrew word *kaphar,* translated "atonement," literally means to cover. It refers to the covering or hiding of sin with the blood of a sacrifice, thus providing forgiveness and alleviating the judgment of God on His people. The innocent animal took judgment of death as a substitute for the person. The Day of Atonement, known today by the Hebrew phrase *Yom Kippur,* literally means the "Day of Covering."

📖 Look at Leviticus 4:20, 26, 31, and 35. Notice the last phrase of each of those verses. What promise did God give His people when they dealt with sin God's way?

When the children of Israel acknowledged their sin and came to Him offering the sacrifice as He directed, God promised their sin would be "forgiven." The Hebrew word *salach,* translated "forgiven," literally means "to forgive, to pardon, to spare," indicating that a person has been spared judgment and given the freedom of forgiveness. It is always used on a **divine level** of God forgiving people, never on a **human level** of people forgiving people. It emphasizes the work of God in forgiving us and caring for us.

📖 Fast forward to Jesus in Israel in the New Testament. What vital statements did Jesus make about forgiveness? Read Matthew 9:1–8. What did Jesus boldly declare in verses 2, 5, and 6?

Jesus made it clear that His power to eternally forgive a man's sin was of far greater significance than His ability to physically heal him. Christ's act of forgiveness would last forever. Jesus confidently declared that He has authority on earth to forgive sin, to release the debt any person has accumulated. Jesus' authority is backed by the promise of the Father who sent His Son to forgive sin (John 3:16).

Back to Leviticus. We have noted the various sin offerings in Leviticus 4 and the promise of forgiveness. To fully understand how God wanted the children of Israel to deal with sin, we must see both types of sin offering—the **sin** offering and the **guilt** or trespass offering.

📖 Read Leviticus 5:1–5 and 6:1–5 and summarize what you find there.

According to Leviticus 6:7. What is God's promise to the one who confesses his sin and makes restitution?

Word Study
FORGIVE

The Hebrew word *salach,* translated "to forgive, to pardon, to spare," is rooted in an ancient Semitic word meaning "to sprinkle" for the purpose of purification. When *salach* is used, it is always God who is acting in forgiveness, pardon, and restoration where there has been confession, repentance, and restitution for sin (Isaiah 55:7). The sin and guilt offerings provided a meeting place for man to confess and for God to forgive sin, providing the heart was rightly directed. Simple sacrifices alone would not provide forgiveness without a repentant heart. *Salach* also carries the idea of release from an obligation. In the case of sin, the obligation would be death if there were no sacrifice made for the sin. The goal of all forgiveness is the restoration of the relationship between God and man and between man and man so that they walk in fellowship and oneness.

Did You Know?

CAN YOU AFFORD GOD'S FORGIVENESS?

A vital truth comes through in the requirements given to the people of Israel regarding the sin offerings mentioned in Leviticus 5:5–7, 10—forgiveness was available to anyone, rich or poor, who was willing to admit sin and come in confession to the Lord. God provided that various sacrifices could be offered for sin so that no one was denied forgiveness based on what he or she could or could not afford. For instance, some could offer a lamb or goat, others only two turtledoves or two pigeons. One's social status or economic level was never to be a barrier. There was always a way for even the poorest to offer an acceptable sacrifice. God made a way for anyone to experience His forgiveness, cleansing, and restored fellowship.

People are naturally self-centered and can easily seek to promote and protect "self" even if it means sinning against someone else. God was well aware of this and made provision for dealing with it. He wanted right relationships among His people of Israel—a righteous walk in every area of their lives—business, community, and family. God considers such entities as community and family to be essential to life, not just a part of or even separate from the "spiritual" dimension of life. Under God's laws for Israel, if a neighbor gave false testimony or failed to tell the truth about some matter, that person was guilty. If a man stole something, extorted money from someone, deceived his neighbor concerning a deposit entrusted to him, or even hid something that he had found which belonged to another, he stood guilty before the Lord and was required to confess his transgression, make restitution for the wrong, and offer a guilt offering. God promised His forgiveness to the one who did this. If we are to walk rightly with God, we must walk rightly with one another.

📖 What did Jesus say about getting things right with others? Read Matthew 5:23–24 and record your answer.

____

____

____

According to Jesus, more important than any gift or offering given at the Temple was a right relationship with others. If one was about to give his offering or gift at the altar and there remembered an offended brother, he should immediately leave the offering at the altar and go find that brother. Jesus made it clear; of first priority is being *"reconciled to your brother"* (or sister)—make right whatever wrong has been done. The Greek word for *"be reconciled"* is *diallássomai*, which refers to a quarrel that can be either two-sided or one-sided. From Jesus' point of view, in either case, where there is an offense, every effort should be made to make things right. What if one refuses to receive our efforts? That one stands before God for his or her heart response. Each of us is responsible to do what each can do. Then, all is in order for one to worship with gifts and offerings at the altar. Whether in the Old Testament or the New Testament, the heart of God is the same—He wants us to walk rightly with Him and with one another.

Did You Know?

A BLAMELESS CONSCIENCE

The apostle Paul knew the importance of walking right with God and with others. In giving his testimony before Felix, he spoke of the resurrection to come when all will stand accountable to the Lord. Then he stated, *"In view of this, I also do my best to maintain always a blameless conscience both before God and before men"* (Acts 24:16).

📖 What if we have something against someone else? What does Jesus want us to know about that issue? Read Matthew 6:12 with 6:14–15. What does Jesus command and teach in those verses?

____

____

____

____

____

Jesus taught His disciples to pray, *"and forgive us our debts, as we also have forgiven our debtors."* We will sin, we will need forgiveness, and God is ready and able to forgive. That is a wonderful reality, to be forgiven, cleared of any sin-debt, living in an openhearted relationship with our Father. But, there is more. We will have those who will sin against us, who will come into that sin-debt arena where they "owe us," and we will have a choice—to forgive and release them from the "debt" or to hold on and try to "make them pay." God is calling us to forgive and is watching to see what we will do.

If we forgive from our hearts, releasing the bitter barb and with it releasing the one who put it there, our hearts will be free of the "gotta get even" syndrome. Our hearts will be open then to receive the forgiveness we so desperately need for our own sins—all those debts, trespasses, and failures. We will also be open to the fullness of prayer God's way. If we close our hearts to others, we are closing our hearts to God's work, to God's forgiveness, and to effective prayer. God wants us to have open, tender hearts not only to receive His love and forgiveness, but also to give that kind of love and forgiveness to others and to pray with a clear heart (see Ephesians 4:31–32 and Colossians 3:12–14).

"Let all bitterness and wrath and anger and clamor and slander be put away from you, along with all malice. Be kind to one another, tender-hearted, forgiving each other, just as God in Christ also has forgiven you."

Ephesians 4:31–32

We must always remember that we do not have the power to love and forgive within ourselves. We must depend on the energy and ability of the Spirit of God in us to love and forgive through us. Even in this dependence, we must be in prayer for God's strengthening grace moment by moment. We must cease neglecting prayer. Start where you are. Pray to get right, so you can be right in prayer. As you do, you will walk in the light of God's forgiveness and experience the joy of praying God's way.

At this point in our walk through Scripture, has the Holy Spirit brought to mind someone with whom you need to make things right? Perhaps you need to call that one or meet him or her and deal with whatever God has brought to your attention. Don't delay. Deal with it as soon as you can. The burden of it may feel like weights on your shoulders now, but obedience to God will bring the freedom of forgiveness and make you feel like you have wings after you have obeyed.

What does all this mean for New Testament believers? There is no tabernacle or temple to go to today where sacrifices can be offered? What does God expect, and how does He deal with sin today? We will see this in Day Three.

Forgiven and Clean

DAY THREE

Something Better

All along, God has wanted to fellowship with man and wants man to fellowship with Him. He created Adam and Eve to bear His image on earth, walking in oneness with Him. That means agreement on every level, in what we think and feel, in the choices we make, and in the attitudes and actions of daily life. How is that to become real today with so much sin all around us (and battling within us)? We have seen God's provision for forgiveness through the Old Testament sacrifices, but is there a better way? What does the New Testament reveal? We will start our journey today in the book of Hebrews and see what God says.

📖 There is a very important truth we need to see in this matter of forgiveness. Read Hebrews 10:1–4. What is the one problem with the sacrifices of the Old Testament, according to verse 4?

Word Study

TAKING AWAY SINS

Aphairéō is the Greek word translated "take away" in Hebrews 10:4 and is used in several verses in the New Testament such as Luke 1:25 and 10:42. In Romans 11:27 and Hebrews 10:4 it refers to taking away sins. It is made up of two Greek words, *apō* meaning away from, emphasizing removal, separation and distance, and *hairéo,* meaning to take. *Hairéo,* is related to *aírō*, meaning to lift up or carry away, to take away. *Aírō* is used by John the Baptist, speaking of Jesus taking away sins (John 1:29). Paul used *aírō* in Colossians 2:14 to speak of the canceling of the certificate of debt by Christ's death on the cross—*"He has taken it out of the way, having nailed it to the cross."* First John 3:5 affirms about the Son, *"And you know He appeared in order to take away sins; and in Him there is no sin."*

Extra Mile

SUFFERING SERVANT

Read Isaiah 53, a prophecy of the Suffering Servant. See how the Lord Jesus suffered, died and paid for our sins. Thank Him and praise Him.

How did God deal with that problem, according to Hebrews 10:5–12? (You may want to read John 1:29 for further insight.)

All the sacrifices of the Old Testament, especially those offered on the Day of Atonement (*"the blood of bulls and goats"*), could not *"take away sins."* In fact, it was "impossible" for them to do so. God sent His Son, the Lord Jesus, to do His will, specifically to offer His body *"once for all"* to take away our sins for all time and eternity. John the Baptist prophesied that Jesus would take away the sin of the world. That was a revelation of great magnitude. The blood of bulls and calves and goats could not take away sin, but this man, this Lamb, would accomplish that forever.

What do we find about Jesus' mission in the Scripture? What do you discover in Matthew 1:21?

What did Jesus say His mission was? Look at Matthew 20:28 and Luke 19:10 and record your answer.

From the outset, even before His birth, Jesus' mission was clear. The angel told Joseph that Mary would bear a son who was to be named Jesus, the Greek form of the Hebrew word we translate "Joshua" which means "Yahweh is salvation." He then explained the reason for that name, *"for it is He who will save His people from their sins."* When Jesus began His ministry, He made it very clear that He knew His mission—*"to give His life a ransom for many"* and *"to seek and to save that which was lost."* He came to deal with sin on the cross where He *"offered one sacrifice for sins for all time"* (Hebrews 10:12).

📖 Our sins were placed upon Christ, and He took those sins out of the way. What is the result according to Hebrews 10:17–18? (You may want to read Luke 23:34 and 24:45–49 to see the heart of Jesus concerning forgiveness.)

____

____

____

____

Because of the one sacrifice of Christ on the cross, God has forgiven us of our sins. He promised, *"THEIR SINS AND THEIR LAWLESS DEEDS I WILL REMEMBER NO MORE."* He has forgiven us fully. There is no need for any more sacrifices for sin. Recall what Jesus said on the cross. He prayed, *"Father, forgive them; for they do not know what they are doing"* (Luke 23:34). After His resurrection, He told His disciples their mission, *"that repentance for forgiveness of sins should be proclaimed in His name to all the nations, beginning from Jerusalem."* To paraphrase this verse, Christ essentially said, "Go tell people everywhere about the forgiveness I offer."

What should be our response to this according to Hebrews 10:19–22?

____

____

____

The book of Hebrews speaks about how the Tabernacle of the Old Testament was a picture of the greater Tabernacle in heaven, the very throne of God. For years the priests served in the earthly tabernacle offering sacrifice after sacrifice, day after day, week after week, year after year, but now that Christ has come and died and rose again, there is no need for any more sacrifices. Now we can come with complete confidence into the presence of God by the blood of Jesus. He has opened the way for full fellowship with the Father. We can now *"draw near,"* not timidly, nor apprehensively, nor with any hesitancy, but with confidence and boldness. Why? Because our hearts have been sprinkled clean from an evil conscience by the sprinkling of the blood of Jesus (see 1 Peter 1:2). Now we can stand before Him and fellowship with Him, pray to Him, and follow Him as His child.

Hebrews 4:15–16 says, *"For we do not have a high priest who cannot sympathize with our weaknesses, but One who has been tempted in all things as we are, yet without sin. Let us therefore draw near with confidence to the throne of grace, that we may receive mercy and may find grace to help in time of need."* Why not apply this verse to your life right now? Come before Him, remembering His mercy and His grace. He wants you to talk to Him, and He wants to help no matter how complicated your **"time of need"** is.

There is one other picture we need to see to appreciate the "better way" Jesus came to deal with our sin. Before Christ came to earth to give His life for us, atonement for sins could only be granted on a case-by-case basis through offerings and animal sacrifice. Of course, Jesus' atonement on the cross became the perfect and permanent sacrifice that needs no further improvement. The picture of Christ redeeming us once for all will help us

"For we do not have a high priest who cannot sympathize with our weaknesses, but One who has been tempted in all things as we are, yet without sin. Let us therefore draw near with confidence to the throne of grace, that we may receive mercy and may find grace to help in time of need."

Hebrews 4:15–16

walk in a better way—day by day—and pray in a better way. We will examine this picture in greater detail in Day Four.

Forgiven and Clean

DAY FOUR

PAID FOR!

We live in a better day, a day made that way by the work of Jesus Christ. Still, we are beset with difficulties, trials, weaknesses, the inability to always know which way to go or which path to choose. Sometimes we struggle over sin or over forgiveness of sin—we may have done something that continually haunts us or that Satan uses to accuse and condemn us. We need to see the full impact of what Jesus did on the cross and how what He did more than two thousand years ago impacts us today—especially how it impacts how we pray.

📖 Let's start at the Cross. Read John 19:14–30. What was the technical crime for which Jesus died, according to verses 15 and 19?

____

____

____

____

____

____

The Romans placed a placard over the head of each criminal, declaring the crime for which that person was being executed. From the viewpoint of the Roman army, Jesus died for the crime of claiming to be a king, the King of the Jews. This is why the placard nailed on the cross above Jesus' head identified Jesus as King of the Jews—to publicly mock Jesus and to send a warning to all Jewish subjects that they were in no position to appoint anyone as their king but were to live in subservience to Roman rule under the domain of the Caesar.

"For Christ also died for sins once for all, the just for the unjust, in order that He might bring us to God. . . ."

I Peter 3:18a

📖 From God's point of view, what was the crime for which Jesus died? Read 1 Peter 2:22–24 and 3:18 and record your answer.

____

____

____

____

____

Jesus did no wrong. He never committed sin, nor did He ever speak one deceitful word. When He died, He died for our sins, bearing the weight of our sin and guilt in His body on the cross. He was the just One who died for us, the unjust. He took our death penalty and paid for our sin so that He could bring us into a right relationship with the Father, into an unblemished fellowship with God.

📖 Thinking of what we have seen thus far, what do you find pictured in Colossians 2:13–14?

____

____

____

____

____

____

Colossians 2 reveals that we are all dead in our sins, our transgressions, until Christ makes us alive with Him. That means that in His death on the cross, He took our death and died in our place. He took our sins, *"all our transgressions,"* and paid for them so that we could be forgiven. When He went to the cross, He took our *"certificate of debt"* filled with *"decrees against us"*—decrees of death for our sins. The Greek word *cheirógraphon,* translated "certificate of debt" or literally, "handwriting," was used of the charges against a prisoner. For every time we step over the line in sin against God, a death decree could be issued. Those decrees were *"hostile to us,"* since they meant death for us if no one paid the penalty in our place. Paying the penalty for our sin is exactly what Jesus did, and in so doing, He took our certificate of debt *"out of the way,"* literally, "out of the midst," or out of sight. He "canceled out" or wiped away our debt by nailing it to the cross. The placard on the cross the day Jesus died said *"The King of the Jews"* in three languages, Hebrew, Greek, and Latin, but the placard the Father saw was yours and mine, the certificate of our sin debts, written in every language under the sun.

The placard on the cross the day Jesus died said "The King of the Jews" in three languages, Hebrew, Greek, and Latin, but the placard the Father saw was yours and mine, the certificate of our sin debts, written in every language under the sun.

Around 3:00 P.M., at the time of the evening sacrifice, when Jesus was about to breathe His last breath on the cross, He cried out something. What do you find in John 19:30?

____

____

____

____

____

____

After crying out *"I am thirsty"* and receiving some sour wine from a sponge, Jesus cried out, *"It is finished,"* and then He *"gave up His spirit"* in death. What is significant about this cry from the cross? The Greek word *tetelestai* (from *teléō*) is translated, *"It is finished."* In the marketplace of that day, *tetelestai* was also used on receipts. In this context, it meant "paid in full." In light of that truth, think what Jesus said about your certificate of debt. He paid it in full and cried out in confidence, "Paid in full!" Sin was now **paid for!**

What significance is it that Jesus has paid the debt for all your sins? Do you know His forgiveness? Is His forgiveness a practical reality in your life? Do you see the significance of forgiveness upon your prayer life? How can the reality that your sin debt is paid in full make a difference in how you come to God in prayer? Stop and spend some time thinking about these things and talking to Him in prayer.

"In Him we have redemption through His blood, the forgiveness of our trespasses, according to the riches of His grace, which He lavished upon us."

Ephesians 1:7–8a

Perhaps it would help to look at one more picture. Think of this matter of forgiveness and cleansing in light of the fact that sin is a debt. Sin is transgressing God's law, stepping over the boundary lines He has clearly given. Sin is against God. It is accounted as debt against us, even *"hostile to us"* as Colossians 2:14 says. Now, think for a moment of a credit card. You may accumulate things—groceries, gas, clothes, and so forth by using a credit card, but you also accumulate debt. The credit card does not "pay" for what you buy. It only "covers" a debt until you or someone else can "pay" the bill. When it comes to our sin debt, not only are we in debt, we are also guilty of wrong for each debt; every "purchase" that contributed to the sin debt is declared illegal by a holy and righteous God.

The Old Testament sacrifices gave "credit"; in other words, they "covered" sin for a time. The Day of Atonement (*Yom Kippur*) literally means "Day of Covering," covering for sin now. While God forgave the sin of His people, Israel, He did it provisionally until someone could come and pay the debt in full. A credit card covers monetary debt for one month at a time, dependent upon whether the card user makes at least minimum payments to the debt in timely fashion. However, the card itself never pays the debt. The bill always comes, and eventually someone has to send payment to the creditor for the bill to be "paid in full." When Jesus went to the cross, a certificate of unfathomable debt was looming against us, hostile to us, condemning us to death, for we could not possibly pay such a debt. But Christ took the certificate of debt and paid it in full. He didn't just "cover" the debt for another month or another year—He paid it in full! He took the debt *"out of the way"* (Colossians 2:14) and removed it far as the east is from the west (Psalm 103:12; see also Isaiah 38:17; 43:25). That is forgiveness—the Greek word used most often in the New Testament for forgiveness is *aphīemi,* literally meaning, "to send away." That is what Jesus did with your sin and mine. Now, do you think you have clearer access to the presence of your Father in prayer?

Take some time right now to talk to your heavenly Father about your sin, about His forgiveness, and about your walk with Him.

Forgiven and Clean

DAY FIVE

For Me to Pray God's Way

Knowing the forgiveness of Jesus Christ is essential to walking with God and talking to Him day by day. Now, we must look at two questions: **1)** what happens if we do not deal with sin? and **2)** what happens when we do deal with sin God's way? Scripture is clear about both options. Today, we want to focus on answering those questions and applying the answers to our walk and to our praying. We want to walk and pray, forgiven and clean.

What is it like when a person refuses to deal with his sin? King David knew quite well, and he has written his testimony in one of the psalms. Read Psalm 32 and then record your insights in the chart on the following page.

What happens . . .

WHEN I DON'T DEAL WITH SIN?	WHEN I DO DEAL WITH SIN?
PSALM 32:3–4	PSALM 32:1–2
PSALM 32:9	PSALM 32:5
	PSALM 32:6–11

How does it affect my praying . . .

WHEN I DON'T DEAL WITH SIN?	WHEN I DO DEAL WITH SIN?

David was miserable when he kept silent about his sin. First of all, he faced the hand of God heavy upon his life—in his heart, in his daily walk, and everywhere else he turned. As a result, his *"vitality,"* his strength and energy, was drained away. David knew the sweltering heat of summer. He had lived in the Judean desert and knew how draining the summer sun could be. He described it as *"fever heat,"* the condition one faces with a high fever—feeling drained, lifeless, aching, wanting some relief. A hot summer day or a fever of one hundred degrees or greater—either one could make life miserable. So can unconfessed, un-dealt-with sin.

David began talking to the Lord about his sin. He "acknowledged" his sin, which meant he admitted his sin and agreed with God regarding his sin, hiding nothing. In that confession to the Lord, David experienced the wonderful forgiveness of God, the removal of all guilt, the blessing of knowing that all of the sin is covered. When one is open, honest, and transparent before the Lord, that person finds the Lord open and absolutely ready to forgive and cleanse sin.

We have two options: either to deal with sin God's way and experience the joy of His forgiveness, or not deal with it His way and thus fail to experience His forgiveness and joy.

"If I regard wickedness in my heart, the Lord will not hear."

Psalm 66:18

David's exhortation speaks to each of us—let the *"godly,"* everyone who truly knows and follows God, pray to Him *"in a time when Thou mayest be found."* That phrase can be paraphrased "in a time of finding out" which can point to "finding out" about our sin and its seriousness or about the Lord and His readiness to forgive and cleanse. It could refer to that time when the Lord calls to us about our sin through the stresses and pressures of life—those caused by **personal** sin as well as those caused by **natural** sin, living on a sinful earth where the pressures of "a flood" or "trouble" can touch any of us. In either case, it is a time to seek the Lord and find Him as our refuge, our "hiding place" (32:7), as well as our teacher and guide (32:8). Not only does He forgive and cleanse, but He also restores and leads us in following Him in a renewed fellowship. These truths in Psalm 32 are vital for praying God's way.

Psalm 66:16–20 is also instructive about this matter of dealing with sin, especially as it relates to prayer. Record your answers in the chart below as you look at these verses?

What happens . . .

WHEN I DON'T DEAL WITH SIN?	WHEN I DO DEAL WITH SIN?
PSALM 66:18	PSALM 66:16–17
	PSALM 66:19
	PSALM 66:20

How does it affect my praying . . .

WHEN I DON'T DEAL WITH SIN?	WHEN I DO DEAL WITH SIN?

The psalmist rejoices in the fact that God had heard his cry. In His loving kindness, God listened and gave heed to the psalmist's prayer. The translation *"given heed"* is from the Hebrew word *qashab*, which literally means to prick up the ears (as pictured in a watchful animal). God focused His attention on the prayer of the psalmist instead of turning away. The psalmist considers what would have happened if he had regarded wickedness in his heart. *"Wickedness"* is a translation of the Hebrew word *aven,* meaning emptiness, nothingness, falseness, or vanity. It is often associated with idolatry (regarding empty gods or turning away from the true God and the fullness He offers to something useless and fruitless).

The word "regard" (Hebrew—*raah*) carries the idea of continually viewing something, earnestly or intently contemplating, or permitting something in the heart. *Raah* means looking, inspecting, investigating, seeing, and gaining full understanding. The Latin equivalent is *video* from which we get our modern-day English equivalent. The psalmist understood that to continually harbor wickedness, think wicked thoughts, or nurse wicked attitudes would result in God's silence. In other words, God does not pay close attention to the prayers of one whose heart is wicked until there is genuine repentance (see Psalm 51). Indeed the psalmist appears most grateful that God had indeed heard him and that he could rejoice and call others to rejoice with him, especially *"all who fear God."* We should be equally grateful, for we can rejoice that God hears us if we fear Him!

Extra Mile

TRUE CONFESSION

Look at Psalm 51, David's cry of repentance and confession. Look carefully at his desire for the freedom of forgiveness. Note the results of God's cleansing in one's life.

The New Testament is also instructive about dealing with sin God's way. What do you find about God and His will for each of His children according to 1 John 1:5–9? Record your insights in the chart below.

What happens . . .

WHEN I DON'T DEAL WITH SIN?	WHEN I DO DEAL WITH SIN?
1 JOHN 1:5–6	**1 JOHN 1:7**
1 JOHN 1:8	**1 JOHN 1:9**

How does it affect my praying . . .

WHEN I DON'T DEAL WITH SIN?	WHEN I DO DEAL WITH SIN?

"But if we walk in the light as He Himself is in the light, we have fellowship with one another, and the blood of Jesus His Son cleanses us from all sin. . . . If we confess our sins, he is faithful and righteous to forgive us our sins and to cleanse us from all unrighteousness."

I John 1:7, 9

God is light. In Him there is no trace of darkness, either in His nature or His actions. There is never any consequence of darkness in anything God thinks, says, or does. A walk of fellowship with Him is a walk in the light with the Father and His Son. If we claim to walk in oneness with Him, but exhibit the marks of darkness in attitude, word, and deed, then we are lying, not truly practicing the life in the light we profess. Walking with God is a walk out of that deception into sin confessed, cleansing experienced, and fellowship made real. It is a walk in the truth, a life *"in the light as He Himself is in the light"*—never allowing sin and deception to reign or even shadow our walk.

The Scriptures show that we must walk in the cleansing God provides. That means "coming clean" before Him, confessing our sin, agreeing with Him about anything He reveals as sin and renouncing that sin. The more of His Word we read, the more time we spend in His presence in prayer, the more easily we will see sin and turn from it. He will point it out—specific, exact, clear. He wants us to agree with Him that it is sin, that we will turn from it, and that we will turn to Him to walk in the truth. Every sin is a result of believing a lie. Every sin is our attempt to satisfy a perceived need, maybe a felt need, maybe even a real need in a wrong way. We sin because we are dissatisfied in some way. God wants us to turn to Him, to be content with Him, His will, His ways, and His timing—trusting Him to fulfill His purposes in our lives as only He can.

Let's sum it all up. When we deal with sin God's way...

...David reveals in Psalm 32 that we move from misery and heaviness to joy and being lifted up, with a heart that is free to come to God in any circumstance and experience His guiding hand.

...Psalm 66 shows us that we move from sin and the silence of God to seeing His salvation and being filled with praise. We experience a life that prays often and receives God's blessings.

...In 1 John we discover that we move from darkness and loneliness to the light of God's presence and the joy of His fellowship, a fellowship that welcomes prayer and enjoys practicing the presence of God.

What a treasure it is to be forgiven and clean! What an open door forgiveness provides to praying God's way!

What a treasure to be forgiven and clean! What an open door to praying God's way!

It's Time to Pray—Hebrews 4:15–16 is an open invitation for us to come before the throne of grace and pray. Hebrews 10:19 assures us that we can come boldly by the blood of Jesus. He has opened wide the way, and His heart welcomes us gladly. We have seen how sin must be dealt with, how Jesus Himself paid the debt for our sin, and how God now invites us, even commands us to come with confidence into His presence every day. In the Old Testament, only one man (the High Priest), on one day a year (*Yom Kippur,* the Day of Atonement) could come into the Holy of Holies. Jesus, our atonement, has opened the way for forgiveness every day of the year, for every moment of life. Come before God's throne with confidence that you have been forgiven and cleansed and that you can come boldly into His presence to talk about any "time of need." **Come now!**

Lord, thank You for forgiving me of all my sin. Thank You for Your love, Your sacrifice, Your constant care. You are amazing in Your mercy. May I never treat sin lightly or flippantly, especially in view of the price You paid to forgive me and cleanse me. Thank You for the truth that You have removed the penalty for my sin, taking that debt out of the way. Thank You that Your cleansing is real, that it goes to the depths of my being, to the totality of the inner man, and that it lasts forever. Thank You *"that Christ Jesus came into the world to save sinners,"* and that I am one who *"found mercy"* in Your eyes (1 Timothy 1:15, 16). I praise You that You are *"a God of forgiveness, gracious and compassionate, slow to anger, and abounding in lovingkindness"* (Nehemiah 9:17). May I live in the reality of an open heaven with Your open heart to hear my humble prayer. May I grasp all it means that You are my Father and that Jesus reigns as my Lord, my Savior, and my Redeemer. In the name of Jesus, Amen.

Write your prayer to God or make a journal entry in the space below.

Notes

THE WORD OF GOD AND PRAYER

Letting the Word of God Focus, Frame, and Build Our Prayers

First John 5:14–15 promises us, *"and this is the confidence which we have before Him, that, if we ask anything according to His will, He hears us. And if we know that He hears us in whatever we ask, we know that we have the requests which we have asked from Him."* What a promise! But how do we know God's will, especially in prayer? He must show us His will, and He has done that first through His Word. The more we know of His Word, the more we know His will. Any failure to follow God's Word is a failure to follow God and His will. Learning the value of God's Word, God's Book, is vital if we are to live praying God's way.

Any failure to follow God's Word is a failure to follow God and His will. Learning the value of God's Word, God's Book, is vital if we are to live praying God's way.

What does the Word of God do in our lives? The Word of God allows us to focus our hearts and our thoughts on God and allows Him to guide us along the way with His clear light illuminating our pathway. By His guiding hand, we can see which way to go, what to avoid, how to miss the stumbling blocks, and how to use the stepping stones. The Word of God shows us how to frame and build our prayers on a solid foundation of the will of God.

Without the Word of God, we can easily go astray in prayer and in the life decisions about which we are praying. Many counterfeit words in the world are leading to many counterfeit prayers. Many prayers that are sincere, passionate, and bold are sincerely wrong, passionately flawed, and boldly misleading. The people of the world (and many world-trained people in churches) speak forth deceptive opinions. There are many melodious sounds that seem to soothe the soul, but, in reality, lead people astray in the ways and wisdom of the world. We must beware of deceptive words and ways and be wise with the wisdom of God's Word. As the Spirit of God illumines the Word of God, we come to know the will of God and pray accordingly. Hence, we are **praying God's way**.

The Word of God and Prayer

DAY ONE

God's Word Reveals God's Will

If we want to find out what someone wants, there are two ways to do so. We can ask the person what he or she wants, or that person can simply tell us (whether we have asked or not). There are many things that God has chosen to clearly reveal as His will, things that He wants with all His heart for us to understand and experience. We find many of these things in His Word. However, there are some things He has chosen not to reveal until He is asked. When we ask, He reveals, sometimes quickly while at other times after a long wait and constant searching in His Word. Then, there are some things God has chosen not to reveal at all, at least not until we are in heaven in the ages to come. How does the reality that God reveals His plans and purposes to us in various methods and stages affect our praying? Obviously, we must know His Word, and then, based on what He has shown us, we can pray accordingly. Let's see how this has worked in the lives of some of the people of God.

First, in the life of David, we see him praying several times, especially in the Psalms. One of the prayers he prayed is not in the Psalms but is very important for all God was doing in his life and in the life of Israel as well as in the future of the people of God. It is a clear example of **focused praying** as a result of the **clear understanding** of God's Word.

Look at 2 Samuel 7:1–17. What did David desire to do, and what did God tell David?

____

____

____

____

David desired to build God a permanent house of worship, a temple to replace the portable Tabernacle. The prophet Nathan encouraged him to proceed. Then the Lord spoke to Nathan, informing him that He did not want David building a temple. God instructed Nathan to give a message to David. That message included recalling all the ways God had been with David, giving him many victories. God also gave David many wonderful promises about the immediate future (giving David a great name, a peaceful reign, and an enduring house) as well as the distant future, promising a lasting kingdom and an enduring throne. God promised that David's son would build Him a house and that God himself would instruct and discipline that son who would rule after David. Included in these promises was a pledge to establish an eternal kingdom and a promise of the coming Messiah who would reign supreme forever.

Now look at David's prayer in 2 Samuel 7:18–29. Summarize what you find there.

Did You Know?

ANSWERED PRAYER NEAR AND FAR

God's promise and David's prayer had a fulfillment both near and far, near in that David's son Solomon became king, continuing the line of David over the throne of Israel. The far fulfillment was in David's greater Son, the Lord Jesus. Almost a thousand years after David's reign, the angel Gabriel told Mary that Jesus, her son-to-be-born, would occupy the throne of David and reign in His kingdom forever (Luke 1:32–33).

After Nathan delivered God's message, David *"went in and sat before the Lord."* He began his prayer focusing on his relationship to God. He humbly prayed, *"Who am I, O Lord GOD, and what is my house, that Thou hast brought me this far?"* David spoke of himself as God's *"servant"* mentioning his relationship to God ten times. He praised God, declaring, *"Thou art great, O Lord GOD; for there is none like Thee."* David also spoke of God's relationship to His people Israel. Knowing God for who He is and for what He had promised, David could request with confidence, *"do as Thou hast spoken, that Thy name may be magnified forever."* David was confident because God had revealed His will—*"I will build you a house,"* and so David prayed, *"therefore Thy servant has found courage to pray this prayer to Thee."* David rejoiced in what God had revealed and in what he could request—*"Thou hast promised this good thing to Thy servant. . . . Now . . . with Thy blessing may the house of Thy servant be blessed forever."*

God revealed to David what He would do in the days ahead, and He revealed what David was to do in the immediate future, revealing that David's son would build a temple. What do we do when we do not know what to do? Where do we turn? Let's look at the life of another king, King Jehoshaphat of Judah, as he reveals the answer for us.

Extra Mile

SOLOMON PRAYED THE WORD OF GOD

Read 2 Chronicles 6:12–17, noting especially verses 16–17. Look at the Word God had spoken in 2 Samuel 7:11–17 and 1 Kings 2:4 and compare it with the prayer of Solomon.

Read 2 Chronicles 20:1–4. What were the circumstances, and what did Jehoshaphat do?

Several nations came together against Judah to make war. Jehoshaphat heard the report that the enemies were advancing on Jerusalem. In a state of fear, he immediately sought the Lord and proclaimed a fast throughout Judah. People began to gather to seek the Lord in Jerusalem, the appointed place God had given them for seeking Him.

What did Jehoshaphat pray? Read 2 Chronicles 20:5–12 and summarize what you find.

Jehoshaphat, along with a great crowd from all over Judah, gathered at the Temple and began to call on the Lord. He first focused on who God is, on His power and might, on His rulership over all the kingdoms of the world. He then called attention to Israel's relationship to the Lord, specifically to what God had done for His people in giving them the land of Canaan. Then, he brought the need before the Lord, pointing to the invading army and crying out for the Lord to deliver them. Jehoshaphat readily admitted Judah's lack of power and lack of wisdom, but acknowledged its dependence on the Lord and His great power. Verse 12 could be paraphrased, "Lord, we are helpless in this situation. We have never experienced anything like this before, but our eyes and our expectations are on You."

"O our God, will You not judge them? For we are powerless before this great multitude who are coming against us; nor do we know what to do, but our eyes are on You?"

2 Chronicles 20:12

📖 It is important to see that Jehoshaphat's prayer was based on the Word of God. Note verses 8–9. Compare what you find in 2 Chronicles 6:18–21 and 28–31. What do these scriptures tell you about the Word of God in prayer? Record your findings.

____

____

____

____

____

Jehoshaphat made a request based on the truth of verses 8–9. Look at verses 10–12 and record your insights concerning his request.

____

____

____

____

____

According to 2 Chronicles 6, Solomon made it clear that the Lord was too great to be confined to a temple in Jerusalem, but that God would dwell there to meet with His people. God promised to hear and answer Israel's prayers when the people came to the Temple to seek Him with an honest heart. When any kind of calamity, plague, famine, or invading army came against Israel, the people were to seek the Lord for His answer and His deliverance. If God revealed any sin in the lives, they were to confess and forsake it. Jehoshaphat prayed according to the promise that God would hear in a time of national crisis if His people humbly sought Him. Jehoshaphat also acknowledged that the land of Israel belonged to the Lord and was theirs as a gift from Him. Therefore, Jehoshaphat prayed for the Lord's protection and deliverance. It is interesting to note that his prayer is not a direct quote of Scripture, but the cry of a heart filled with the truth of many scriptures. He was praying in line with the heart, mind, and will of God as revealed in Scripture and expected God to answer accordingly.

God answered Jehoshaphat and the people of Judah with a great victory over the invading armies. Jehoshaphat prayed in line with the Word of God, and God fulfilled that Word. He was not the only one who prayed the Word of God. We find this occurring many times in Scripture. We will see some of these occurrences in Day Two.

The People of God Praying the Promises of God

God is purposeful in all He does. He has a purposeful plan for His people, which He has revealed in many ways throughout Scripture. The more we see this in Scripture, the more we will be able to pray in line with His purposes and His promises for our lives and for His kingdom. Examples of God's guidance will help steer us away from uninformed or misinformed praying and will help us stay on track with the things that are on God's heart and mind.

One of the clearest examples of the promises of God being fulfilled in the lives of His people is found in the events surrounding the Babylonian captivity (605–536 B.C.). Jeremiah prophesied that Israel would be captive in a foreign land for seventy years.

Read Jeremiah 25:8–14 and 29:10–14 and then read Daniel 9:1–2. What was God's prophecy and promise?

____

____

____

____

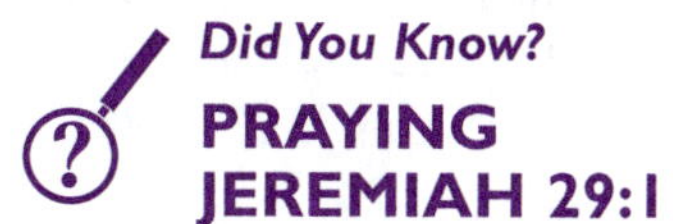

Did You Know?

PRAYING JEREMIAH 29:11

When Jeremiah prophesied about God's work in His people's lives, he remembered God's words of judgment, mercy, and restoration. Jeremiah 29:11 was a reminder to future generations. Daniel later read the words of this verse and prayed for God to fulfill its promise of restoration. "*'For I know the plans that I have for you,' declared the Lord, 'plans for welfare and not for calamity to give you a future and a hope.'*"

The Lord gave a message to Jeremiah for the people of Judah. He would send the Babylonians under Nebuchadnezzar to take the people of Judah captive to Babylon, but He would not leave them there indefinitely. God promised that after seventy years He would restore them to their homeland out of Babylonian captivity. He would also deal with the nation of Babylon for their wrongs. God's promise to His people gave great hope. He reassured them that He had wonderful plans for them—not for ultimate calamity, but for their welfare, their well-being. There was a future for the nation of Israel, something to which the people could look forward with hope and confidence. Seventy-plus years after Jeremiah declared this prophecy, Daniel read it and discovered the promise of a return from captivity after seventy years of captivity in Babylon.

Read Daniel 9:1–19 and record your findings about how the Word of God impacted Daniel's prayer?

____

____

____

____

In the first year of Darius (539 B.C.), some 67 years after the captivity began, Daniel made a careful search of Scripture, and, as he was reading the scroll of the prophet Jeremiah, he discovered the prophecy that the desolations determined for Jerusalem and Judah would last seventy years. Through the prophecies of Jeremiah, the Lord promised a restoration for His people. After Daniel read this in the Scriptures, he began seeking the Lord with prayer and fasting while clothed in sackcloth and ashes. Daniel was confident that the Lord wanted to restore the city and His people there. Daniel began to pray accordingly, confessing the sins of the people that had brought this calamity upon the city and the nation. He noted that all the calamities that Israel and Judah had faced in the last two centuries had occurred just as the Law of Moses said it would if the people rebelled. At the same time, Daniel appealed to the Lord's great compassion and forgiveness and called on Him to fulfill His Word and restore the city of Jerusalem. Daniel focused on the Lord's will and on what God could do for His sake. Daniel asked God to act for the sake of His name so that His will would be fulfilled.

EZRA PRAYED THE WORD OF GOD

When Ezra arrived in Israel, he saw that many were not living according to the Word of God. In Ezra 9:5–15, we read his prayer. In verses 11–12, he prayed the Word of God, not a rote quotation, but a summation from several passages including Exodus 23:32; 34:15–16; Deuteronomy 7:1–6; 23:6; and Proverbs 13:22; 20:7.

In the Old Testament, we find another example of the Word of God guiding one's prayer, this time in the life of Nehemiah. When Nehemiah chapter 1 opens, the year is 446 B.C., about ninety years after Daniel's prayer in Daniel chapter 9. Daniel's prayer had begun to be answered, when around 536 B.C., Zerubbabel took around fifty thousand Jews back to Jerusalem, where they rebuilt the Temple. In 458 B.C., Ezra took a second group of exiles back to Jerusalem, and he began teaching the Word of God in Israel, seeking to rebuild the people of the land. Some attempts had been made at further restoration of the city of Jerusalem, rebuilding the walls for protection, but those attempts were unsuccessful. In Nehemiah 1, we read of Nehemiah, cupbearer to the Persian King Artaxerxes, getting word about the current condition of the city. He began to pray. What can we learn from his prayer?

📖 Read Nehemiah 1:1–11. Note especially verses 7–9. What did Nehemiah use as the basis of his request in verses 8–9?

____

____

____

____

Nehemiah began to pray the burden of his heart. He knew the people of God in Jerusalem were in a difficult and sad state. He began to look to the God of heaven to move in that situation. As he prayed, he acknowledged that their condition was the result of their sin, the rebellion of the people of God, but that God was not finished with His people. God had promised to bring restoration to Judah if His people returned to Him. Nehemiah based his request on the word of God through Moses. He prayed with confidence that God would answer and fully restore His people and the city of Jerusalem.

📖 Look at Leviticus 26:33 and Deuteronomy 12:5–7 and 30:1–5, the verses upon which Nehemiah based his prayer. Compare those with what he prayed in Nehemiah 1:8–9. Record your insights, using the Word of God in prayer.

____

____

____

____

____

____

In the Law of Moses, the Lord warned His people that if they disobeyed Him and surrendered themselves to idolatry and all the corruption that goes with idol worship, He would deal very severely with them, bringing their cities to waste and scattering them among the nations. This is exactly what God did to the nation of Israel, and Nehemiah recounted the judgments in his prayer. He noted not only the warning of God but also the promise of God. If Israel would return to the Lord, then He would bring them back from the nations into which He had banished them. Then, in Jerusalem, the place where He had chosen to establish His name, the people could come and worship Him in gladness of heart.

When Nehemiah thought of the devastation of Jerusalem and how it remained in such a condition of reproach, he also called to mind the promises of God for His people. As he thought of those Scriptures, God's Word framed his prayer, and he offered up his request to God. Nehemiah voiced the heartbeat of God toward His people. This was not a matter of a rote quotation of verses in a "canned" prayer. Rather, it was the cry of the heart, a heart nourished with the Word of God and longing for the will of God to be fulfilled. The Scripture Nehemiah knew so well informed him of the will of God and formed his prayer for God's will to be done in Jerusalem and in Israel.

There is one other truth from which we can benefit in looking at the life and times of Nehemiah. Note in Nehemiah 1:1 that he began praying in the month *"Chislev,"* or December. Then in Nehemiah 2:1, we find it is the month *"Nisan"* or April.

📖 Look back over Nehemiah's prayer in Nehemiah 1:4–11 in light of the fact that this is most likely the essence of his prayer for that four-month period of time. Then look at Nehemiah 2:1–8 to see God's answer to the prayer. What does this tell you about prayer, about praying the Word of God, and about the ways of God in answering prayer?

____

____

____

____

____

____

____

____

If the will of God is to be fulfilled in the lives of God's people, it must be done in line with the Word of God, according to the ways of God, and in the timing of God.

It is evident that Nehemiah continued to seek the Lord for Jerusalem and Judah over this four-month period of time. His prayer was founded on the Word of God, and he consistently prayed in line with that Word, looking to the God of heaven to act. In seeking to help the people of God, one of the factors Nehemiah had to address was the fact that he was cupbearer to King Artaxerxes and could not leave his position or the land without the kings's order. Such an order from the king appeared close to impossible. Therefore, Nehemiah simply prayed, seeking the Lord and the fulfillment of His will as revealed in His promises. Nehemiah was living a truth we must learn: if the will of God is to be fulfilled in the lives of God's people, it must be done in line with the Word of God, according to the ways of God, and in the timing of God. After four months, God opened a door for Nehemiah. The king asked him what he wanted and then granted Nehemiah everything he asked for, a list that was doubtless compiled by Nehemiah as he sought the Lord in prayer over that four-month period of time. Nehemiah began to see the Word of God being fulfilled before his eyes.

We can pray as Daniel did, as Nehemiah did, and as many others have done through the years—"Lord, act according to Your will for the sake of Your name, for Your sake, work in this situation or in this person's life. Do as You have written in Your Word. Fulfill Your desire and Your will in this life." We can seek the Lord for His will in our lives and in the lives of those around us. Pause and pray for a need you see. Pray in line with God's Word.

Is praying the promises of God a truth reserved only for Old Testament saints? What do we find in the New Testament? We will see in Day Three.

The Word of God and Prayer

DAY THREE

PRAYING THE WORD OF GOD IN NEW TESTAMENT DAYS

What do we find in the pages of the New Testament concerning praying the Word of God? How did people pray in the days of Jesus and the apostles? We will see today some clear similarities to the ways of God in the Old Testament, and we will begin to see how those examples can encourage and equip us in our praying.

In the opening pages of the New Testament, we find a man of prayer seeking the Lord, and we are given a glimpse of his prayer life. Look at Luke 2:22–35, the event of Joseph and Mary bringing Jesus to the Temple to present Him before the Lord as the firstborn. Note especially Simeon's prayer in Luke 2:25–32. What do you find about his prayer?

____

____

____

____

____

How did Simeon use the Word of God in his prayer?

____

____

____

Simeon prayed all his life for the coming of the Messiah, and the Spirit of God revealed to him that he would not die until he had seen the Messiah. When he came into the Temple, the Spirit revealed to him the infant Jesus as that Messiah. Simeon took the Christ Child into his arms and began to pray to the Father, thanking Him for fulfilling His Word. Simeon rejoiced that the Messiah had come, and in his prayer quoted from Isaiah pointing to the Messiah as *"A LIGHT OF REVELATION TO THE GENTILES"* as well as *"the glory of*

Your people Israel." The Word of God informed Simeon of God's will so that the Word of God could form Simeon's prayer. He could pray with confidence that God would fulfill His will and in this case had fulfilled His will before Simeon's own eyes. Simeon rejoiced greatly and prophesied over this Child.

📖 Where did Simeon find this Scripture to pray? Look at Isaiah 9:2; 42:1–6; and 49:5–6 and compare those verses with Luke 2:32. What connections do you see to the Messiah and to how Simeon prayed when he saw the infant Jesus?

____

____

____

____

____

____

What can we learn from him for our own praying? Write any insights you discover in how we can know what to pray as we seek the fulfillment of the will of God?

____

____

____

____

____

____

____

The Lord gave the prophet Isaiah several prophecies about the coming Messiah and how He would bring light to a dark land, to a darkened people. He would be a light to the nations. It is evident that Simeon had read and/or heard these many prophecies and that he prayed in line with them through the many years of his life. Again we find that this prayer of Simeon was not a rote quotation of Scripture. Rather it was the outpouring of a heart filled with the Word of God, seeking only the will of God, and delighting in the ways of God. For Simeon, he had waited a lifetime. However, the timing of God was worth the wait as is seen in the way Simeon blessed the Lord for fulfilling His will in bringing the Messiah for Simeon's eyes to see.

We can learn much from Simeon's short prayer. In those few words we see a lifetime of walking with God, hearing and meditating on God's Word, and then in prayer, pouring out the longing of his heart for the fulfillment of that Word. We see here a truth that comes up time and time again in Scripture. It is this: prayer is the outflow of a personal relationship with our Father, the cry of a heart surrendered to our Lord. It is not a combination or formula of magical words said in a mystical way, nor is it a religious ritual performed by a select few. It is a child talking to the Father, a subject talking to the King, knowing God has spoken His Word revealing His will. We can pray that Word and wait expectantly for Him to answer. Simeon did, and we can do so as well.

FORETELLING OF THE MESSIAH

Isaiah prophesied about the coming Messiah:

"And now says the LORD, who formed Me from the womb to be His Servant, to bring Jacob back to Him, in order that Israel might be gathered to Him (for I am honored in the sight of the LORD, and My God is My strength), He says, 'It is too small a thing that You should be My Servant to raise up the tribes of Jacob, and to restore the preserved ones of Israel; I will also make You a light of the nations so that My salvation may reach to the end of the earth.'" (Isaiah 49:5–6)

Jesus said—"For I have come down from heaven, not to do My own will, but the will of Him who sent Me" (John 6:38).

📖 In the pages of the New Testament, we also see our Lord Jesus praying the Word of God. Look at Hebrews 10:1–10, especially verses 5–9. Write your insights concerning this prayer of the Lord Jesus?

____

____

____

____

In this very unique testimony of the work of Jesus Christ in His death on the cross, we are allowed to hear the heartbeat of our Savior. In particular, we have the opportunity to hear the essence of His prayer to the Father concerning His mission in life. The foundation of this prayer is Psalm 40:6–8, and most of the words are a direct quotation of those verses. Jesus took the words the Holy Spirit inspired David to pen and prayed them to His Father. These words expressed the will of the Father, and Jesus always and only wanted to do the Father's will. Therefore, He prayed these words to His Father. We are called to follow Jesus in doing the Father's will, and we too can pray Scripture as we seek to do His will and see His will done in the lives of those around us.

📖 Members of the early church era also knew the importance of praying in line with the Word of God and of letting the Word of God form their prayers. First, read Acts 4:1–31 to see the setting of a prayer meeting that occurred in Jerusalem. How would these people respond to the threats of the authorities in Jerusalem? Reread the prayer in verses 24–30. How did they pray?

____

____

____

____

____

____

What do you see about how they used the Word of God in prayer?

____

____

____

____

Peter and John had an opportunity to tell others how the power of Jesus Christ made the lame man well and how He could change the life of anyone willing to repent of sin and turn to Christ, trusting Him as Lord and Savior. The religious authorities in Jerusalem did not want these two men speaking about Jesus or about His death and resurrection, so they arrested them. When questioned, Peter and John simply told them their eyewitness testimony of the life and power of Jesus Christ and the salvation He alone could bring. The authorities told them to speak no more of this or of this Man, Jesus. They threatened them harm if they did. Peter and John confidently declared that they must tell what they had seen and heard.

Doctrine

OBEYING GOD

Peter and John focused attention on the priority of obeying God in proclaiming the message of Jesus' death and resurrection. When government authorities stood against that message, they knew God must be obeyed. This was not a demonstration of anarchy or rebellion against governmental authority. Romans 13:1–7 instructs us to honor government leaders. Peter himself wrote *"submit yourselves for the Lord's sake to every human institution. . . . honor the king"* (1 Peter 2:13–17). Peter and John told the Jewish leaders of their obligation *"to give heed . . . to God"* and testify of what they had seen and heard concerning Jesus.

Peter and John went to their companions and told them the whole story along with the details about the threats of the chief priests and elders. Those gathered began to pray. They first focused on the Lord as Creator, quoting Scripture that showed Him to be the ultimate authority over all creation. Then they began recounting the testimony of David in Psalm 2 about how the nations had taken their stand against the Lord God and His Christ. They applied Psalm 2 to the crucifixion of the Lord Jesus, acknowledging that all had been done under His sovereign hand. They acknowledged the threats of the authorities in Jerusalem and called on the Lord to *"take note of"* those threats and to give them boldness to declare the Word of God as God worked His miracles to exalt the name of Jesus.

What applications do you see for your prayers from the lives of people like Simeon, the Lord Jesus, or the early disciples? What burdens or needs are on your heart? What aspects of the will of God make you concerned right now? Is there something in your life, your family, your church, your community or in the life of someone else for which you desire the will of God to be done? What can you pray? Spend some time in Scripture and in prayer. Ask the Lord to show you scriptures that apply in some way to your prayer burden and lift those before the Lord.

We have seen how the believers of old prayed in the Old and New Testaments. Their lives **and their prayers** are an example to us. We can learn to pray as they did. We will see that in Day Four.

The Word of God and Prayer

DAY FOUR

Knowing Jesus' Words, Praying in Jesus' Name

We saw in Day One that the Word of God reveals the will of God. Our praying always must be in line with the Word of God. The more we know and pray the Word of God, the more we pray in line with the will of God and see answers His way. We have seen examples of this in the lives of many in the Old and New Testaments. When Jesus talked to His disciples, one of the things He revealed concerned the inseparable link between abiding in Him, His words abiding in the heart, and experiencing answered prayer. Abiding in Him includes knowing His words, a vital link we need to apply to our daily praying. We will see that in today's lesson.

The more we know and pray the Word of God, the more we pray in line with the will of God and see answers to our prayers—His way.

Final instructions can be of extreme importance. The night before Jesus was crucified, He gave His disciples some of the most important truths of His entire ministry. We know these words as the "Upper Room Discourse" (John 13–16). During this time with His disciples, Christ spoke of many things—His going to the Father, the coming of the Holy Spirit, the ministry of the Spirit in their lives, the future He had planned for them, and He revealed more about His approaching death and resurrection and what that would mean to them. In the midst of those very weighty words Christ uttered, He revealed some vital truths concerning prayer. We need to understand those truths, especially as they relate to praying the will of the Father.

📖 First of all what do we find about the words of Jesus in the Scriptures. Read the verses given below and summarize what they reveal.

John 3:34–36

____

____

____

____

John 6:68

____

____

____

____

John 8:47

____

____

____

____

John 14:10

____

____

____

____

The Father sent His Son, our Lord Jesus, to speak His word, to reveal His will, to show His love, and to give eternal life to all who would believe in Him. As the disciples began to follow Jesus, they listened intently to His words; words the Father gave Him to speak. Some who heard Jesus chose not to believe, and they withdrew from Him. After Jesus asked the disciples if they, too, wanted to leave, Peter spoke for those who believed, *"Lord, to whom shall we go? You have words of eternal life."* Those words Peter spoke were the words of God. The Father was teaching the disciples as Jesus spoke words of wisdom to them.

📖 The night before Jesus was crucified, what did He promise about the days ahead? Read John 14:16–18, 25–26 and 16:7, 13–15. What was to be the ministry of the Holy Spirit in the lives of the disciples (and now in our lives)?

____

____

____

____

____

Jesus would be leaving, but He would not leave the disciples as orphans. He promised to send the Holy Spirit to indwell them and continue the teaching ministry Jesus had begun. The Father would send the Spirit of Truth to teach and bring to remembrance the things Jesus had said. We have Christ's teachings written in the Scriptures of the New Testament. The ministry of the Spirit then and now is to guide into the truth, taking the words of the Father and the Son and revealing them to His children. As we read or hear the Scriptures, the Spirit of God gives us illumination and understanding. He speaks to us through the Word of God and always guides us in line with that Word.

We gain additional insights from 1 Corinthians 2:6–16, where Paul speaks of the ministry of the Spirit in giving us spiritual understanding. The Spirit teaches us the truths of the mind of God. Indeed, we have the mind of Christ, thus the spiritual ability to hear from God, to be taught by God, and to know the thoughts and wisdom of God.

📖 How does this ministry of the Spirit relate to prayer? Look back at John 15:5–8. What does Jesus say about His words?

____

____

____

What link do you see between His words, our asking, and His answers?

____

____

____

When we come to Jesus and believe in Him and His Word, we enter into an inseparable relationship with Him, a relationship of mutual abiding, like a branch related to the vine. As we live linked to the vitality of the Vine (Jesus), we bear the fruit Christ produces. In that relationship, He speaks to us, and we speak to Him. As we hear His words and allow those words to abide in us, we know His heart and His will. Then, we can know how to pray in line with His will, praying His desires. Since we are surrendered to Him and His will, His desires are becoming our desires. When we pray *"whatever* [we] *wish,"* it is not a matter of seeking something for selfish use, never praying contrary to His will, but of seeking what will be for His use, for His will, and for His kingdom. The answer to such a prayer will be for our use and our fulfillment as we walk with Him in His will. The Father is glorified in that kind of living and praying and answering because His kind of fruit is continually born, fruit that lasts forever and reflects His character, power, and love.

As we walk with Jesus abiding in Him, He teaches us by His indwelling Spirit. As we know His words, we know how to pray, how to ask, and how to expect Him to answer. He promises to answer prayers in line with His heart and His words because they are the expression of His will. The more we know Him and His Word, the more we will know His specific will for the things we face each day and the more specific we can pray and see answers from Him. That is the heart of praying God's way. How is your relationship with Jesus? Are you spending time in His Word and allowing that Word to frame and build your prayers? Pause and talk to the Father about these things.

Did You Know?

FULLNESS OF JOY

Jesus' desire for His disciples is that they know fullness of joy in knowing His Word and experiencing answered prayer. His desire is related in the following verses:

> *"These things I have spoken to you, that My joy may be in you, and that your joy may be made full" . . . "Ask, and you will receive, that your joy may be made full."* He Himself prayed, *"But now I come to Thee; and these things I speak in the world, that they may have My joy made full in themselves."* (John 15:11; 16:24; 17:13)

What additional insights do you gain from John 14:12–15; 15:16, and 16:23–27?

Doctrine

A DIVINE GUARANTEE

In John 14:13, Jesus promised that if we ask in His name, He would answer—*"that I will do."* He said in John 16:23 that if we *"ask the Father for anything, He will give it to you."* In John 15:7, He promised, *"it shall be done for you."* Jesus will do it, the Father will give it, and it shall be done—a triple guarantee. We can pray with confidence when we want the will of the Father, when we seek the desire of the Son, and when we pray with dependence on the Spirit.

Believing in Jesus is the start and the heart of our relationship with Him—a relationship of living faith. Because He now lives in us by the work of His Spirit, we have His nature. We love the Father and the Son and want to keep Jesus' commandments. That is why we can ask the Father in Jesus' name, as though Jesus Himself were asking. Since we are following Him, loving Him, desiring to obey Him, we have His desires more and more in our hearts, so we can ask for things that match His heart. As we have seen in other Scriptures, the Spirit Himself helps us in prayer; He teaches us and guides us so we know the words of Jesus and so we can know what to ask. Asking according to His Words is the same as asking in His name since His words reveal who He is and what He wants. The results are the answers the Father delights to give, answers that make our joy full. Fruit is borne—eternal fruit—and joy is experienced, the joy only God can give.

The Word of God and Prayer

DAY FIVE

For Me to Pray God's Way

How can we pray the Word of God day by day? What truths can we apply to our daily lives and our daily prayers? The Word of God is alive and just as powerful today as the day it was written. God's Spirit still speaks through His Word. He illumines our minds and fires our hearts for His will and His ways. His Word can still guide us in all kinds of prayer, whether praise or thanksgiving or confession of sin, whether petition for our own needs or intercession for others. The Word of God discerns our thoughts and our motives and guides us in line with the thoughts and the heart of God. Today, we want to see how we can apply this living Word to our daily praying and discover the power of prayer God's way.

Let's take Psalm 1 as an example. Read and meditate on Psalm 1:1–6. You may want to read it in several translations to catch the fuller meaning. Then, pray Psalm 1 and write any reflections on your prayer. You may want to write your prayer in the space given below.

Below is an example of praying Psalm 1 for yourself. (You could adapt this and pray it for someone else just as easily.) Read through or pray this prayer and write any additional insights in the space given.

Put Yourself in Their Shoes

WAYS TO WALK WITH THE WORD

- Read the Word
- Listen to the Word
- Meditate on the Word
- Memorize the Word
- Study the Word
- Obey the Word
- Speak the Word
- Pray the Word

> Lord, I pray that I will be a blessed person, blessed by You, that I will never *"walk in the counsel of the wicked, nor stand in the path of sinners, nor sit in the seat of scoffers."* May my delight be in Your law, and may I learn to meditate on it day and night. May Your Word feed and nourish my thoughts every day so that I think more and more like You. Lord, I desire to be *"like a tree firmly planted"* and rooted *"by streams of water"* so that I yield fruit in season and never wither from lack of water, the water of Your Word. May I prosper Your way with Your blessing and not be like the wicked who are driven like chaff in the wind, worthless, useless, not planted, without roots, and out of Your will. Lord, I want to stand in the assembly of the righteous knowing Your righteousness in my heart. You know all about my way and are pleased when I walk in righteousness following Your Word, Your will, and Your ways. Thank You for delivering me out of *"the way of the wicked,"* the way of destruction. I am truly blessed in knowing You, Your Word, and Your will. Amen.

Your reflection:

____

____

____

____

____

PRAY Now, you take another psalm or a portion of a psalm and pray it to the Lord. Some suggested psalms are Psalms 5, 8, 13, 16, 18, 23, 25, 27, 34, and 37. Write your prayer or your reflections in the space below.

____

____

____

____

____

____

____

The book of Psalms is the prayer book of the Old Testament, but it is not the only place from which we can pray. There are many prayers throughout Scripture that show us how to pray and that can be used to frame the prayers of our heart. They can express the burdens we have, or the confession of sin we need to make, or the praises that are filling our hearts, or the thanksgiving we want to express. Look at the psalm and the other passages of Scripture given below and see how others prayed. [As an historical note and an encouragement, it was said of George Müller, Christian leader in nineteenth century England, that he made it a practice to read and meditate on the Bible on his knees, allowing the Word of God to guide him in prayer.] Use the passages below to guide you in prayer.

A Burden—Psalm 22 and Matthew 27:45–50—Your insights or your prayer . . .

A Confession—Nehemiah 9:1–37—Your insights or your prayer . . .

D. L. Moody once noted that prayer and the Word of God are like the wings of a bird in a Christian's life. Both go together, and to lose either one is to be crippled and unable to soar as God intended.

A Praise—Exodus 15:1–18—Your insights or your prayer . . .

A Thanksgiving—2 Corinthians 2:14 (see 2:12–13) and 2 Corinthians 9:15 (see 9:6–14)—Your insights or your prayer . . .

Psalm 119 is the longest of the psalms, 176 verses. It is a beautiful portrait of the Word of God and Scripture's benefit and blessing in one's life. The psalm also teaches us much about prayer. As a matter of fact, verses 4–176 form a prayer. The last 8 verses, 119:169–176, form one of the clearest pictures of the link between the Word of God and prayer found in the Bible. Read these verses several times. Note the different aspects of prayer (asking, praising, singing, etc.) and how the Word of God relates to them. In the space below, record any insights you glean.

The psalmist cried out to the Lord and prayed for insight into His Word. Crying out to the Lord and praying for insight go together; as we humbly cry out, God responds, and as we are taught His Word, we cry out with greater understanding. From the Word, we learn how to ask according to God's will. When God teaches us His Word, our praise is praise in truth, and our singing is a song of righteousness. Whatever the need, the Word shows us how to call on the Lord, how to seek His help, how to find our way, how to pray God's way, and how to experience Him working in our lives, answering our cries.

Close your study with a time of prayer.

Lord, thank You for Your Word. Thank You that You have expressed Your heart so clearly. I appreciate the examples from so many lives through the ages, lives that have hearts much like mine, struggles similar to mine, opportunities for praise and thanksgiving like I have. Thank You for showing us the honest expressions of need, of wonder, of awe and adoration, of thanks, of confession, and even of questions and confusion that some faced. Thank You that I can pray Your Word, continuing to look to You and learn from You about how to pray and how to look for Your answers. Father, I ask You to fulfill in my life Your will as expressed in Hebrews 13:20–21, that You as *"the God of peace, who brought up from the dead the great Shepherd of the sheep through the blood of the eternal covenant, even Jesus our Lord, equip* [me] *in every good thing to do* [Your] *will, working in* [me] *that which is pleasing in* [Your] *sight, through Jesus Christ, to whom be the glory forever and ever. Amen."*

In light of all you have seen in this lesson, write a prayer to the Lord. Or in a journal entry record your insights or some personal application about praying the Word of God.

Put Yourself in Their Shoes

PRAYING GOD'S WORD

George Müller, noted for his ministry to orphans in Bristol, England in the nineteenth century, was a man of fervent prayer. One of his regular practices was reading and meditating on the Bible on his knees as preparation for and guidance in prayer. He first heard of the practice when reading a biography of the eighteenth century evangelist George Whitefield. Müller copied that practice. He found the Word coming alive as God spoke through His Word. Müller found his prayers filled with that Word as he spent time in praise, thanksgiving, and in pleading for the needs of so many. (For further testimony, see Arthur T. Pierson. *George Muller of Bristol*. Grand Rapids: Zondervan Publishing House, 1984.)

Notes

HONORING THE FATHER

VALUING GOD OUR FATHER FOR WHO HE IS AND WHAT HE DOES

Our God is LORD, Lord of heaven and earth, Creator of all that is. He is perfect, righteous in all His ways, without blemish in every detail, and marked by absolute integrity in every thought, word, and deed. God is worthy of great praise and adoration. He is brilliant; His wisdom goes light-years beyond human comprehension. God's strength is unparalleled, able to support the universe with a word—from the faintest electrons, atoms, and molecules to massive planets, solar systems, and galaxies.

The Father is worthy of great honor, abundant praise, and continued thanksgiving and adoration.

Our God is also a father. His care and love for His creation is documented throughout history and is real and tangible in this moment. He has given His only Son to rescue sinful, rebellious men and women to bring into existence a holy family of sons and daughters—all in the image of Christ. That sacrifice of His Son is the greatest expression of His love, grace, and mercy, but not the final expression. Ephesians 2:7 declares that *"in the ages to come He* [will] *show the surpassing riches of His grace in kindness toward us in Christ Jesus."* The Father is worthy of great honor, abundant praise, and continued thanksgiving and adoration.

But are we giving Him the honor He deserves, the true praise and thanksgiving He has earned? Do our requests for ourselves and for others reflect a heart that honors Him? Is our praise adequate? Are we truly showing our love and surrender to Him? How are we expressing our thanksgiving, our true gratitude for all He has done (and continues to do) for us? How are we responding to all He has promised to do in this life and in the ages to come? Through prayer, we can begin to express our hearts to Him. We can tell Him of our love. We can say, "Thank You," and praise Him with our lips, but we must do so with a right heart, not just with "lip service." We must look at our hearts, our attitudes, and our daily practices. In this lesson and in the lessons that follow, we will see what the Scriptures say about these things and seek to make real life applications. This is all part of **praying God's way** and is sure to help us know Him and honor Him more than ever.

Honoring the Father

DAY ONE

WHAT DOES IT MEAN TO HONOR OUR FATHER?

We saw in Lesson Two that knowing and loving the Father is at the heart of true prayer. Prayer is part of the relationship we have with God the Father. Prayer is not a religious ritual, rite, or spiritual task, but it consists of talking and walking with, listening to and learning from our Father. Jesus wanted His disciples to understand this. When Jesus began talking to His disciples about true prayer, He revealed to them "The Lord's Prayer," which is really "The Disciple's Prayer." This prayer is a pattern for all other prayers. That pattern begins, *"Our Father who art in heaven, hallowed be Thy name."* What key truths was Jesus showing His disciples (and us) in this pattern about prayer and about our relationship with the Father? We will look at various parts of this pattern in several of the lessons in *Praying God's Way,* but today we want to focus on what the Scriptures say about honoring the Father.

First, we need to see some scriptural truths about honoring God and about prayer in the Old Testament. One of the early examples in the history of the people of God occurred in the first days of the Tabernacle worship era, and it is connected to one of the Old Testament symbols of prayer.

📖 Look at Leviticus 10:1–3 and summarize what you find.

____

____

____

____

____

What was at the heart of the sin of Nadab and Abihu? On what did the Lord focus in verse 3?

____

____

____

____

____

In the Tabernacle, the incense offering was offered twice a day on the golden altar of incense, using coals taken from the bronze altar in the outer court where the various sacrifices were offered. The incense was symbolic of prayer. The coals of the outer court serve as a picture of the fires of judgment on sin, a judgment ultimately fulfilled in Jesus' gruesome death on the cross. Nadab and Abihu ignored the very clear regulations of the Lord and placed ordinary coals on their fire pans and then offered incense on those same coals. This dishonored the Lord's Word and distorted the message and symbolism God intended in the activities of the Tabernacle. Their actions especially distorted the message of dealing with sin through the fires of the bronze altar. In failing to appropriate God's way of dealing with sin—only in the fires of the bronze altar, not with just any fire—Nadab and Abihu did not treat God as holy. Thus they failed to honor God before their fellow priests and before the people. For us today, the coals of the bronze altar speak of coming before the Lord through the merits of Christ's death, through His blood. Coming to God through the blood of Christ honors both the Father and the Son (see Hebrews 10:19–22). We will see the truths about the incense as a symbol of prayer in greater detail in next week's lesson.

Word Study
HONOR

The Hebrew word translated "*honor*" in Leviticus 10:3 is ***kabad,*** meaning "to be heavy or weighty," the idea being conveyed is of one who is weighty in influence, wealth, or integrity, and so worthy of great honor. ***Kabad*** is sometimes translated "*glory*" and often refers to the awesome appearance of the glory of God.

Our view of God and His Word determines our voice in prayer. If we do not honor His way to pray and His way to worship, we dishonor Him. Nadab and Abihu did not honor God. Their view of God and His Word was so flawed that it corrupted their worship of God. How we value the Father (or fail to value Him) comes out in how we pray. To better honor Him, we need to see what Scripture shows us about God and His worth, His value.

What do you discover in Isaiah 46:5–10?

____

____

____

God calls Israel to compare the idols of Babylon with Him, the true God. Their idols may be of silver or gold, but they have to be carried around. The true God carries His people; His people do not have to carry Him. Idols are useless—*"though one may cry to it, it cannot answer; it cannot deliver him from his distress."* By contrast, God hears the cry of His people and is able to deliver them from distress. The Lord is God and there is no other. There is no one, no so-called god like the one true God. He knows all about time and the events of all creation and can tell the details of the end *"from the beginning."* He knows tomorrow as well as He knows today or yesterday. With that knowledge, He assures us that His purpose will be established and that He *"will accomplish all* [His] *good pleasure."*

Doctrine
HONORING AUTHORITY

"Render . . . honor to whom honor" is due, declares Romans 13:7. That chapter speaks of God putting authorities in place. In honoring them, we honor God and His rule over all. Honoring authorities includes obeying them, obeying the laws of the land, and paying the various taxes that are due (Romans 13:1–7 and 1 Peter 2:13–17).

What insights do you glean from Psalm 115:1–8, 13 and 135:5–7?

____

____

____

____

____

To God belongs all honor and glory. His greatness, His lovingkindness, and His truth are evident. He is God, and He does as He pleases. Idols can do absolutely nothing. They cannot speak; nor can they see, hear, smell, feel or walk. They cannot respond to anyone or to anyone's deepest needs. God, however, rules over all creation and knows the ways and needs of man in every detail. He can hear, see, and speak, and He gladly turns to the heart that fears Him, whether small or great, rich or poor. He loves and cares greatly and is worthy of great honor.

📖 Look at Romans 11:33–36 and summarize what you find about God.

____

____

____

____

God's wisdom and knowledge are unfathomable, going far beyond our limited understanding and comprehension. We cannot conceive all His ways, for His judgments—the decisions of His mind and heart—are impossible to fully grasp. He is never at a loss as to what to do. He does not need, nor does He ask for our counsel or opinion. He is never dependent on us for anything; nor does He seek from us any clearer understanding on any given topic or any resources or riches from us to complete any given task. We can never say He owes us anything. We must simply declare that He is the source of all things, that through His hands passes all that comes to us, and that to Him all things ultimately answer. All glory and honor and praise goes to Him.

📖 What if we fail to honor God? What is the result? How does such a failure affect our praying? What do you discover in Romans 1:20–21 about these things?

____

____

____

____

____

____

📖 What kind of "worshiping," "serving," and "praying" would go with failing to honor God as God? Look at Romans 1:22–25 and record your insights.

____

____

____

____

The evidence for the existence, the power, and the character of God are scattered throughout His creation. When a person looks around and fails to acknowledge God as the Creator, that person will fail to honor Him as the true God. That means this person will fail to see God as the source of life and all that supports life. Therefore, such a person will not offer any **prayers of thanks** for all God has given. Sadly, this is not the end of the downward spiritual spiral. Human beings were made to worship. If they will not worship the true God, then they will worship false gods in one form or another and walk in lies and superstition. They will pray superstitious prayers. When people do not honor the one incorruptible, eternal God, they will have a thousand lesser gods and idols vying for their attention and affection. They will begin surrendering their **worship, service, and prayers**—their hearts, their minds, and their choices—to false gods. False gods encompass many forms, ranging from images of the corruptible creatures around us—man (and the inventions of man), animals, birds, and even *"crawling creatures."* If we are to worship and pray God's way, we must start by honoring God as God.

How about you? Are you honoring God as your God? Are you living and praying with an awareness of His eternal power, His abilities? What about His divine nature or His holy and loving character? Are these truths affecting the way you pray? Are they real in your heart and mind? Stop for a moment and pray. Ask the Lord to search your heart? Perhaps you could pray the prayer of Psalm 139:23–24, *"Search me, O God, and know my heart; Try me and know my anxious thoughts; and see if there be any hurtful way in me, and lead me in the everlasting way."*

Jesus viewed His Father with honor. That is the foundation of all He did, of how He prayed and how He taught prayer. In John 8:29 Jesus testified, *"I always do the things that are pleasing to Him,"* and in John 8:49 He declared, *"I honor My Father."* He valued His Father and the relationship they had. It was at the heart of everything He prayed. When Jesus taught His disciples about prayer, honoring His Father was at the center of everything He said, so when He commanded His disciples, *"Pray, then, in this way. . . ."* we can be sure He would show them what it meant to value and honor the Father. We will see more of Jesus' teachings concerning prayer in Day Two.

Honoring the Father

DAY TWO

"Our Father Who Art in the Heavens"

How did Jesus view His Father? What does He show us about honoring the Father in "The Disciple's Prayer," especially in the first part of this prayer? As we look at each phrase in that first part, we can begin to see how important it is to truly understand who our Father is and how we can begin to **pray God's way** more consistently and wholeheartedly.

📖 In the prayer pattern Jesus gave, notice first the phrase *"who art in heaven"* in Matthew 6:9. Where is the Father's position, and what does this mean, especially for our praying?

____

____

____

____

____

OUR GOD IS A FATHER

In so many religions of the world fear is the motivating factor, whereas, for the Christian, it is love. That is because God is a Father, and He is the one who first loved us. First John 4:10 says, *"In this is love, not that we loved God, but that He loved us and sent His Son to be the propitiation for our sins."*

Our Father is *"in heaven,"* or literally *"in the heavens."* Our Father is not bound by earthly limitations. He is not limited by time and space as we are. He can work in time and space, but He can also work beyond it. There is a significant truth in the phrase *"in the heavens."* Scripture shows that "the heavens" consist of three areas. The first area is the atmospheric heaven or sky where the birds fly and clouds and rain abound. Then there is the stellar heaven where the sun and stars reside, and then there is the heaven where God's throne and the angels reside. In 2 Corinthians 12:2, Paul speaks of his vision of the third heaven—where he saw and heard unspeakable, indescribable things. Our Father is Lord of all the heavens, including the atmosphere, outer space, and Heaven—our ultimate home. But the phrase, *"who art in heaven,"* is far more than a lesson on where the Father is. *"Who art in heaven"* does not focus mainly on the place, but more on the person—His holiness and power, His exalted and honored position as the God of heaven. When we pray to Him, we are speaking to the Most High God and proclaiming that there is none higher than the God we are worshiping.

Now let's look at those first two words, *"Our Father."* Write your insights into the significance and meaning you see in those two words?

____

____

____

____

____

Extra Mile

THE FATHER'S WORK

Read 2 Corinthians 1:2–5, 8–10. In those verses, how does Paul describe the Father's work on his behalf, especially verses 8–10?

The words *"our Father"* tell us two things. The first truth we must not miss is that this holy and awesome God who rules over the heavens and the earth is our **Father**. We are in a supernatural family with a holy, loving, and powerful Father. Those in a personal relationship with the Father through Jesus Christ can pray to this "Father," their "Abba" or "Daddy." In other words, we are **children** of this Father. When Jesus thought of the Father, He thought in the most personal, intimate, and loving terms. In Mark 14:36, He cried out *"Abba! Father!"*—the term we have already seen as our heart's cry by the power of the Spirit of God (Romans 8:15; Galatians 4:6). As followers of Christ, we are in a unique relationship to God the Father. We are in a relationship with the Father that no one else can claim. For instance, we are in a relationship of comfort and security, knowing His loving presence and His willingness to hear. We are also in a relationship in which we show Him the utmost respect, reverence, and obedience. The second truth is this: we are part of a family of brothers and sisters. He is *"**our** Father,"* referring to the whole family of God.

Our Father is ruler of the heavens and the earth. We saw in an earlier lesson that He is called *"the Father of Mercies and God of All Comfort"* (2 Corinthians 1:3). What else do we learn in other scriptures about our Father?

📖 What do you find about the Father in James 1:17–18?

____

____

____

____

James 1:17–18 speaks of God as *"the Father of lights,"* the Creator, and the one who birthed us into His family. Just as *"the Father of lights"* spoke and created all things, declaring the creation "very good," so in working in our lives, He chose to bring us forth *"by the word of truth,"* the message of Christ and His salvation (see Ephesians 1:13; Colossians 1:5). The word translated *"brought forth"* is the Greek word *apokuéō,* meaning "to give birth." The Father spoke and revealed the truth to us. He birthed us into His family (as a new creation), and He is now working to bring us to maturity. Those verses assure us *"every good thing bestowed and every perfect gift is from above,"* from *"the Father of lights."* Unlike the variations and shadows that come with the light of the sun, moon, and stars, the Father is unchanging and stable, totally dependable. He continually cares for us. We who are *"among the first fruits of His"* creation especially belong to Him, and we can rely on Him throughout life.

Word Study

"FIRST FRUITS"

First fruits in Scripture refer to the firstborn son, the firstborn of the flock or herd, and the first of the harvest that belongs especially to the Lord. It is brought to Him and given to Him. He owns it as His special possession. Believers are the Father's first fruits, set apart as holy and belonging to Him as His treasured possession. (Exodus 13:2; 23:16; 34:22, 26; Leviticus 19:23–25; 23:10).

📖 We find another name for the Father in Ephesians 1:17. How does Paul describe the Father in that verse?

____

____

____

Paul refers to the Father as *"the God of our Lord Jesus Christ"* and *"the Father of glory"* (or as some translate, *"the glorious Father"*). This name, "Father of glory," paints a beautiful picture when we take a deeper look at the word "glory" in Scripture. First, consider the Greek and Hebrew words for "glory." "Glory" is a translation of the Hebrew word *kabod* in the Old Testament, while in the New Testament, it is a translation of the Greek word *dóxa*. The Hebrew word *kabod* literally means "heavy" or "weighty" and was used to speak of a person's honor, esteem, or influence. Among its uses, it can be translated "wealthy" (heavy with possessions or money), "honored" (heavy with influence or position), or "great" (heavy with power). We convey these ideas when we speak of someone in phrases such as, "his words carry a lot of weight" or "He has a weighty influence." So, when we think of "the Father of Glory," we know He is deserving of greatest honor and worship. The root idea of the Greek word *dóxa* is "to form an opinion about," and so its English translation of "glory" or "glorify" points to honoring someone because one has a good opinion about that person. The more we understand who the Father is and what He has done, the greater our opinion of Him becomes. But there is more to this title, "Father of glory."

The more we understand who the Father is and what He has done, the greater our opinion of Him becomes—we "glorify" Him and His Son, our Lord Jesus Christ.

The Father of glory is the revealer of truth. When Paul wrote the letter to the Ephesians, he also understood a connection to the Old Testament that we often miss.

📖 Thinking of *"the Father of Glory,"* read Exodus 40:34–35 (Moses and the Tabernacle) and 1 Kings 8:1–11 (Solomon and the Temple) and record what you find.

____

____

____

____

____

Doctrine

JESUS IS THE WAY

John 1:14 says, *"And the Word became flesh, and dwelt among us."* The word translated "dwelt" can literally be translated "tabernacled" or "tented." Jesus, who is God Himself, came and "tabernacled" on earth in order to reveal the Father, showing the "*glory*" of the Father. Jesus revealed Himself and the Father *"full of grace and truth."* The Father showed us His grace in sending His Son to die for us to forgive us. Not only does God desire to forgive us; He also gives us His grace in everyday situations so we experience His enabling power and presence. He is full of truth, absolutely trustworthy, completely reliable. He wants us to walk with Him in truth. What a privilege that Jesus Christ opened the way for us to come to the Father, to know Him, and to pray to Him."

In the building of the Tabernacle in Moses' day and in the finishing of the Temple in Solomon's day, the Cloud of Glory came and filled both structures, manifesting the presence of the Lord in such a powerful way that the people were awed. That Glory Cloud is sometimes called the "Shekinah Glory" Cloud, from the Hebrew word *shakan,* meaning, "to dwell." This points to the dwelling of God with His people. God's desire to dwell with His people was His overarching purpose for having Moses build the Tabernacle (Exodus 25:8). Solomon built the Temple as the meeting place where God would meet with His people. It was the tangible house of prayer, the place to which they came to meet God and seek Him in prayer. This name, "Father of Glory," reminds us of the way God revealed Himself in the Old and New Testament periods so that people could truly know Him and pray to Him. Such a father who reveals Himself in this fashion is *"our Father who art in the heavens"* (Matthew 6:9 [literal translation]).

This Father *"in the heavens"* is *"our Father," "the Father of lights,"* our Creator who wants us to belong to Him. He cares deeply for each of us. He is *"the Father of Mercies and God of All Comfort"* who comforts us in all kinds of afflictions and pressures. He is *"the Father of Glory"* who reveals Himself through Jesus and wants us to know the riches of a personal relationship with Him through Jesus. As the Father of our Lord Jesus, *"full of grace and truth,"* He is always giving and always trustworthy.

Paul prayed to a Father who is *"full of grace and truth."* Jesus told us to pray to this same Father. Why not spend some time now in prayer to your Father.

Honoring the Father

DAY THREE

"HALLOWED BE THY NAME"

When Jesus spoke of the Father, He first spoke of hallowing His name. We hear that word at times when someone speaks of a hallowed event, an occasion usually viewed as serious or significant in some way. We are to view our Father and our relationship to Him as both serious and significant. Jesus told us to "hallow" the Father's name, to take Him seriously. How are we to do this? We will see in today's lesson.

Jesus called us to pray, *"hallowed be Thy name."* What does it mean to hallow someone's name? You may want to look up "hallow" in an English dictionary or in a Bible dictionary and write what you find.

____

____

____

____

____

Word Study

"HALLOWED"

"Hallowed" is a translation of the Greek word *hagiázō,* which means to treat as holy, as set apart, to honor, thus to treat God as honored and exalted in a class unique to Himself.

The English word "hallow" or "hallowed" is not frequently used today. *Webster's Ninth Dictionary* defines "hallow" as "to make holy or set apart for holy use," or "to respect greatly." To hallow the Father's name means to treat Him as He deserves, to speak of Him with the honor due Him, and to help others do the same. So when we hallow the Father's name, we show great reverence and respect for Him, and that in turn issues in a life of trust and obedience. To hallow or revere the Father's name is a part of honoring Him.

Praying God's Way

"HALLOWED BE THY NAME"

Jesus hallowed His Father's name when He prayed. In John 17, we hear Him say, *"Holy Father"* and *"O Righteous Father"* (John 17:11,25). Jesus did more than just repeat the Father's name. Jesus declared in His prayer, *"I manifested Thy name to the men whom Thou gavest Me out of the world"* (17:6). The Son revealed and honored His Father's name in His lifestyle and His words.

📖 Sometimes the best way to understand a truth is to see its opposite. Read Exodus 20:7 and summarize your insights into this all-important command.

____

____

____

____

The third commandment of the Ten Commandments tells us not to take the name of the Lord in vain or use it in an empty, thoughtless manner. To take His name in vain is not simply a matter of using His name in profanity or in jest or mockery. To take His name in vain is to treat Him as nothing or as worthless, to ignore Him or His Word. That would also mean not trusting Him for who He truly is, not listening attentively to His Word, not seeking Him in prayer, and therefore living a life that fails to depend on Him.

"You shall not take the name of the Lord your God in vain."

Exodus 20:7

How do we treat the name of our heavenly Father in a holy manner, showing His true worth and the respect due Him? What does it really mean to hallow our Father's **name**? We know that in Scripture a person's name is more than a label. It refers to all a person is as well and signifies that person's reputation and character. Even today, we talk about "a name you can trust," referring to a product or service worthy of purchase or to an individual that will uphold his word. To truly honor the Father, we must know His name in truth.

📖 In Exodus 33:18, Moses requested of God, *"show me Thy glory!"* God promised to make His goodness pass before Moses and to **proclaim His name** before Him. Read that promise in Exodus 33:19 and then look at Exodus 34:5–6. What do you discover about the Lord and His name in this encounter? Look for ways that can apply to your life.

____

____

____

____

____

____

The Lord descended in the cloud and stood with Moses. Moses called on the name of the Lord and *"the LORD passed by."* He **proclaimed His name,** declaring and revealing His character as *"compassionate and gracious, slow to anger and abounding in lovingkindness and truth."* These words are more than labels. They describe **who the Lord is.** God's names are more than the words "Lord," or "God," or "King." God's names are the totality of who He is and what He does. In this experience, Moses learned more fully about who God is and could therefore relate to Him more fully, more closely, with more understanding. Knowing the Lord's names is the foundation of each part of the relationship we have with Him. When we understand He is compassionate and gracious, we can come to Him with our weaknesses and failures, our sin and disobedience. We can experience His loving kindness. We have the opportunity to see things correctly, as He who is the truth shows us the truth about our situation or ourselves—or even about our sin. Responding truthfully then to the Lord is part of hallowing His name.

What is the result of knowing God's name according to Psalm 9:9–10? What do these verses imply about prayer?

When we are oppressed or facing trouble, where do we turn? Those who know the name of the Lord turn to Him, put their trust and confidence in Him, and find Him to be a stronghold of protection. Knowing His name means knowing who He is, of what He is capable and how He works. Putting trust in Him includes seeking Him in prayer. That is part of what it means to hallow or reverence His name. To trust the Lord is to show dependence on Him by seeking Him in prayer, knowing He will live up to His name.

Psalm 91 is a psalm of trust in the Lord. Read this psalm and complete all exercises pertaining to it.

Note the names of God used or the way the protection of God is described (especially verses 1, 2, 4, 9). What does this psalm reveal about the difference knowing God's name makes in a person's life?

What do you find about knowing God's name in Psalm 91:14? What promise for prayer do you find in verse 15?

One who knows the Lord as the Most High runs to Him for protection. As the *"Most High,"* He rules over all. There is none greater. The one who knows this comes to Him and recognizes Him as sovereign Lord. He is also *"the Almighty"* in whom is all power. *"The Almighty"* is a translation of *shaddai* and can be described as "the all-sufficient one." It is a word that speaks of the suf-

Doctrine

"FATHER, GLORIFY THY NAME"

Jesus prayed this just days before He went to the cross. To *"glorify"* is a translation of the Greek word *doxá*, which literally means, "to form an opinion about." When we "glorify" someone, we have seen some truth about that person and have formed an opinion to praise that person in some measure. Jesus revealed the truth about the Father so that all could see and form an opinion, which in turn would lead to great praise, adoration, and trusting obedience. When we obey the Father and follow Jesus as Lord in the daily decisions of life, we are glorifying the Father through His Son.

Did You Know?

THE NAMES OF GOD

In Scripture, every name of God is a revelation of God. He revealed Himself to Abraham as Jehovah or *Yahweh* ("the LORD"), then *El Elyon* ("God Most High"), as *El Shaddai* ("God Almighty"), and then as *Yahweh Jireh* ("the LORD Our Provider"). (See Genesis 12:1, 7; 14:18–20, 17:1; 22:14.) Every revelation brought forth a new name, and every name brought forth clearer revelation. With increased revelation came the opportunity for God's people to develop a deeper faith, a stronger trust, and a greater love. Every name for God gives us an opportunity to hallow God, to honor and trust Him in some area of our lives. In the case of Abraham, he grew in his knowledge of God and in his faith and confidence in God. He grew so much that he trusted God to give him and Sarah a child, even though they were past childbearing years (see Romans 4:13, 16–25).

ficiency of a mother nursing her child with the child finding all the nourishment he needs in the arms of his mother. This God is able to deliver from the traps and deceitful schemes of others (including the temptations of the evil one, Satan). In addition, the Lord is pictured as a mother bird, covering and caring for her young who run to her for protection. The Most High is a refuge, like a cave in the wilderness. God promises that the one who loves and trusts Him will find His protection because that person knows His name; hence, God *"will set him on high"*—safe and secure. Such a person knows the value of calling on the Lord in prayer and the experience of the Lord's presence. God promises to *"answer him,"* to be *"with him in trouble,"* to *"deliver him and honor him."* What a treasure to know the name of the Lord!

When we pray *"hallowed be Thy name,"* we are asking that God be treated with the respect and honor due to Him as our Father. We are also asking that others come to see Him for who He is and that they love, trust, and obey Him accordingly. This is a prayer for others to know and honor the Father as their heavenly Father. In light of these truths, pause and pray to your Father.

If we know who God is as our Father, we also need to know that He is King over all. What does it mean to be a part of His kingdom and to know Him as our King? We will begin to see in Day Four.

"Because he has loved Me, therefore I will deliver him; I will set him securely on high, because he has known My name. He will call upon Me, and I will answer him; I will be with him in trouble; I will rescue him, and honor him.

2 Corinthians 5:17

"Thy Kingdom Come, Thy Will Be Done on Earth, as It Is in Heaven"

Honoring the Father

DAY FOUR

When Jesus instructed us to pray, *"Thy kingdom come,"* He linked that with hallowing the Father's name and His will being done on earth. How do all these elements tie together? What are we praying when we pray "Thy kingdom come"? We will examine this aspect of "The Disciple's Prayer" further in today's lesson.

📖 The first thing to understand about a kingdom is that it is always inseparably linked to a king. Read and meditate on these verses and record what you find about God as King.

Psalm 47:2; 95:3 and Jeremiah 10:7

____

____

____

____

Psalm 99:1–5

____

____

____

____

"Now to the King eternal, immortal, invisible, the only God, be honor and glory forever and ever. Amen."

I Timothy 1:17

Isaiah 6:1–5 and 44:6

Psalm 5:2

Psalm 10:16–18 (Note what kind of King the Lord is.)

The LORD Most High is a great king who reigns over all the earth, over all nations and over all "gods." He is to be feared, reverenced, and honored as God and King. All should exalt and worship this King whose name is worthy of great praise. He is holy and awesome in all He does. He loves justice and righteousness. When Isaiah saw Him, he was awestruck in His holy and majestic presence and deeply convicted of his sin. This King alone is God and Redeemer, the first and the last, over all time and eternity. He listens to the desire and the cry of the humble. He is eager to come to the aid of the fatherless and the oppressed and to stop the wickedness of man. God our King is also God our Father, the one who hears our cries when we call on Him in prayer.

📖 What are the marks of God's kingdom and those who belong to His kingdom? Read and meditate on these verses and describe some of the characteristics of God's kingdom.

Psalm 45:6 and 145:13

Psalm 145:11–12

Matthew 7:21

____

____

____

____

Romans 14:17

____

____

____

____

Colossians 1:13–14

____

____

____

____

God's throne and God's kingdom endure forever. His kingdom is marked by righteousness; He always upholds **His** standard of right. His kingdom is marked by glory, majesty, and power, and those who belong to His kingdom are marked by righteousness, joy, and peace because of the presence and the work of His Spirit. When one enters this kingdom, he or she moves from the domain of darkness and deception into the kingdom of Jesus, the beloved Son of the Father, and that one receives redemption—all sins are forgiven, paid for by the Lord Jesus. One who lives in the kingdom of heaven does the will of the Father, obeying Him from the heart. What a wonderful kingdom! It lasts forever and is marked by righteousness, glory, majesty, joy, peace, light, forgiveness, and obedience to the Father. Who wouldn't want to live forever in that kind of kingdom!

What a wonderful kingdom! It lasts forever and is marked by righteousness, glory, majesty, joy, peace, light, forgiveness, and obedience to the Father. Who wouldn't want to live forever in that kind of kingdom!

Sometimes, it helps to see the opposite of something. The contrast helps define what we are looking at. What do you discover about the kingdom and the conditions out of which we came in contrast to being in the kingdom of God? Read these verses and record your answer.

Acts 26:18

____

____

____

____

Colossians 1:13–14

____

____

____

____

Galatians 5:19–21 with 1 Corinthians 6:9–11

____

____

____

____

Ephesians 2:1–3, 12 with 5:5–8

____

____

____

____

Titus 3:3–7

____

____

____

____

Once we were under the dominion of Satan and his deceptions, walking in darkness and disobedience, indulging our lusts. We were also dead in trespasses and sins, destined to receive the wrath of God. The marks of one in this condition, a person outside the Kingdom of God, can include immorality, idolatry, stealing, coveting, drunkenness, dishonesty, and all kinds of impurity, both mental and moral. One who practices these sins as a lifestyle has never entered the kingdom of God and cannot expect to inherit any part of the kingdom unless he turns to God in repentance and faith, yielding to Him as King and Savior. One existing outside the kingdom of God walks in darkness and is separated from Christ—with no hope. Before God saved us and placed us in His kingdom, we were like those described in Titus 3:3—*"foolish, disobedient, deceived, enslaved to various lusts and pleasures,"* full of malice, envy, and hate. But God changed us through the work of Christ by His Spirit so that we could know His forgiveness and the joy of His life within.

In the Scriptures, often when the kingdom of God is mentioned, it is in relationship to individuals. Jesus once told a scribe, *"You are not far from the kingdom of God"* (Mark 12:34). One night, Nicodemus, a *"ruler of the Jews,"* came to Jesus with some questions concerning the kingdom of God.

"Truly, truly, I say to you, unless one is born again, he cannot see the kingdom of God."

—Jesus in John 3:3

📖 What did Jesus tell Nicodemus about the kingdom of God? Read John 3:1–16, noting especially verses 3 and 5. How does one enter the kingdom of God?

____

____

____

____

____

____

Nicodemus came to Jesus at night with some questions about all that Jesus was doing and teaching. Jesus talked to him about the kingdom. He began explaining to Nicodemus that in order to *"***see** *the kingdom of God,"* one must be born again or be born from above. The idea of being "born again" did not make sense to Nicodemus. Jesus added that one must be birthed by the Spirit in order to **"enter** *into the kingdom of God."* Being born again is a supernatural event, a supernatural entrance into God's kingdom. Jesus went on to explain about what it means to believe in Him and receive eternal life and a place in God's kingdom. Kingdom subjects know and walk with God as their Father and King.

Access to the kingdom of God is all about matters of the heart. When one enters the kingdom of God, that person's heart changes, as well as that person's relationships with God and others. *"Righteousness, and peace and joy in the Holy Spirit"* are things of the heart that come out in the lifestyle, especially in relationships with others (see Romans 14:13–21). Kingdom subjects walk in righteousness before God and with one another. They have a heart to do what is right, and the Holy Spirit who resides within leads them in that right living. They walk in peace with God and peace with one another. They walk in the joy of the Holy Spirit as they follow their Father-King and do His will.

To pray "Thy kingdom come" is first to pray for the rule of Jesus Christ and the Father over one's own heart and life. That life, surrendered to Jesus as Lord, no longer has to be dominated by Satan, by deception, darkness, disobedience, and condemnation. Those who are in the kingdom of God are no longer hopeless and no longer need to be ignorant of the forgiveness of sin that God provides. To pray "Thy kingdom come" is also to pray for people on earth to come under the kingship of Jesus Christ and to know God as their Father-King.

Pause and thank God that you are part of His kingdom. Then pray for someone who needs to know God as their Father and Jesus as their King and Savior.

What more does it mean for God's kingdom to come? Ultimately, praying "Thy kingdom come" is to pray for the true reign of Christ over all the earth. Revelation 20:1–10 speaks of the future reign of Christ on earth. At the close of Christ's earthly reign, He will usher in new heavens and a new earth. Peter declared concerning the final goal of God, *"But according to His promise, we are looking for new heavens and a new earth, in which righteousness dwells"* (2 Peter 3:13). Revelation 21—22 speaks in broader detail of these new heavens and the new earth. But for now, we see the kingdom advancing one heart at a time.

Jesus also said to pray, *"Thy will be done on earth as it is in heaven."* If we are to truly honor our Father, we must honor His wishes, His will. To say we are honoring Him and then ignore what He wants is to deceive ourselves **and** to greatly dishonor Him. To do His will we need to know His will. We have all asked, "What is God's will?" and heard others ask it as well. What do we need to discover about God's will, particularly *"as it is in heaven"*?

How is God's will done in heaven? Psalm 103:19–22 gives us some clues. Read that passage and record what you find.

____

____

____

Put Yourself in Their Shoes

BORN TO FOLLOW

What a difference we see between being part of the kingdom of God and being outside the kingdom! How does one become a part of the kingdom of God? Jesus told Nicodemus that one has to be born again or born from above to see and enter the kingdom of God (John 3:3, 5). Being born from above comes with placing one's faith and trust in Jesus Christ as Lord and Savior, believing in Him (John 3:16). This is more than mental assent. It is repenting of one's sin, trusting His death on the cross as payment for sin, entrusting one's life to Him as Lord and Savior, and relying on Him to give His resurrection life, eternal life. One born into the kingdom not only receives eternal life, but will one day reign with Christ the King (Revelation 5:10; 20:4).

Doctrine

WHO IS A KINGDOM MEMBER?

Jesus spoke about the nature of a true son. The one who does the will of the Father belongs to Him, is part of His family, and is a subject of His kingdom. In Matthew 7:21, Jesus said, *"He who does the will of My Father who is in heaven"* enters the kingdom. In Matthew 21:28–32, Jesus spoke the parable of the two sons. He told of the son who said he would obey, but did not, and of the son who said he would not, but did. The conclusion: the one who does the will of his Father is the one who is a kingdom member.

The psalmist David acknowledged that God is enthroned in the heavens and rules over all. His angels obey Him at all times and in all places of His dominion. Their mighty strength is ever at His command and call to fulfill all His word and all His will. **All** the hosts of God do His will. The atmosphere of heaven can be described as a place filled with creatures (both human and supernatural) that are entirely devoted to honoring God and carrying out His will. In heaven, God the Father is praised the way He should be. His name is hallowed the way it should be, and the kingdom order is as it should be. We could sum up this truth by saying that God's will in heaven is done promptly, continually, fully, and gladly. Everyone there does His will; there are no marginal people or angels, no "fence-straddlers." His will is done in every part of heaven; there are no pockets of resistance. All is done with love and honor to the Father. God wants His will done on earth in this same, unanimous fashion. Though the earth is filled with imperfect people and is generally populated with those who walk *"according to the prince of the power of the air"* (Satan), we can still pray that God's will may be done promptly, continually, fully, lovingly, and gladly here on earth—for as His will is done in heaven, so may it be on earth. This is why Jesus taught us to pray that the Father's will be done *"on earth as it is in heaven."*

In light of the truths found in Psalm 103, pause and pray *"Thy will be done . . .* **in my life** *. . . on earth as it is in heaven."* Then, pray for the salvation of those you know who have not yet placed their faith in Jesus as Lord and Savior—that they too could know and do the Father's will in their lives.

How can we apply all the truths we have seen from Days One through Four so that our lives and our prayers honor the Father in the way He deserves? We will see in Day Five.

Honoring the Father

DAY FIVE

FOR ME TO PRAY GOD'S WAY

When we speak of honoring our Father, it is important to understand what the Scriptures say about "honor." The Greek word for "honor" is *timḗ* or *timáō,* which means "to value," "to prize," "to honor or "to esteem." These words are rooted in the word *tíō,* which means "to pay (a price)" and are sometimes used of money paid for something. We find these words often in the New Testament (see 1 Corinthians 3:12) and in the Greek Old Testament (also known as the Septuagint), speaking of costly jewels or precious stones like those the Queen of Sheba brought as a gift to Solomon (1 Kings 10:2; 2 Chronicles 9:1, 10). Understanding that honoring someone involves placing high value on that person and seeing that individual as of great worth helps us evaluate how we are honoring God our Father. He is of ultimate value and worth, and we need to honor Him accordingly.

God our Father is of ultimate value and worth, and we need to honor Him accordingly.

First, it is important for each of us to know **what** God values so we can properly line up our hearts with His heart and His values. Look at each of these verses and record what God values.

Psalm 116:15

____

____

____

____

Psalm 138:2

____

____

____

____

Proverbs 3:13–15 and 8:11

____

____

____

____

John 5:23 (22–24) and 8:54

____

____

____

____

As we search the Scriptures, we discover Jesus in the Gospel of John clearly revealing the values of His Father and Himself. God the Father values and honors His Son, our Lord Jesus, and the Son honors His Father. God the Father honors our trust or belief in His Son and in the words His Son says. Psalm 138:2 also points to the high value God places on His Word. The Lord sees the death of His saints as *"precious,"* a word used of the most precious jewels. God sees His saints as treasures of great worth. When we value our brothers and sisters in Christ, we are honoring our Father (see 1 John 4:20–21). Proverbs makes it clear that the wisdom of God and the Word of God are of inestimable value. God highly values His Son, His redeemed children, His wisdom and His Word—and so should we.

The "things," activities, events, or people you value can be seen in your investment of time, money, thought, and care.

APPLY What do you value—put a high price on, see as worth your investment? The "things," activities, events, or people you value can be seen in your investment of time, money, thought, and care. Let's pause and evaluate. On a scale of one to five (**1** representing very little value and **5** representing very much value) rate how valuable the following items are to you today.

having a daily quiet time in Scripture and prayer_____

owning a home _____

involvement in world missions_____

getting an education_____

owning a car_____

involvement in politics_____

making more money_____

being more successful in my job_____

getting plenty of exercise_____

seeking opportunities to share the gospel with others_____

being well dressed_____

friends_____

community activities_____

the approval of others_____

extra time reading and meditating on God's word_____

family relationships/ family activities_____

being involved in sports_____

seeking God's wisdom for daily decisions_____

extra time in prayer_____

fellowshipping with other Christians_____

other priorities (you name it…) ______________________________

APPLY In light of the truths we have seen in Day Five, what are some ways you can honor the Father, especially in prayer? Read each of the verses given below in the light of hallowing the Father's name, seeking His kingdom, and following His will. Record any personal applications you see.

His name

"In God we have boasted all day long, and we will give thanks to Thy name forever" (Psalm 44:8).

"As is Thy name, O God, so is Thy praise to the ends of the earth" (Psalm 48:10a).

My thoughts or personal applications . . .

____

____

____

____

____

His kingdom

"But seek first His kingdom and His righteousness, and all these things shall be added unto you" (Matthew 6:33).

My thoughts or personal applications . . .

____

____

____

____

____

His will

"That you may stand perfect [complete or mature] *and fully assured in all the will of God"* (Colossians 4:12).

"You ought to say, 'If the Lord wills, we shall live and also do this or that" (James 4:15).

My thoughts or personal applications . . .

God wants His will done promptly, continually, fully, lovingly, and gladly.

Close your time of study with a word of prayer.

Father, I hallow Your name. You are honored above all. In many ways I have just begun to see the value of who You are and all You have done, all You are doing, and all You will do. You are worthy of all praise. Your name I honor and praise. Thank You for calling me into the kingdom of Your Son, making me a kingdom subject and allowing me to follow Jesus as my King. May Your kingdom come in more and more hearts, leading up to that great day when your kingdom shall rule over all the earth. Give me the wisdom and boldness to tell others how they can come into Your kingdom. May the life of the Lord Jesus be clearly seen filling and controlling me in my everyday living so that Your will is done more fully in my life. I know You desire that Your will be done promptly, continually, fully, lovingly, and gladly. Thank You that Jesus lives in me to make that a reality. Thank You that one day we will see Your will fully accomplished in the new heavens and new earth and we will see You honored fully as You deserve. In Jesus' name, Amen.

Record your prayer or a journal entry in the space below.

Notes

MY PRAYERS AS INCENSE

OFFERING TO GOD THE INCENSE OF PRAISE AND THANKSGIVING

In both the Old and New Testaments, we read of incense being offered up to God. The incense of the Tabernacle (and later the Temple) is a picture of the prayers of God's people—all kinds of prayer, prayers of praise and thanksgiving, as well as prayers of petition and intercession. When we picture prayers offered up "as incense" we discover a beautiful expression of worship. The fragrant aroma of incense marked the Tabernacle and Temple of old, and the fragrant aroma of prayer should mark each Christian, each "temple of the Holy Spirit," today.

When we picture prayers offered up as incense, we discover a beautiful expression of worship.

Just as there were many ingredients that went into the incense in the Tabernacle, so there are many kinds of prayer that daily ascend to the Father. We have seen how prayer encompasses calling on the name of the Lord, crying out to Him over one's need for salvation, and then crying out in dependence on Him in a thousand other ways. We have seen the importance of humility before our Lord, the place of confession of sin, the wonder of discovering our Father's forgiveness, and the essential role of the Word of God in praying (learning the value of God's guidebook for praying God's way). These truths have led us to understand the necessity and privilege of honoring our Father and His will. In this lesson, we will see the scriptural picture of incense, particularly the incense of praise and thanksgiving.

In the lessons to follow, we have more offerings of incense to view—the incense of petition, which is asking for our personal

"...There shall be perpetual incense before the LORD throughout your generations."

Exodus 30:8b

needs, and the incense of intercession, which is learning what it means to pray for others. Then, there is the incense of anguish, that warfare in prayer. There we become aware of the battles in prayer and of the Lord, our warrior and victor in those battles. We will look at the incense of praying together and discover the dynamic that too many Christians miss in their walk with God. Finally, we will see the incense of Jesus' prayer life, the most costly and precious of all incense, the incense of His holy life.

In this lesson, we will look at the incense of praise and thanksgiving that flows from a heart that knows and honors the Father. Because of the work of Jesus, we can know the Father and experience His Life as well as His ongoing love and forgiveness. Knowing His love leads to offerings of praise and thanksgiving. We have much to praise and thank our Father for, and in the days ahead we will see what it means to offer up our sacrifices of praise and thanksgiving to Him. First, let's seek to get a good understanding of the incense of the Old Testament.

DAY ONE

A Look at Pure Incense

When we enter into the environs of the Tabernacle in Exodus, we find a holy structure set apart for the worship of God. We see a place where God promised to dwell and speak to His people. We experience a place where hundreds of sacrifices were offered in the years in the wilderness and then in the land of Israel. We also see the place where daily incense arose to God, a picture of the people's prayers to their Lord. We saw some of these truths in last week's lesson. What more can we see? What was this incense like? What can we learn from such a simple picture? We will begin to develop answers to these questions as we proceed with this lesson.

Read Exodus 30:1–8. What do you learn about the incense offering? Where and when was it to be offered?

____

____

____

____

____

Did You Know?

THE COALS OF THE ALTAR

Incense was placed on the golden altar. The coals upon which the incense was placed came from the bronze altar in the outer court of the Tabernacle. Those coals were part of the fires that burned the sacrifices. The blood of those sacrifices touched those coals. God prescribed that the coals for burning incense must come from the bronze altar. He considered any other coals unclean. These coals represent the blood shed in the righteous sacrifices of the offerings, especially the twice-daily burnt offerings. The offerings and the blood of the outer court touched the offering of incense; the offering of incense was connected to the truths of forgiveness and surrender pictured in those offerings at the bronze altar. When Nadab and Abihu offered up incense using *"strange fire,"* coals from some other fire, the fire of God struck them dead. God declared at that time, *"By those who come near Me I will be treated as holy, and before all the people I will be honored"* (Leviticus 10:1–3).

God made provision for the incense to be offered on the golden altar of incense in the Holy Place in front of the veil separating the Holy Place from the Holy of Holies. Every morning and every afternoon, the priest was to burn incense on that golden altar, a perpetual burning of incense in the Tabernacle (and later in the Temple). That daily practice was for every generation of Israelites, not just for those who first came out of Egypt.

To better understand what this meant, it would be good to describe the daily routine of the priest. Every morning around 9:00 A.M. and every afternoon around 3:00 P.M., the priest would offer the burnt offering on the bronze altar in the outer court of the Tabernacle. After offering that burnt offering and washing in the laver of water, the priest would come into the Holy Place, the first indoor room of the Tabernacle. This room had walls of gold and was lighted by seven olive oil lamps on the seven-branch lampstand, a lampstand made of over one hundred pounds of gold. Within that first room, the lamp stand shone its light on the gold covered table of showbread (or the bread of presence) and on the golden altar of incense.

After trimming the lamps, the priest would go to the golden altar, carrying the hot blood-soaked coals he had brought from the bronze altar. He placed those coals on top of the golden altar and then took a handful of incense from a golden pan beside the golden altar and placed that incense on those coals. (We read about these golden pans in Numbers 7:14, 84, 86.) The smoke and the aroma of the incense ascended up in front of the veil and symbolically lifted before the enthroned presence of God. All of this pictured a walk with God in the light, fellowshipping with Him in the light of His presence, experiencing a walk characterized by the incense of prayer every morning and every afternoon. What can we learn from this experience of the priests?

📖 Look at Exodus 30:34–38. List the characteristics of the incense that was acceptable to God.

____

____

____

____

____

What do the characteristics given in verse 35 tell you about this incense?

____

____

____

____

The incense that pleased God contained the **exact ingredients** He prescribed and, when combined, made a fragrant perfume. He allowed no substitutes in ingredients or procedures. The ingredients, which were to be beaten very fine, included the spices of stacte, onycha, galbanum, and frankincense, along with salt. This incense was to be **salted** so there would be no decay in it, no stench of rottenness. The incense was to be **pure** with no added mixtures put in (and none taken out). It was **holy** incense, set apart to God and His use, for the proper worship of Him. The priests took some of this incense and placed it in golden pans or dishes in the Holy Place ready for the priests use each day.

In the Old Testament and in the New Testament, we see incense symbolically associated with prayer. Look at the characteristics of the incense in Exodus 30:34–37. List the four characteristics given in verse 35.

____

____

____

____

The Spices of the Incense were stacte, onycha, galbanum, frankincense, along with salt. **Stacte** is an aromatic gum. The Hebrew word for **"onycha"** means to peel off or scale and possibly refers to an aromatic mussel. **Galbanum** is also an aromatic gum. **Frankincense** literally means "to be white" and is a white or yellowish gum or resin obtained from slitting the bark of the Boswellia Serrata tree, a tree native to central and southern India. Once the fragrant sap is harvested from the trees, it hardens. The frankincense used in the Tabernacle probably came from Arabia, having been imported from India. **Salt** was added to the fragrance of the incense and served as a preservative for these spices, keeping the incense free of decay and ready as a "fragrant aroma" before the Lord.

If incense is symbolic of a prayer to God, what do these characteristics tell us about prayer that is pleasing to God? (Look at Proverbs 15:8 for additional insight. As a help in describing that which is "pure" and "holy," you may also want to read James 3:14–17 and 1 John 2:15–17.)

____

____

____

____

____

Put Yourself in Their Shoes

GOD WANTS HOLY PRAYER

Just as the incense of the Old Testament was considered holy, so in the New Testament we find the Lord's instructions through Paul in I Timothy 2:8: *"Therefore I want the men in every place to pray lifting up holy hands, without wrath and dissension."* Holy hands speak of hands whose actions please the Lord, hands guided by a heart free of selfish motives, wrong relationships, or disruptive actions. Wrath refers to an angry or revengeful disposition toward someone else, and dissension points to quarreling, disputing, open opposition, even backbiting and divisiveness between believers. Those things corrupt prayer and are not a pleasing offering to the Lord. He wants holy, pure prayer marked by His character, His concerns, and His heart.

Just as incense is to be God's recipe, with the ingredients God orders, so prayer is to be God's recipe. We are not to come up with our own ideas for prayer and offer them to God. Prayer starts in the heart of God. What we are to pray must agree with His heart and mind. That is the meaning of praying according to His will. Prayer should be as **"a perfume,"** a fragrant offering to the Lord. That means prayer should be pleasing to God. It should not be offensive in any way. When we pray God's way, He is glad. Proverbs 15:8 says, *"the sacrifice* [or offering] *of the wicked is an abomination to the LORD, but the prayer of the upright is His delight."* Prayer must also be **"salted"** or protected from decay. Prayer must have no unrighteousness in it—no decay of the flesh and no self-centered elements. In previous lessons, we have seen that God does not want any fleshly show, nor any fleshly formulas offered to Him. Fleshly praying is unacceptable to God.

The Father also wants **"pure"** prayer, prayer that has no added mixture, nothing of the world's wisdom or the world's desires. James 3 tells us *"the wisdom from above is first pure,"* just so, the prayer God accepts must be pure. God leads us in pure prayer; it comes from above. It has nothing of the world's wisdom, that which is *"earthly, sensual, demonic"* (James 3:15 NKJV). The prayer that God delights to hear is not marked by the limited opinions of the earthly realm, nor the corrupt, decaying thoughts of the sensual realm, nor the deceptive thoughts of the demonic realm. He wants no prayer marked by the world's desires—*"the lust of the flesh and the lust of the eyes and the boastful pride of life"* (1 John 2:16). God wants to hear prayer that is marked by the things that agree with His thoughts, His Word, His wisdom from above, and His will that "abides forever" (1 John 2:17).

The prayer God in which God delights is also **"holy"** like the incense of the Tabernacle. That means it is set apart for His use, without sin or selfishness or rebellion. It is prayer that worships God in spirit and truth and that is marked by the beauty of holiness. It is also submitted to His will and for His glory. One other characteristic of this prayer is its exclusive use for the purposes of God. Therefore, prayer is never for selfish use but for the fulfilling of God's will. That does not mean prayer cannot include personal requests. We have seen how God wants us to call on Him for personal needs, and we will see that in greater detail in future lessons. Are personal needs and requests acceptable to God? Yes, of course they are! Are selfish wants acceptable to God? Never!

There is more to see about this incense in the pages of Scripture. We will examine more of these characteristics in Day Two.

The Incense Offered Up

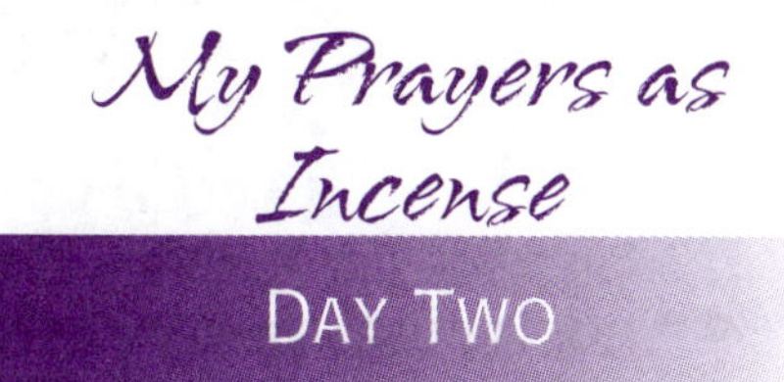

What did this incense mean to the people of God? What significance did it play in their worship of God? Of even more importance, what did this incense mean to God? How did He view the incense offered up before Him?

King David, known as a man after God's own heart, understood what it meant to walk with God. What did he say about prayer and incense in Psalm 141:1–2? You may want to look at the verses that follow to see the fuller prayer David offered.

____

____

____

____

David called upon the Lord in a time of great need. He wanted God to *"hasten"* to him and listen to his prayer. David desired that his prayer be *"counted as incense"* before the Lord, like the evening offering before His presence. The Hebrew word translated "counted" can also be translated "fixed" or "established." Like the incense offering was fixed or established as an offering that was acceptable before the Lord, so David desired that his prayer be fixed before the Lord as an acceptable request. He asked the Lord in Psalm 141:3–4 to stand at the door of his lips ready to hear every word, making sure those words had no evil intent or evil request. He only wanted to walk in righteousness and know the Lord's protection from all wickedness.

How did people in the New Testament view this incense? We find a clue in the Gospel of Luke. Read Luke 1:5–13, especially verses 9–10. What did the people do during the time of offering incense?

____

____

____

____

In Luke 1:10, we find the people at the Temple associating the offering of incense with a time of prayer, a time to call on the Lord in thanksgiving and praise. Luke 1 presents to us the story of Zacharias and Elizabeth and the miraculous birth of their son, John. This couple had prayed for years that God would give them a son, but eventually gave up on their request since Elizabeth had long exceeded the natural childbearing age. The announcement of the delayed answer to their prayers and the coming birth of John occurred when Zacharias was offering incense in the Temple. While he was completing that duty, the people were outside in prayer in the Temple area. It was the custom of the day for those who could do so to come to the Temple for a time of prayer every morning at 9:00 and every afternoon at 3:00 when the priests were carrying out the offering of the burnt offering along with the incense offering. Worshipers associated this time of offering as a time of prayer before the Lord, symbolically offered in the incense and actually offered in the prayers of the people at the Temple.

Put Yourself in Their Shoes

THE POSTURE OF PRAYER

With what posture are we supposed to pray? Must it always be with head bowed and eyes closed, or is there another way? When we survey Scripture, we find a number of postures in prayer. In Psalm 141:2, David speaks of **lifting up his hands** before the Lord. When Solomon began praying at the dedication of the Temple, *"he stood before the altar of the Lord . . . and spread out his hands"* (2 Chronicles 6:12). Then **he knelt.** First Kings 8:54 adds that when he finished praying, *"he arose from before the altar of the Lord, from kneeling on his knees with his* ***hands spread toward heaven."*** Paul says in I Timothy 2:8, *"I want the men in every place to pray lifting holy hands without wrath and dissension."* David is pictured **sitting** before the Lord in 2 Samuel 7:18, while John 17:1 reveals Jesus ***"lifting up His eyes*** *to heaven."* In all these postures, it is not the posture but the heart that counts before God. Often the heart will determine the posture, but regardless of the posture, we need to pray.

Look at Revelations 5:1–8, especially verse 8. What do you discover about incense? (You may want to read Numbers 7:1–2, 12, 14, and 84–86 for an Old Testament picture of the golden bowls.)

____

____

____

____

____

____

____

Put Yourself in Their Shoes

INCENSE AND PRAYER

Several significant prayers were offered at the time of the offering of the evening sacrifice/incense offering. Elijah prayed for God to bring down fire on the sacrifice in front of the prophets of Baal (1 Kings 18:36). Ezra offered his prayer for the people of God at the time of the evening sacrifice (Ezra 9:5–15), and Daniel lifted his prayer for the people of God during this time (Daniel 9:20–21).

When God gave the apostle John a vision of heaven, He showed him twenty-four elders, representative of the saints of the ages. They had white garments and gold victors' crowns (Greek—*stephanos,* the victor's crown). Each one held a harp and a golden bowl filled with incense. This incense represents the prayers of the saints. When the elders saw the enthroned Lamb that was also the Lion of Judah, they fell before Him in worship.

What is the expression of their heart, that which fits with the use of a harp and incense? What do you find them singing before the Lord in Revelation 5:9–10?

____

____

____

____

____

____

Did You Know?

HARPS IN PRAISE AND PROPHECY

In the Old Testament, we find the harp used in times of praise (1 Chronicles 15:16; 25:6; Psalm 33:2). It was also used at times when a prophetic word came from the Lord (1 Samuel 10:5; 1 Chronicles 25:1). In Revelation 5:8, the elders are each holding a harp and a golden bowl of incense. The harp fits with the song they sang in praise of the Lamb as well as the prophetic word about the future reign of the saints on the earth.

In this vision, each of the elders has a harp (an instrument of praise) and a bowl of incense (a picture of prayer). Their voices begin to express the praise of their hearts. Their offering of prayer is an offering of praise to the Lamb. He alone is worthy to take the scroll and break its seals because He was slain, and by His death purchased people from *"every tribe and tongue and people and nation."* He is the Lamb on the throne, indicating that He is Lord of all heaven and earth. Therefore, He has the right to take the scroll and carry out the decrees written on it. The focus of the elders' praise is the Lamb, the price He paid to redeem man, and the place of reigning He gives to all the redeemed. Their praise and thanksgiving is a sweet offering, a glad song, a song worthy of the Lamb to whom it is sung.

The offering of incense is a picture of pure prayer, a visual representation of the sweet aroma of worship coming from surrendered, praise-filled, grateful hearts. What does Scripture show us about this worship? There are many expressions of prayer in the Scripture. In this lesson, we will look at two of the most joyful, the offerings of praise and thanksgiving. In the next lesson, we will look at the incense of asking, seeking from the Lord His answers to our petitions. Then, we will look at intercession, the incense of praying for others. For now, what can we learn about the offering of praise to God? We will see in Day Three.

The Incense of Sincere Praise

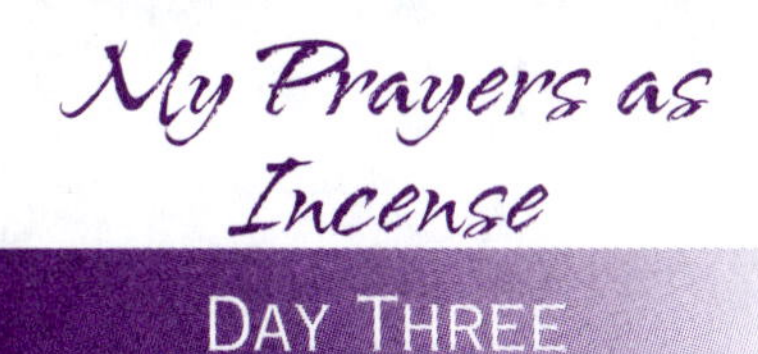

The Scriptures are full of praise for our God, for His character, for His wonderful works, for His gracious and merciful ways, and for His awesome plans both in time and in eternity. We saw in Day Two how the twenty-four elders offered their incense of praise for the redemption provided by the Lamb of God. Today, we will look at several offerings of sincere praise and examine ways we can offer that incense more effectively and more whole-heartedly.

Sincere praise begins when we understand the infinite value and worth of God, including His perfect character and far-reaching love as well as His power and ability to accomplish all His good purposes. We will look at an example of one who offered sincere praise in the life of King David. Though David was Israel's greatest king, he was also the psalmist who understood many elements of sincere, heartfelt praise.

📖 Look at these expressions of praise in the Scriptures listed below and summarize what you find, especially about offering up sincere praise.

Psalm 34:1–8

____

____

____

____

____

Psalm 63:1–8

____

____

____

____

____

Psalm 34 was written after David escaped from the Philistine king Abimelech and possible death. David's heart expressed praise for the Lord for hearing him when he sought Him, for delivering and protecting him. David called on all who would read or hear his words to *"magnify the Lord with me, and let us exalt His name together,"* and then urged, *"taste and see that the Lord is good; how blessed is the man who takes refuge in him."* David's cry and call is one of sincere, heartfelt praise. Psalm 63 is the heart cry of David when he was in the wilderness of Judah, a dry and deserted land. He focused on God, praising Him as God, as the quencher of his thirsty soul. David praised and blessed the Lord, declaring that His merciful lovingkindness was *"better than life."* This was no empty flattery or showy prayer. The Lord was the satisfaction of David's soul, so David could offer praise with joyful lips even in a barren land. Like a mother bird protecting her young, so the Lord protected David—and David, like those young birds, could sing for joy in His presence, offering abundant praise to the Lord.

Did You Know?

SINGING IN SCRIPTURE

There are over two hundred verses in Scripture containing the words "singing," "sing," "singer," "song," and "songs." Most of these verses refer to singing to the Lord as an act of worship. We find a beautiful example of singing praise in Exodus 15 after the Lord miraculously led the children of Israel through the Red Sea, delivering them from the armies of Pharaoh. In Judges 5, the Song of Deborah and Barak expressed great praise for the victory God gave over Jabin and the Canaanites. The Psalms speak often of singing a *"new song"* to the Lord for the salvation and victory He has given (Psalm 33:3; 40:3; 96:1; 98:1; 144:9; 149:1). The titles of 56 psalms give directions to *"the chief musician"* (KJV), indicating the author intended that they be sung by the people of God. Paul spoke of the expression of the Spirit-filled believer in Ephesians 5:19 as *"speaking to one another in psalms and hymns and spiritual songs, singing and making melody with your heart to the Lord."* God is a God of song, and His people are meant to sing in their hearts alone as well as with one another, celebrating who He is and all He has done.

For what can you pause and praise God? Is there a situation from which He has delivered you, or are you in a barren land where, in spite of the circumstances, you can praise God for who He is and for how He can quench your "thirst"? Pause and praise the Lord.

How many ways can we praise God? Look at each of these verses and give the expression of praise about which the Scripture passage speaks.

Psalm 30:10–12 and 149:1–3

Psalm 33:3

Psalm 47:1–2, 7–8

Psalm 98:4–6

Psalm 150:1–6

Ephesians 5:18–19

Did You Know?

INSTRUMENTS OF PRAISE

Instruments of praise given in Scripture include the trumpet, a long metal (silver) horn flared at the end, the harp (played with a plectrum or pick), the lyre (a stringed instrument played with the fingers without use of a pick), the timbrel (similar to a tambourine), the pipe or flute, and other stringed instruments, as well as cymbals of various sizes (Psalm 150). The Hebrew word *mizmor,* translated "psalm" in the Old Testament, and the Greek word *psalmos* in the New Testament both refer to a song sung with instrumental accompaniment such as a harp or lyre or other instrument.

Word Study

PRAISE

Halal is the Hebrew word translated "praise" in the Old Testament. The word's primary meaning is "to be bright or to shine" and carries the basic idea of radiance. Thus praise or boasting belongs to God who is light, who is radiant in His glorious splendor (Psalm 145:5). *Halal* is the root for *tehillah,* which refers to a hymn or song of praise, a psalm, or simply the praiseworthiness of certain deeds (145:21). *Halal* is found in the word ***Hallelujah,*** which is a command meaning "praise the LORD," or "praise JAH" (Yahweh, Jehovah [Psalm 148:1; 149:1; 150:1, 6]). It is noteworthy that "hallelujah" is transliterated directly from the Hebrew into many different languages. It is a universal word to praise the God who reigns over the universe.

The Scriptures call us to *"***sing** *for joy in the* L*ORD,"* to "**clap your hands,** *all peoples."* Then there is the call to "**shout** *to God with the voice of joy."* We can *"sing praises with a* **skillful psalm"** to our God who reigns over all the nations. We can praise the Lord with a celebrative **dance;** the Hebrew words for dance refer to skipping or whirling about much like one would do when celebrating a great victory. The Scriptures call us to praise the Lord with **instruments** such as the trumpet, harp, lyre, timbrel, stringed instruments, pipe or flute, and cymbals. Giving praise to God is not just singing or playing music. Ephesians 5:18–19 shows us it is a matter of the heart. It is the fruit of the Spirit's fullness, and Paul points to a person controlled by the Holy Spirit as *"singing and making melody with your heart to the Lord."* There are many ways to praise, and each expression of praise can bring honor to the Lord when offered from a right heart.

Pause and praise the Lord. Perhaps you could sing a song to Him, a hymn or chorus, or even shout to the Lord. Remember, praise is not as much about the **songs** we sing as it is about the **heart** that sings (or speaks, shouts, claps, or dances) before the Lord.

Often we find praise and thanksgiving together in Scripture. In Day Four, we will look at the incense of thanksgiving.

My Prayers as Incense

DAY FOUR

The Incense of Thanksgiving

We have much for which we should be thankful. When Paul was talking to the Athenians, he pointed to the true God and declared, *"He Himself gives to all life and breath and all things"* (Acts 17:25). God is the one to be thanked for *"life"* and *"breath"* and *"all things."* We certainly want to avoid the pitfall of those in Romans 1:21 who knew about God but failed to honor Him as God or give Him thanks. Today we will see some of what the Scriptures reveal about offering thanksgiving to the Lord.

"Enter His gates with thanksgiving, and His courts with praise. Give thanks to Him; bless His name. For the Lord is good; His lovingkindness is everlasting."

Psalm 100:4–5

📖 What do you find from these Old and New Testament Scriptures concerning thanksgiving?

Psalm 50:7–15 (note verse 14)

____

____

____

____

Psalm 92:1–4

____

____

____

____

Hebrews 13:15

____

____

____

____

Since God owns all that exists, including the cattle on a thousand hills, to sacrifice a bull or goat or any number of cattle does not meet a need in His life. He has no needs. Nor do sacrifices impress Him. He is interested in what comes from the heart, not mere religious duty or ritual offerings. God calls to His people to offer that which pleases Him: *"a sacrifice of thanksgiving."* God wants us to think about all He has done and all He has given and thank the One responsible—God Himself. In Psalm 92, the psalmist calls us to consider these things, to think of God's loving kindness each morning as we face the day, to think of His faithfulness each night when we look back on the day. As we think in the morning, we should thank Him. As we think in the night, we should thank Him. *"It is good to give thanks to the LORD, and to sing praises to Thy name, O Most High"* (Psalm 92:1). When we come to the New Testament, we find that Jesus died for us to open the way for a personal relationship with the Father. Through Jesus, we can come before the Father, continually bringing a sacrifice of praise with heartfelt thanksgiving.

Put Yourself in Their Shoes

EATING AND GIVING THANKS

In I Corinthians 10:23–33, we find Paul's answers to some basic questions the believers had. These questions encompassed various issues, one of which was eating meat that had been sacrificed to idols. The main issue to Paul was not offending another person by what one did (in this case, in what one ate), especially not causing a Christian to stumble in his walk or to cause confusion in someone considering coming to Christ. Paul made it clear that he was free to eat whatever he wanted as long as it did not harm relationships or cause a person to stumble. For Paul, the one certainty in eating was partaking with thankfulness and giving thanks. That was part of glorifying God, and to Paul, even eating and drinking should show others what God is like and the difference He makes in one's life. That is an example all of us can follow.

📖 In the New Testament, we find Paul as a man marked by gratitude. What are some of the things for which he was grateful? Read these verses and record your findings.

Romans 1:8

____

____

____

____

Philippians 1:3–5

____

____

____

____

1 Thessalonians 1:2–5 and 2:13

____

____

____

____

Paul was thankful for the believers in Rome because their testimony of faith in Christ was being proclaimed from Rome *"throughout the whole world."* Paul expressed His gratitude to God for the believers in Philippi as well. Their faith and their participation in the ministry of the gospel was the cause for many thanks to God. Paul said the same thing about the Thessalonian Christians, noting their *"work of faith and labor of love and steadfastness of hope"* in the Lord Jesus. He was grateful they received the message of God that he proclaimed, believed it as the word of God, and came to know Christ as Lord and Savior. Paul focused on the things that lasted forever—having an eternal relationship with God the Father through Jesus Christ and joining together to get that message out to the world so that others could come to know Christ.

Praying God's Way

PAUL GAVE THANKS

Paul often gave thanks for others, for the churches he ministered in, and for the testimony they bore. We find his thanks expressed in Romans 1:8; 6:17; 16:4; 1 Corinthians 1:4; Ephesians 1:16; Philippians 1:3; Colossians 1:3; 1 Thessalonians 1:2; 2:13; 3:9; 2 Thessalonians 1:3; 2:13; 2 Timothy 1:3; Philemon 4–5. He also often offered thanks for God's gifts and God's work of grace and victory. We find that in Acts 27:35; 28:15; Romans 7:25; 1 Corinthians 15:57; 2 Corinthians 1:11; 2:14; 4:15; 8:16; 9:15; Colossians 1:12; 1 Timothy 1:12. He exhorts others to give thanks in Ephesians 5:4, 20; Colossians 3:15, 16, 17; 1 Thessalonians 5:18.

📖 What added insights into the matter of thanksgiving do you uncover in 1 Timothy 4:1–5, especially in verses 4 and 5?

____

____

____

____

____

In the last days, some will take what God has given as the normal course of life, daily blessings such as marriage and food, and seek to twist the truth about them, making things like marriage and even certain foods off limits. Paul warned that many teachers would use this line of false reasoning as part of their false doctrines. Such reasoning may include abstaining from marriage, food, and other comforts as a way to merit salvation or sanctification. Paul focused on the fact that God has created marriage and foods *"to be gratefully shared in"* and enjoyed. All of God's creation is good. He declared it so in Genesis 1. He wants us to receive His many gifts with gratitude. As we allow the Word of God to instruct us and as we pray in line with His Word including offering thanks, God will guide us in what pleases Him and what makes our lives more fully set apart for His purposes.

📖 What truths do you find in 1 Thessalonians 5:16–18?

____

____

____

____

____

____

"Rejoice always; pray without ceasing; in everything give thanks; for this is God's will for you in Christ Jesus."

1 Thessalonians 5:16–18

One of the clearest evidences that we are walking in the will of God is practicing a walk of rejoicing in the Lord. Even though circumstances can be difficult or even sorrowful, we can rejoice in who the Lord is, what He has done, and what He has promised us about His grace for the day's needs. As we face the situations of each day, including the trials, the people, and the relationships we must deal with, we can be in a mode of continual prayer. That does not mean we are to walk around on our knees with our head bowed. It means we are to walk with and talk to our Father about the day, about the trial, about those we care for, or those we are dealing with in some matter—whether it's a family matter, a business matter, or an issue dealing with our daily lives in general. We can give thanks in the midst of each day for what He has provided, how He has guided, and that He is sufficient for that day.

📖 Paul did not just talk about giving thanks. He lived what the Lord had revealed to him. Read Acts 27:14–36. What do you discover about Paul and thanksgiving in these verses, especially verse 35?

___

___

___

___

Paul was on his way to Rome on board a ship with 275 other passengers. The ship was caught in a *Euroquilo,* a strong northeastern wind similar to a typhoon or hurricane. The ship was blown about for many days. Most of the passengers, if not all of them, had not eaten for fourteen days. Paul encouraged them to eat, and then *"he took bread and gave thanks to God in the presence of all"* and began to eat. Paul practiced true thanksgiving to God, even in the middle of a storm.

If Paul could give thanks to God in the midst of a hurricane-like storm, then it is possible for us to do the same in the everyday matters of life. Pause now and give thanks to the Lord for something in your life, perhaps something He has brought to mind, even if it is some part of a "storm" you are going through.

My Prayers as Incense

DAY FIVE

We need to make sure any hindrances to praise and thanksgiving are removed.

For Me to Pray God's Way

Offerings of praise and thanksgiving have always marked the people of God, whether praying alone or in worship with others. The atmosphere of heaven is filled with praise and thanksgiving. When *"Thy will be done on earth as it is in heaven"* is fulfilled in one heart or a thousand hearts, praise and thanksgiving are evident. The same should be true in our lives if we are praying God's way. Today we want to make some applications of this to our praying and our daily walk.

Sometimes we fail to give thanks. There may be many reasons for this failure. Yet the first thing we need to do is make sure any hindrances to praise and thanksgiving are removed. Anything clouding our vision of God or road blocking our way needs to be out of the way. Which of these hinder you sometimes (or often)?

- ❐ Forgetting that God is God, that He has all wisdom and knows what is best for me.
- ❐ Failing to see God as my loving Father who knows my true needs.
- ❐ Not understanding that God is a gracious Giver who is willing, ready, and able to give at the right time but also willing to withhold what is necessary.
- ❐ Failing to grasp that because God loves me, He will guard my paths and my direction in life.
- ❐ Forgetting that sometimes God withholding from me is far better than God giving to me.

Your hindrance:

____

____

____

____

In Day Four, we mentioned Romans 1:21, where Paul spoke of those who did not honor God as God nor gave Him thanks. Honoring God and giving thanks go hand in hand. When we fail to see God as God, we forget that it is He to whom we should be thankful and give thanks. How are you doing in the "giving thanks" category? Perhaps you need to rethink who God is in your life. Read the following verses and record what they tell you about God. Then offer thanks based on the truth you see.

SCRIPTURE	WHO GOD IS...	MY RESPONSE...
1 Chronicles 29:10–14		
Acts 17:24–25		
1 Corinthians 8:9 with John 3:16		
1 Corinthians 9:15 with Ephesians 2:8–10		

David recognized the Lord as God, as the owner and giver of riches and honor. God is all powerful and able to make one great. He gives strength and blessing to His people. Even the gifts we give to the Lord have first come as gifts from Him. He deserves all blessing and honor, praise and thanksgiving. In Acts 17:25, Paul told the Athenians that God is the Creator of all and of everyone, that He needs nothing, and that He *"gives to all life and breath and all things."* That covers every area of life—spiritual, mental, physical, and material. Of greatest significance is the gift of eternal life that comes from Jesus Christ. The great grace of God shown to us and given to us by faith in Christ is a gift of indescribable worth. (See also 1 Peter 1:18–21.)

Knowing who God is helps us know how to praise Him. Knowing God's many names is one way of better knowing Him. Read some of the names below and write a statement of praise to God. (To help you offer praise, some of the Scriptures giving that name are listed beside the name.)

Alpha and Omega (Revelation 21:6; 22:13)

___

___

___

Creator (1 Peter 4:19)

___

___

___

___

Father (2 Corinthians 1:2–3)

___

___

___

___

Extra Mile

PRAISE HOMEWORK

Read Isaiah 9:6–7 and 40:9–31 for a further look at our God who is worthy of honor and praise and thanksgiving.

King (John 1:49; Revelation 19:11–16)

___

___

___

___

Lord/Master (1 Corinthians 8:4–6)

___

___

___

___

Redeemer (1 Corinthians 1:30; Ephesians 1:7)

___

___

___

Savior (Matthew 1:21; Luke 2:11; Titus 3:4–7)

___

___

___

___

Sometimes it is good to write a letter to someone to express all that is on your heart and mind. Write a letter to God offering your praise to Him. Perhaps you could begin by addressing Him with a name from Scripture that is very meaningful to you.

"Dear ____________________,

I have found it helpful to write specific notes of thanks to the Lord. For example, "Lord, I thank You for the gift of sight today, for the sunrise I saw this morning," or "I thank You for the encouragement a friend gave me," or "I thank You for Your gift of our children," or "Thank You for the meal we shared with friends yesterday." Write some "Thank You" notes to God about these things.

Father, I thank You for . . .

a spiritual blessing . . .

a person(s) . . .

a material blessing . . .

a physical blessing . . .

____

____

____

____

a trial or delay or detour . . .

____

____

____

____

It can be a great boost to your attitude of gratitude to practice such examples of thankfulness to the Lord each day. Be specific about the things for which you are thankful. Bring your study time for this lesson to a conclusion with a final word of prayer.

Father, I thank You and praise You for being so good to me. Thank You for the opportunity to offer up the "incense" of praise, for You are worthy of much praise. Your greatness and goodness are beyond description. Your power and ability are awesome. You are also worthy of continual offerings of thanksgiving. Thank You for being my God and my Savior, my Redeemer and King, my Father and Friend. Thank You for the salvation You brought through Jesus Christ and then for bringing that salvation to me through Him. Thank You that I can know You and walk with You. May my life—my thoughts, words, and deeds—be a continual offering of praise and thanksgiving to You. *"You are my God, and I will praise You; You are my God, I will exalt You."* (Psalm 118:28 NKJV) Amen.

Write a prayer to the Lord or record a journal entry in the space below.

____

____

____

____

____

____

____

____

____

____

____

____

____

____

____

Notes

Notes

ABOUT ASKING

Humbly Asking Our Father to Meet Our Needs

We all have needs—physical needs, spiritual needs, emotional needs, as well as needs for wisdom, for understanding, and for insight into the situations we face each day. God knows all about these needs. He knows whether a particular need came as a result of poor planning on our part or if it came as a result of someone else's failure in some way. He knows how deep the need is, how extensive it reaches, how many lives it touches, or if it only touches one life—yours. How are we to address these needs? How do we know which needs are worthy of bringing to our Father?

We have seen that true prayer starts by acknowledging the Lord as God and calling on Him with a whole heart. The heart of true prayer is found in knowing and loving the Father, making our relationship with Him more important than any need we might have. We have looked at the necessity of humility and how God responds both to deceitful pride and honest humility. We have begun to understand the place and the privilege of a forgiven and clean heart in our walk with God, and we have seen how vital it is to properly honor our Father, giving Him the allegiance, adoration, respect, and submission that is due Him. All of these aspects of prayer are vital to know and live if we are to know how to ask our Father for the needs we face.

This is not to say the Father is looking over a checklist every time we pray to see if we got it right or said it right. What He is looking for is the heart of a humble, loving child seeking his Father, knowing his Father loves him and is able to help him.

SEEING GOD FOR WHO HE IS

The Father wants us to ask, and then He meets the need, so that we see Him for who He is. Every need is an opportunity to know Him better, perhaps to know Him in a new way we had never seen before.

Because He wants to see a humble heart and because He knows there are several things that can get in the way of that kind of heart attitude, God has graciously given us clear instruction about asking, about making our petitions known to Him, and about avoiding frivolous or foolish asking.

The Father wants us to know Him as He truly is, not as He is often mistakenly presented, and He wants us to truly understand prayer as He desires it, not as it is sometimes erroneously offered. The Father wants us to ask and then meet the need, so that we see Him for who He is—every need is an opportunity to know Him better, perhaps to know Him in a new way we had never known before. So, how do we ask our Father about the needs we see in our lives? We will examine this question further throughout this lesson. Then, we can ask knowing how pleased God is to hear us **asking His way.**

About Asking

DAY ONE

Asking Is Admitting a Need

Asking is admitting that we have a need (or several needs). It is coming before our Father and talking to Him about the need, not just seeing Him meet the need but finding out what He thinks about the need. It may not be a need after all, but we may not be able to see that truth until the Father shines the light of His Word and the wisdom of His Spirit on that "need." How do we know what is truly a need, and then how do we ask Him to meet that need? We will see in today's lesson.

Did You Know?

DAILY BREAD AND MEAL TIMES

In a typical Jewish home, the housewife made bread cakes each day for the family meals. She would ground barley or wheat to make dough, let it rise, then shape it into flat cakes and bake it in a fire in a hole in the ground or in a small clay oven located in the house or courtyard. In most homes, there were two basic meals. Breakfast would have been only a small snack eaten on the way to work or carried and eaten as the mid-morning or mid-day meal. It could have consisted of bread cakes along with fruit or olives or even some salted fish. At supper the family had a more substantial meal that could include a vegetable stew (lentils, beans, corn, onion, garlic, etc.) eaten with the bread cakes. Other items eaten in the home included salted fish, cheese, eggs, chicken, honey, nuts, fruits (figs, grapes, dates, pomegranates, etc.) and occasionally some meat (usually goat or lamb). The meat would have been more likely eaten during one of the feast times. Bread cakes were the everyday food.

Look at Luke 11:1–4. Jesus responded to His disciples' request to teach them to pray. What do you find Jesus saying about needs in these verses?

____

____

____

____

What types of needs are addressed in these verses?

____

____

____

What does this tell you about Jesus' attitude toward needs? What about the Father's needs?

____

____

____

____

Jesus first directed His disciples toward fixing their focus on the Father, especially on hallowing His name and desiring His rule above all else. Then, Jesus addressed a very basic need, daily bread. He instructed His disciples to ask the Father each day for their necessary bread. In addition, they were to talk to the Father about the need for forgiveness, remembering also their need to forgive others. Along with the need for forgiveness is the need to be led step by step in avoiding temptation and tempting places.

Jesus and the Father are not surprised that we have needs, and He makes it clear that we must honestly and readily admit those needs. He welcomes our coming to Him. The fact that Jesus says to ask for daily bread tells us the Father wants us to come to Him **daily**. It is also clear that the Father wants us walking submitted to Him and His rule as we depend on Him for our needs. He wants us acknowledging we are very capable of sinning and need forgiveness and that we must guard our relationships, ready to show genuine forgiveness. He wants us admitting we need His wisdom and guiding hand all along the way.

Immediately after teaching the disciples this pattern for prayer, He told them a parable about prayer. Read Luke 11:5–10. What is the situation presented in this parable (verses 5–7)

____

____

____

____

What does the neighbor with the bread do according to verse 8?

____

____

____

In the culture of Jesus' day, it would not be uncommon for a person to travel to a friend or relative's house for a visit or as a stop along the way. Since there was no way to tell the exact time a guest might come, it was not unusual to be surprised, in this case, at midnight. The one needing bread would be very determined to be a good host. That was expected. In this case, in order for this man to be a gracious host, he had to disturb the sleep of his friend and neighbor. The neighbor was reluctant, not wanting to be bothered and certainly not wanting to wake up his children—which was bound to happen in what was likely a one-room house. As soon as a lamp was lit and the neighbor moved about getting some loaves of bread, everyone would be awake. The neighbor said, "No!" but the host would not take "no" for an answer. He was persistent, a translation of the Greek word *anaídeia,* meaning "shamelessness or impudence." He was so persistent that we would say he embarrassed himself. This is not the persistence of a selfish heart, but the urgency of a needy heart. He wanted bread for his friend and kept asking. Because of this, the neighbor gave him all the bread he needed.

How did Jesus apply this to the matter of us asking the Father for our needs (verses 9–10)?

____

____

____

____

Word Study

DAILY BREAD

Epiousios arton, translated "daily bread" in Luke 11:3, gives us a clear picture of our need. The word *epiousios,* translated "daily," is made up of two Greek words (*epí* and *ousía*) which can literally be rendered "for" and "being." In other words, what is necessary for our physical being or well-being to carry on daily life. It is a clear admission of our daily need. How many times have we begun to feel weak or tired simply because we are in need of some food? We need daily bread, and we can ask our Father who is glad to provide it.

Did You Know?

YOUR TYPICAL ISRAELI HOME

Most homes in Israel consisted of a single room with walls built of mud bricks or of roughly cut stone. The roof was made of wooden poles laid across the walls and covered with layers of woven branches and packed clay. This roof was surrounded by a parapet and served as an extra "room." It could be reached by an outside stairway or a ladder and was used as a place for working during the day (where there might be a breeze), drying fruit, grain, or flax, enjoying a meal together, sleeping on a hot night, or storing certain things. The inside of this one room house was divided into two basic areas. The first area near the door would house any family animals. The family stayed in the second area, which was usually a raised platform (about 18 inches) where they ate and slept together. At night they unrolled animal skins or woven mats, and for covering they used tunics, cloaks, or perhaps a goathair blanket. Most homes had very little, if any, furniture, perhaps a few stools and a small wooden table. Small oil lamps provided lighting, and the daily bread cakes were baked in a clay oven either in the house or outside perhaps in a courtyard. There would be few windows, and they were small and high, covered with some sort of latticework. The low doorway was covered with woven branches or perhaps wood hung on leather hinges.

Jesus made a connection to prayer—*"I say to you, ask . . . seek . . . knock."* The verb tenses are in the present. Like the persistent man, we are to keep on asking, keep on seeking, keep on knocking. As a result, Jesus promised we will receive; we shall find; and it shall be opened to us. Jesus wanted His disciples to understand the importance of continued asking, a heart-felt, even desperate cry for a need. That cry would not fall on deaf ears. The Father would respond.

📖 The Greek word for "ask" in Luke 11:9 is *aitéō,* which means to ask, or even to beg. It was used of one in a lower position asking from a superior. *Aitéō* is used several times in the New Testament. The apostle John recorded Jesus' instructions about prayer in John 14:11–17, where He used the word *aitéō* (specifically in verses 13 and 14). What do you find out about prayer, especially about asking in this passage?

____

____

____

____

____

When Jesus met with His disciples the night before His crucifixion, what He told them was of the utmost importance. He wanted them to know the essentials for walking with Him and the Father after He had ascended to heaven. He promised them that as He had faithfully been with them, so He would not leave them as orphans. Speaking of the Spirit, Jesus said in John 14:17, *"you know Him because He abides with you, and will be in you."* The Holy Spirit was present with them and in their midst during Jesus' ministry, but soon He would **indwell each of them.** Another factor in their relationship with Him and the Father would be a new day in prayer—they could ask the Father in the name of Jesus and He would grant their request.

"In Jesus' name" is a phrase so familiar in many churches. Here we must note that this matter of asking in His name has **everything to do with our relationship** to the Father and to Jesus. It is not just a way to end a prayer. Nor is it a carte blanche to get one's every wish, no wish-list granted by saying some magical words like "in Jesus' name." Praying in Jesus' name is inseparably tied to an ongoing relationship of loving the Father and Jesus, believing, trusting in Jesus, and obeying His Word. At the heart of this praying is seeking to bring glory, honor, and recognition to Him by the power and presence of His Holy Spirit. We cannot pray, nor do we have the wisdom to utter one syllable in the will of God without His guiding us—He is the Spirit of truth who enables us to pray in truth.

📖 Read 1 John 3:21–24 (the word *aitéō* is used in verse 22) and record any additional insights.

____

____

____

____

____

John wrote this at least forty years after Jesus' resurrection, but he still points to the inseparable link between relationship and prayer—a relationship of trust, love, and obedience as the foundation for a true prayer life. Knowing and recognizing Him as Lord and Savior means humbly asking those things in His will, confident He will grant them in His way and in His timing. Such humility is always linked to pleasing Him, walking in faith. Not only must we walk believing in Jesus Christ, believing all He is, all He has done, and all He has promised to do, we must also walk in right relationship with one another, with genuine love for one another. Again, John points to the ever-present ministry of the Spirit indwelling each believer, empowering each one to love and obey Jesus.

How is your relationship to the Father? To others you know? Is there anything that is keeping you from asking with confidence? Has something in today's lesson encouraged you to come to your heavenly Father and ask about a very real need? Spend some "asking time" with the Father.

What else do we need to understand about this matter of asking? We will see still more in Day Two.

Asking Starts with Abiding

About Asking

DAY TWO

What more can we learn from Jesus about prayer and its inseparable link to our relationship with the Father? What did He tell His disciples? There is one special passage in which Jesus focused on a personal relationship both to the Father and to Himself and on the matter of asking and receiving answers. This passage of Scripture is at the heart of being a disciple of Jesus Christ. We begin today's lesson looking at that passage.

"If you abide in Me, and My words abide in you, ask whatever you wish, and it shall be done for you. By this is My Father glorified, that you bear much fruit, and so prove to be My disciples."

John 15:7–8

📖 Read John 15:1–8. What is the picture presented by Jesus in these verses?

____

____

____

____

____

What is the key to a healthy relationship and abundant fruit according to verses 4 and 5? How important is this in Jesus' eyes?

____

____

____

____

____

____

Jesus pictures the relationship between His disciples and Himself as that between the branches and the Vine. The Father is the Vinedresser who cares for the branches, making sure they bear fruit—more fruit—much fruit. The matter of fruit in the life of the branches is always connected to the matter of abiding in the eternal life of the Vine. No abiding equals no fruit. Constant abiding equals certain fruit. Apart from an abiding relationship with Jesus, a believer can do nothing to produce real fruit.

What are the marks of an abiding relationship according to John 15:7? What do you learn about asking in that verse? (Note: *aitéō* is the Greek word used here and translated "ask.")

____

____

____

____

____

Apart from an abiding relationship with Jesus, a believer can do nothing to produce real fruit.

What link do you see with John 15:8?

____

____

Abiding in Jesus means depending on the Life of the Vine in all we do. It is looking to Him and listening to Him in all of life. Abiding means keeping all of life connected to Him, allowing Him to live in and through us as the Vine Life lives in and through the branches to produce His wonderful fruit. Only Vine Life can produce Vine Fruit, the fruit Jesus wants to see in and through our lives, and Jesus reveals a vital link between abiding and fruit bearing. Asking the link between the need and God's answer.

Only Vine Life can produce Vine Fruit, the fruit Jesus wants to see in and through our lives, and Jesus reveals a vital link between abiding and fruit bearing. It is asking, the link between the need and God's answer.

As we listen to Him and hear His words with a heart ready to obey, He changes our hearts and our desires. We come to know Him, His Life, and His will more consistently. We understand which way He wants us to go, where He wants us to start or turn or stop. As we walk this way, we are better able to ask in line with His will. His will has become the desire of our hearts, and we can ask what we wish (since it lines up with what He wishes). It is the same thing as asking in Jesus' name. Since we are walking in agreement with Him, we can experience the joy of answered prayer. Those prayers answered to the delight of the Son are also the delight of the Father. The Father and His will are more clearly revealed in those answers, and so the Father is glorified. As fruit, more fruit, and much fruit are born in answer to prayer, we are seen as His disciples, learners of Him and His will and followers of Him and His Father.

We find in the Scripture an excellent testimony of this matter of right relationship and right praying. James the Apostle (and the half-brother of Jesus) understood about right relationships and the link to right praying. James was a man of prayer. It is said that he was known in the early church as "camel knees" because he spent so much time in prayer on his knees. While prayer was important, even crucial in the life of James, he did not focus on prayer as the centerpiece of the Christian life in the epistle that bears his name. James knew what we have been discovering in our journey of praying God's way—right relationship is the centerpiece of our walk with God.

James penned his letter to reveal what true faith is, because true faith is essential for true righteousness, and true righteousness is absolutely necessary for a right relationship with God. While not the centerpiece of his epistle, James does talk often about prayer—in James 1:5–8; 4:1–3; 4:7–10; 5:13–15; and 5:16–18. What can we learn from James that complements and connects with what Jesus said?

📖 Read James 5:16–18. What does James say about the prayer of a righteous man?

____

____

____

____

____

What example does James give of a righteous man who asked God for something? How does he describe this man in verse 17?

____

____

____

____

____

The effective prayer or the "energized personal request" (Greek—*energeo deesis*) of a righteous man is very strong and capable of producing righteous results. One who is walking with God having been made righteous by faith in Christ and daily walking in that right relationship is energized by God to pray the will of God. As a result, he or she sees God answer prayer, like Elijah in the days of Ahab. Elijah was a man like any of us, with fears and failures, weaknesses and weariness, but he had a right heart toward God. He surrendered himself to do the will of God and listened carefully to the word of God, so God could use him to accomplish His purposes in Israel. He can use us to do the same today and see His purposes accomplished in our personal lives, in our families, in our churches, and in our communities.

EFFECTIVE PRAYER

"The effective prayer of a righteous man can accomplish much. Elijah was a man with a nature like ours, and he prayed earnestly that it might not rain; and it did not rain on the earth for three years and six months. And he prayed again, and the sky poured rain, and the earth produced its fruit." (James 5:16–18)

What was the result of Elijah's praying? (You may want to read the full account in 1 Kings 17 and 18.)

____

____

____

____

____

God directed Elijah to pray that there would be no rain except at his word, which would always be in line with the Word God revealed to him. Elijah told Ahab about the coming drought (1 Kings 17:1), and it did not rain for three and a half years. Then, at the Word of the Lord, Elijah appeared with the message that God would send rain once again (1 Kings 18:1) Elijah prayed for that rain and it came in abundance so that *"the earth produced its fruit"* (literal fruit). As Jesus promised His disciples in John 15, much fruit is born through right praying, praying that flows out of a relationship of abiding in Jesus and allowing His word to abide in us. We see the same truth in the life of Elijah. As we abide in Jesus and allow Jesus' words to abide in us, we too will ask the Father and see the fruit of the Father in our lives in answer to prayer.

Now is a good time to evaluate where you are in your relationship with the Father and with Jesus. How is your abiding in Him, your life-link dependence on Him? Of vital importance is how well His word is abiding in you. Are you reading and meditating on the Scriptures? Are your desires His desires? For what are you praying, or perhaps it would be better asked, for what are you praying and seeing answers? Pause and spend some time with the Lord.

Prayer is part of a growing relationship with the Father. We don't learn a few basics and then stop. As the ABC's and the 1-2-3's of first grade are the building blocks to such responsibilities as writing essays, letters, job applications, business proposals, checks and checkbooks, so it is in our relationship with the Father. As we grow in our prayer lives, God the Father takes us into new areas of prayer, wider applications of prayer, greater opportunities to ask and trust Him to answer. We will see in Days Three, Four, and Five some of those dimensions of asking.

About Asking

DAY THREE

WHAT'S YOUR WORRY?

Do you ever worry? For some, that's like asking, "Do you ever breathe?" What does God have to say about worry and what does that have to do with praying God's way? If we can grasp what God says and the significance of it for our daily lives, then worry will be seen with a whole new insight, and our praying will take on a whole new life.

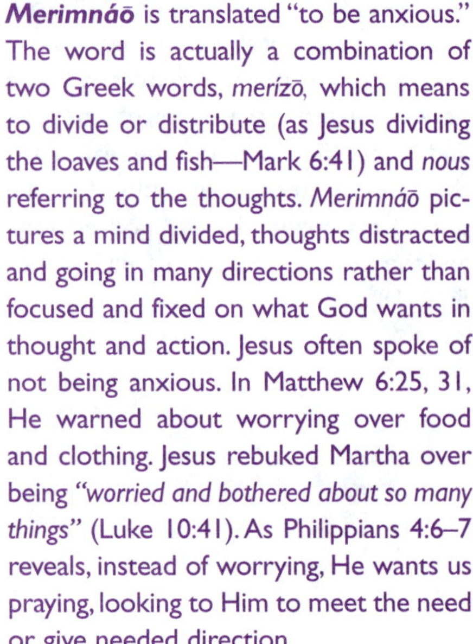

Word Study

BE ANXIOUS

Merimnáō is translated "to be anxious." The word is actually a combination of two Greek words, *merízō*, which means to divide or distribute (as Jesus dividing the loaves and fish—Mark 6:41) and *nous* referring to the thoughts. *Merimnáō* pictures a mind divided, thoughts distracted and going in many directions rather than focused and fixed on what God wants in thought and action. Jesus often spoke of not being anxious. In Matthew 6:25, 31, He warned about worrying over food and clothing. Jesus rebuked Martha over being *"worried and bothered about so many things"* (Luke 10:41). As Philippians 4:6–7 reveals, instead of worrying, He wants us praying, looking to Him to meet the need or give needed direction.

Look at Philippians 4:6–7. What do you discover about worry?

What is the answer to worry?

Scripture commands us to *"be anxious for nothing,"* or "do not worry about anything." The verb used in this statement is present imperative, which means it is a command. It can be translated "do not worry," "do not start worrying," or "stop worrying." In any case, it is clear that God does not want us to worry or to be anxious. The word translated "anxious" is *merimnáō*, which literally pictures a divided mind, one drawn in different directions, distracted and bothered. How do we overcome that? We must focus our attention on God, coming before Him about the need that had caused us to be so distracted and filled with anxiety.

Specifically, how are we to bring this worry-causing need before our Father? Philippians 4:6 tells us, but first, it may be helpful to see the various words for prayer there. *Proseuchḗ* refers to "prayer" in general and emphasizes our devotion to God, bowing before Him as Lord. *Dḗēsis,* translated "supplication," points to specific requests with a strong sense of personal need, *eucharistía* is the word for "thanksgivings," and *aítēma* is the word for "requests" (rooted in *aitéō*), pointing to what one needs to be given and acknowledging one's inability to meet the need.

Look at Philippians 4:6 word by word and answer these questions…

What things should we bring to the Father?

____

____

____

With what attitude should we bring them to the Father?

____

____

How specific should we be?

____

____

____

How personal can we be?

____

____

____

God wants us to bring everything before Him, especially those things that distract us and worry us. When we come in prayer (*proseuchḗ*), we are humbly acknowledging our allegiance to God and our dependence on Him. This is part of our devotion and love for Him, not a business transaction or a "grocery list" given to Him. In walking with God, we can talk over our needs and point to specific, personal matters (*dḗēsis*) and ask Him to meet those needs (*aítēma*). We are to always be grateful, expressing our thanksgiving to Him—literally, "thanksgivings" (plural), or the many ways He has blessed us and given to us.

What is the result of such praying, according to Philippians 4:7?

____

____

____

____

Put Yourself in Their Shoes

THE ANXIETY ALARM CLOCK

Let worry or anxiety be like an alarm clock in your walk with God. When you start to worry, let that wake you up to prayer. Wake up spiritually and mentally and then lift up the matter to the Lord in prayer. It will make a difference in your worry and your walk.

If we lack wisdom, if we don't know which way to go or which option to choose in the midst of a trial, we need to humble ourselves and pray looking to our Lord, asking for His wisdom.

God promises us that as we pray this way, He will give His peace, that peace that goes beyond human comprehension, deeper and richer than we can explain. We cannot explain all there is to know about God's peace, but we can experience that peace. His peace will act as a guard over our hearts and minds, our meditations and choices. Instead of acting as a nagging distraction, raining in on us and pulling us in many directions, His peace will surround us and protect our thoughts by the power of Jesus Christ. When the anxious thoughts approach, the Spirit catches sight of the bothersome distraction, and He reminds us of who our God is and what He can do. As we continue to pray, peace continues to guard, and we are enabled to choose the right course.

One of the places worry quickly crops up is in the midst of trials. How does God want us to handle trials, and what prayer provision is there for those times? We noted in Day One that the Greek word for "ask" in Luke 11:9 and John 14:13–14 is *aitéō,* which means to ask, or even to beg. Recall that it is often used of one in a lower position asking from a superior. That word, *aitéō,* is also used in James 1:5–6 in the discussion on handling trials.

📖 Read James 1:2–8. What do you discover about trials and asking from the Father, especially in verses 5 and 6?

____

____

____

____

James instructs us about how to face trials—not "if" we face them, but "when" we face them. We are to count them "all joy," evaluating them as a test of faith and ultimately valuing them for bringing us to greater endurance in faith. However, that endurance is not the end. God wants us to grow and mature through those trials so that we are *"perfect and complete, lacking in nothing."* The term "perfect and complete" does not mean sinless, but rather mature in Christlikeness, reaching closer to the goal God has for each of us. Our words "perfect" and "complete" are translations of the Greek words *téleios*, meaning mature or reaching the overall goal, and *holóklēros*, meaning complete in each and every part.

In order for God's goal to be accomplished, He wants us to know how to face the difficulties along the way, the perplexities of each and every trial. We cannot handle them alone. Therefore he points us to prayer for each of the specifics we face. If we lack wisdom, if we don't know which way to go or which option to choose in the midst of a trial, we need to humble ourselves and pray, looking to our Lord, and asking for His wisdom. He faced every kind of trial a man could face—yet without sin, Hebrews 2:18 and 4:15 tell us. If we humbly admit our need and ask, He will answer and give us the specific wisdom we need for the specific trial we face.

When we ask God for wisdom, we should trust Him to answer and give that wisdom. We need to be looking for God-given wisdom, expecting Him to guide us specifically. If we doubt Him, wavering back and forth, doubting the character or conduct of God, we should not expect God to answer. God works on the basis of our trust relationship with Him. He wants us to know and love Him as a Father, thus humbly seeking Him and depending on Him as a trusting child. Our asking is never separated from our walk with Him. When we separate the two, our relationship is in trouble and our prayer life is in double trouble—we are unable to pray rightly, and we fail to see His answers to our prayers.

How about you? Are there any trials or worries you are facing? What needs do you have that you have failed to bring to the Father? Many times, the simple answer is the best answer—just pray! Spend some time talking to the Father.

For Example

About Asking

DAY FOUR

How did people in the Scriptures face the many needs that arose? How did they deal with physical needs, times of anxious worry, and trials that came to them on their journey of following God? Today, we are going to look at some examples from Scripture, examples that can give us some clear direction and a more thorough understanding about asking the Father concerning the needs we face.

The first example is found in Genesis 32. Jacob and his family had left Haran and his father-in-law Laban after twenty years of hard labor in the fields. Laban chased and overcame them at Mizpah, where they entered into a covenant not to harm one another. Then Jacob faced the possibility of confronting Esau when he returned to Canaan. That is where we pick up the story.

Remember four elements in making a request from God:

***Relate** to God first—Know who God is, and know that your relationship with Him is the basis for your request

***Request** from God—Recognize that He is the one who can meet this request

***Reason** with God—Talk to Him about the request, what it means to Him and to you

***Rejoice** before God—Celebrate His promises and His answers

📖 Read Genesis 32:3–8 and then Jacob's prayer in Genesis 32:9–12. What dilemma confronted Jacob according to verses 3–8?

____

____

____

God told Jacob to leave Haran and the home of his father-in-law Laban and return to Canaan. Since he faced the prospect of going back to Canaan **and back to Esau** in that land, he sent messengers to inform Esau. When the messengers returned, they told of Esau and his four hundred men coming to meet Jacob. This news caused Jacob to be *"greatly afraid and distressed,"* knowing that Esau had vowed twenty years before to kill him. Jacob divided his family and goods into two companies as a stopgap way of protecting at least one company. Then, he prayed.

When we look at asking God for specific requests, there is a basic pattern often found in Scripture. There are four elements often seen in petitions—

- **Relating** to God—who He is, what His name reveals, how I am related to Him. (Praying God's way is always linked to our relationship to Him.)
- **Requesting** from God—what need is there, why I am calling on Him.
- **Reasoning**—why this request should be answered, why this matters to God or to me.
- **Rejoicing**—celebrating what God has done or promises to do.

🕮 Now, look at Jacob's prayer in Genesis 32:9–12 and see which of these four elements you can find. Summarize his prayer and list the elements as you find them.

____

____

____

____

Jacob began his prayer by **relating** to God as the *"God of my father Abraham and God of my father Isaac."* His **request** was clear. He asked God to deliver him from the hand of his brother Esau. Why did Jacob request this; what was his **reasoning**? From a human point of view, he feared Esau, that is, he feared Esau's vengeance, and the potential for harm to him and his family. From God's view, Jacob pointed to the Lord's command to return to Canaan and His promise to prosper him not only in the present, but also in the days ahead for all his descendants. Jacob admitted that he was unworthy of all God had done in giving him a family and the wealth of servants and livestock. At the same time, Jacob **rejoiced** over all God had done for him and called on God to fulfill His will in the present situation.

After that, Jacob arranged a large gift of livestock to be sent before him to his brother, Esau. Perhaps God gave him the wisdom to do this since this happened immediately after he prayed. Proverbs 19:6 says, *". . . every man is a friend to him who gives gifts."* In any case, the Lord did answer Jacob's prayer, and he and Esau had a warm, memorable, and safe reunion.

🕮 We see this pattern of petition again in 1 Kings 18. Look at 1 Kings 18:21–24 to see the situation between Elijah and the prophets of Baal. What did Elijah propose in verses 23 and 24?

____

____

____

____

Word Study

CRY OUT TO GOD

The Hebrew word *qara* translated "call" in I Kings 18, refers to a specific cry to a specific person expecting a specific response. It is most often referring to a loud cry, even a desperate cry, seeking God to answer the need."

Elijah proposed a prayer meeting and an altar of sacrifice. The prophets of Baal would call on their god and Elijah would call on *"the name of the LORD."* The God who answered by fire and consumed the sacrifice would be recognized as the true God. Elijah carefully chose his words when he made this proposal. When he spoke of calling on the Lord or on Baal, he used the Hebrew word *qara,* which is a specific cry to a specific person expecting a specific response. The prophets of Baal would call on their god by name and ask him to send fire. Elijah would call on the Lord by name and ask Him to send fire—specific fire on a specific sacrifice at a specific time and specific place.

🕮 Look at the actions of the prophets of Baal in 1 Kings 18:25–29 and summarize their prayer meeting and their way of making requests to their god.

____

____

____

The prophets of Baal prepared their sacrifice on the altar and began calling on the name of Baal. They called from morning until noon but received no answer. They leaped about the altar and cried out to Baal. Elijah mocked them, their cries, and their god. They began crying out even louder and cut themselves in an attempt to get Baal to hear and answer, but *"there was no voice, no one answered, and no one paid attention."*

Look at Elijah's actions in 1 Kings 18:30–35, then read his prayer in verses 36–37 and its results in verses 38–39. Record what you discover, especially any of the four elements of asking you see in his prayer.

____

____

____

____

Elijah properly prepared the altar for the sacrifice and even poured twelve containers of water on the sacrifice, the wood, and the altar. Then, he called on the name of the Lord—a specific cry for a specific response. He focused first on who this God is and his **relationship** to this God, *"O LORD, the God of Abraham, Isaac and Israel,"* and spoke of himself as *"Thy servant."* He **requested** that God make Himself known as God in Israel, and that Elijah be clearly seen as God's servant. He **reasoned** that if God answered by fire as he had proposed, it would then be known that Elijah had done all this at God's word, not out of his own imagination or planning. He also **requested** that God would answer with fire and **reasoned** that the people would then know that God is God and Baal is not. He asked God to answer and turn the heart of the people back to Him.

Anytime we make our requests to God His way, His answers ultimately lead to rejoicing before Him.

God answered Elijah's prayer, and the fire of God fell—consuming the sacrifice, the wood, and the stones of the altar. The people responded immediately, *"The LORD, He is God; the LORD, He is God."* This was a time of great victory and **rejoicing** for the people of God, a time of answered prayer when God revealed Himself in great power. Anytime we make our requests to God His way, His answers ultimately lead to rejoicing before Him.

God wants to work in our lives as He did with His people in the Scriptures. How can we apply these truths and examples to our own daily walk? We will see some ways in Day Five.

FOR ME TO PRAY GOD'S WAY

About Asking

DAY FIVE

As we have seen in what Jesus taught His disciples about prayer, in what James said about righteous praying, in what Paul said about worry versus praying, and in what we have seen in the examples from people like Jacob and Elijah, everything depends on our relationship with God. We know that prayer starts with acknowledging the Lord as God and calling on Him as our God. That includes knowing and loving Him as our Father, humbling ourselves before Him, dealing with any sin He reveals in our lives, and always maintaining an attitude of honor, respect, and gratitude to Him. In addition, the Scripture is clear that He wants us to come to

Him with the needs we face, needs that He already knows about and that He is ready and able to meet.

📖 It is important to remind ourselves of the things about which Jesus reminded His disciples. Look back at Matthew 6:6–8, especially verse 8. We have looked at this passage in a previous lesson, but it is important not to forget the vital truth Jesus presented. What central truth about our needs do you find in those verses?

____

____

____

"For your Father knows what you need, before you ask Him."

Matthew 6:8

The Father knows what we need before we ask Him. That should never stop us from asking. On the contrary, it should encourage us to come running to our Father, knowing His care is so deep and His concern so genuine that we can bring to Him any need that arises. We do not have to have fancy words or "just-right" formulas or exact phrases to get Him to hear us. He already wants to hear us and waits for us to come in the confidence and neediness of a child. Remember, real prayer is all about real relationship with the Father and a real relationship with Him will mean heart-felt prayer before Him.

It is helpful to remember that the Father knows what we need even before we ask. That keeps our focus on the Father more than on our needs. There are some other things that we must watch if we are to ask appropriately. Of particular importance is our relationship with others. There is a very important passage we need to quickly look at and make sure that the relationship lines are clear if we are to expect the prayer request lines to be clear.

📖 Look at 1 Peter 3:7–12. What can hinder prayers according to verse 7?

____

____

____

"FOR THE EYES OF THE LORD ARE UPON THE RIGHTEOUS, AND HIS EARS ATTEND TO THEIR PRAYER, BUT THE FACE OF THE LORD IS AGAINST THOSE WHO DO EVIL."

I Peter 3:12

Understanding that 1 is addressed to "all"—all those Peter has been talking to (subjects under government, servants under masters, wives and husbands)—what specific applications could be made first to a husband and wife, then to the wider scope of relationships in daily life? Summarize what you find about prayer based upon your reading of these verses.

____

____

____

____

In 1 Peter 3:7, Peter focused specifically on the husband's responsibility to seek to understand and be sensitive to his wife's needs, recognizing her weaknesses physically and honoring her as an equal heir of the grace of life. If the husband fails in this relationship essential, he will greatly hinder his prayer life (*proseuchḗ*—the word for prayer in general). Peter widens the scope of relationships in verses 8–12 and makes another vital application to prayer. All are responsible to live in relationships marked by harmony, being sympathetic toward others, caring for one another, acting like brothers (and sisters) in a family, being kindhearted and humble toward one another. Any relationship can deteriorate where vengeance rules or where the tongue starts lashing out. Don't go the way of returning evil for evil or insult for insult. Instead, bless those you encounter day by day, especially those closest to you. God designed life to be a joy not a pain. When a person follows these relationship guidelines, he will find God watching and listening carefully to his or her prayers (*dēesis*—specific, personal requests). Where relationships are faltering, God is less likely to listen until the relationships are made right.

How about your relationships? Are there any barriers you have raised by your words or actions? Every barrier to another person is a brick wall in the way of your prayer life. Stop and consider any thing on which the Lord has placed His focus. **Whatever is significant enough for God to call to your attention is significant enough for you to address.** Let this list help you evaluate where you are.

Whatever is significant enough for God to call to your attention is significant enough for you to address.

- Am I harmonizing with others or sowing discord? Am I an irritating noise or a welcome sound? Is there anyone with whom I am not in harmony, with whom I am not seeking to walk together?
- Am I acting sympathetic toward others or ignoring their needs?
- Am I loving like a true brother (or sister) or acting like a distant stranger?
- Am I being kindhearted or hardhearted toward others?
- Am I being humble in spirit willing to meet people where they are or proud and arrogant, looking down on them?
- Do I have a "get even" mentality along with a ready-to-fight, war-of-words mindset? Or am I ready to bless others (not "bless them out") with my words, to speak well and to encourage?
- Do I look for ways to hurt or tear down others? Or do I turn from evil and look for ways to help, to do good for others, and to build up others?
- Do I speak deceitfully with others to get my way or to trip them up? Or do I try every way to make peace and keep peace?
- Do I see God listening and answering my prayers, my personal requests? Or does God seem distant and deaf?
- Am I loving life and seeing good days?

Do I see God listening and answering my prayers, my personal requests? Or does God seem distant and deaf?

Remember, the sooner you deal with roadblocks in your relationships, the sooner you will remove hindrances to prayer!

We saw in Day Four that often in asking God for specific requests, there is a basic pattern found in Scripture, with four elements often seen in petitions. Let's apply this to a request that is on your heart right now. Look at these four elements and write out how your request fits these elements.

First—**Relating** to God. Relate to who God is, to what His name reveals about Him, to how you are related to Him. (Remember, praying God's way is always linked to our relationship to Him.) This is how I relate to God and how my request relates to God:

____

____

____

Second—**Requesting** from God. What need do you have? Why are you calling on Him? This is the request that I have:

____

____

____

____

____

Third—**Reasoning.** Why should this request be answered? Why does this matter to God or to me? This is my reason for asking this of God:

____

____

____

____

____

Fourth—**Rejoicing.** About what can I celebrate? What has God done or promised to do? This is why I can rejoice on the promise upon which I am making my request and rejoice in God's answer:

____

____

____

____

Make your requests known to God!

Use this pattern as you seek God's answer to your needs, your worries, your trials, and your questions. **Make your requests known to God** (Philippians 4:6)!

Why not close your study time with prayer?

Father, thank You for the privilege of asking You to meet my needs. Thank You for Your care and concern, for Your awesome power and ability, and that You already know every detail of every need. I praise You for calling me to follow You and to begin a walk of delighting in Your desires and then discovering how to pray those desires. Thank You for the joy of answered prayer Your way. I sincerely thank You for not answering many of my prayers, prayers that were off course, short of the goal, or even opposite Your will. I am grateful for the way You are teaching me to pray Your way, to listen more carefully to Your word, and to wait on You and Your timing. You are forever to be blessed and praised for Your ways. Thank You for the many believers found in Scripture who encourage by their example. Thank You for the way Your Word equips me in asking the right way for the right requests. Thank You for showing me the wrong ways as well so that I might better avoid the missteps and stumbling stones of self-centered, self-agenda praying. As I walk with You, may I learn more clearly how to ask, how to persevere in asking, and how to wait in faith. I thank You for the answers to come in the days ahead. In Jesus' Name. Amen

Thinking back over all we have seen about asking the Father to meet our needs, write a prayer to the Lord, perhaps with some of your needs highlighted. You may also want to make a journal entry about what the Lord has shown you about asking in the lessons of the past few days.

Notes

9

THE WARFARE IN PRAYER
WINNING BATTLES GOD'S WAY

Have you faced any battles lately? Certainly you have if you are a follower of Jesus Christ. Some days are more war-torn than others, but everyday has its struggles. How should we handle those, especially in prayer? How do we face battles in our prayer times? When we realize that just setting aside time to pray can be a battle, we know that the prayer time itself will not always be an easy ride.

If we are to ever win the battles of life and walk in the victory of answered prayer, we must depend on the Lord; we must "be strong in the Lord and in the strength of His might."

We find the battle comes at us from several fronts. There are struggles with when to pray; then when we make the time and begin to pray we sometimes struggle with what to pray or how to pray. Add to that the struggles with the "Big 3"—the world, the "flesh," and the devil—plus all that can distract and discourage us in prayer. We soon realize that if we are to ever win the battles of life and walk in the victory of answered prayer, we must depend on the Lord; we must *"be strong in the Lord and in the strength of His might."* He alone is strong enough and wise enough to fight each battle we face. Like David of old when fighting the Philistines, we must pray, asking the Lord what He wants us to do. David did *"just as the LORD had commanded him"* and won the battle (2 Samuel 5:17–25). Jesus instructed us to pray, *"Lead us not into temptation, but deliver us from evil."* That includes all kinds of evil including the evil one, the devil, the world system under his deception, and the flesh. Remember, our flesh, in order to get its own way, will quickly ally with the world and the devil in an effort to please self. This is the spiritual warfare we face.

This lesson will make clear the war we face, walk us through the battlefield, show us the armor we must wear, and enable us to be more dependent on the Lord and experience His victory. Are you ready to do battle . . . and claim victory?

The Warfare in Prayer

DAY ONE

THE LORD IS A WARRIOR WINNING BATTLES

"The LORD is a warrior; The LORD is His name."

Exodus 15:3

The earth has been a battleground almost from day one. Soon after Adam and Eve were created, the serpent came tempting, seeking to kill, steal, and destroy. On the day this first temptation took place, Adam and Eve lost the battle, but the Lord came seeking them, dealing with their sin, and promising a Seed to come to overcome all evil. The Lord began showing Himself to be the Overcomer, the Victor. We must understand that He is the one upon whom we must focus if we are to walk in His victory. We do not focus on the enemy or even on the battle, but on the Lord in the midst of the battle. What are some examples in Scripture that especially reveal Him in answer to prayer?

What do you discover about the Lord in Exodus 14:1–31? What did He do?

____

____

____

____

The Lord made Himself known to the Israelites and the Egyptians. Moses told the children of Israel, *"Do not fear! Stand by and see the salvation of the LORD. . . . the LORD will fight for you"* (14:14). The Angel of God went before the camp of Israel. Then, with Pharaoh and his army approaching, He moved and stood between the camp of Israel and the camp of Pharaoh. The next day the Lord divided the Red Sea, and Israel marched through on dry land. Pharaoh's army pursued, and the Lord *"brought the army of the Egyptians into confusion"* (14:24). The army cried out, *"the LORD is fighting for them against the Egyptians"* (14:25). Then Pharaoh's army was drowned as the sea came crashing in around them. The Lord revealed Himself as a mighty warrior fighting for His people.

How did the people respond in Exodus 15:1? How did they speak of the Lord in Exodus 15:1–21, especially in Exodus 15:3?

____

____

____

____

The people began to sing to the Lord, declaring, *"He is highly exalted."* The Lord showed Himself far above Pharaoh and the army of Egypt and brought a great song to the hearts of Israel. When the enemy came against God's people, God overcame them. Israel confidently praised the Lord, *"Who is like Thee among the gods, O LORD? Who is like Thee, majestic in holi-*

ness, awesome in praises, working wonders?" God in His mercy and loving kindness led His people to victory and safety. They rejoiced in the great victory He gave. On that day, the Israelites proclaimed, *"The LORD is a warrior; The LORD is His name"* (15:3).

This was not the only time the Lord fought for His people. We find this happening again and again throughout Scripture. In one well-known incident, we find David declaring his confidence in the Lord as he dealt with the intimidating enemy giant, Goliath. He said to Goliath, *"The LORD does not deliver by sword or by spear; for the battle is the LORD'S"* (1 Samuel 17:47). As we have seen in a previous lesson, when three enemy armies came against Judah, King Jehoshaphat cried out to the Lord, *"We are powerless against this great multitude who are coming against us; nor do we know what to do, but our eyes are on Thee"* (2 Chronicles 20:12). The answer came from the Lord through the Levite Jahaziel, *"Thus says the LORD to you, 'Do not fear or be dismayed because of this great multitude, for the battle is not yours but God's"* (20:15). Isaiah prophesied about the Lord, *"The LORD will go forth like a warrior, He will arouse His zeal like a man of war. He will utter a shout, yes, He will raise a war cry. He will prevail against His enemies"* (Isaiah 42:13). In the Old Testament, we see the Lord is indeed a warrior, but the Old Testament is not the only place where the Lord is shown as a warrior. We also see the Lord Jesus in the New Testament, fighting for His disciples in prayer.

When Jesus was about to go the cross, He talked with His disciples and told them that He had prayed for them. The prayer He prayed had to do with overcoming defeat. Read Luke 22:31–32 and record what you discover there.

___

___

___

___

At the time of the Lord's Supper, Jesus was talking to His disciples about the coming crucifixion and about the characteristics of His followers, those who would be a part of His kingdom. In the midst of that, Jesus turned to Simon Peter and told him that Satan had demanded permission to sift all the disciples like wheat (the verb is in the plural). The phrase *"demanded permission"* carries the idea of obtaining permission by asking, not by ordering God to give permission. Jesus knew that His Father was in charge. Then, He encouraged Simon specifically, *"but I have prayed for you* (singular)." Jesus prayed that Peter's faith not fail and that once he turned back to following Christ, he would strengthen and encourage his brothers. Jesus knew how to fight and win. We see that most clearly in His victory on the cross.

Two passages help us see the extent of the Lord's victory on the cross. First, read Colossians 2:13–15, the account of what Jesus did on the cross. We have seen the extent of the forgiveness described in verses 13–14 in Lesson Four. Verse 15 paints a picture of our Lord as a warrior. Read that verse again and describe what Jesus did.

___

___

___

___

Put Yourself in Their Shoes

OVERCOMING DISTRACTIONS

Nehemiah 1—6 records Nehemiah and the people overcoming numerous obstacles in rebuilding the walls of Jerusalem. In his devotion to God, Nehemiah started the rebuilding process with prayer, first in Susa in the Persian kingdom and then in Jerusalem. God then gave him clear direction as to what should be done. When he began rebuilding the walls, he faced several distractions from the enemies of Israel. For every distraction, Nehemiah prayed, seeking God, and God gave fresh direction. Devotion—Direction—Distraction—Devotion—This was the pattern Nehemiah and the people followed to overcome the devastation of Jerusalem. The wall was successfully completed, and all said, *"this work was done by our God"* (Nehemiah 6:16). The same can be true in our lives as we pray in our devotion to God, seeking to fulfill the will of God. God will give us direction and overcoming grace for each distraction.

Did You Know?
PUBLIC TRIUMPH

In Colossians 2:15, when Paul speaks of Christ making a public display of the rulers and authorities, he is referring to Satan and the demon hosts being soundly defeated at the Cross. Paul first says Christ *"disarmed"* them. The original Greek word translated "disarmed," *apekdúomai*, was used to refer to a soldier stripping the armor and weapons off a defeated enemy. Paul said Jesus *"made a public display"* (Greek—*deigmatízō*). Paul's triumphant language here is reminiscent of a triumphant Roman commander. When a victorious general won a victory, he brought his army to Rome followed by his defeated enemies tied to his chariot as prisoners. He publicly displayed them in a processional, a Triumph, through the streets of Rome, showing himself as the victor. Christ did that on the cross, triumphing over sin, death, hell, Satan, and all the demons, *"the rulers and authorities."*

Now, look at Hebrews 2:14–15 and record what His death accomplished.

____

____

____

Jesus went to the cross to die for our sins, and there He defeated sin, death, Satan, and all the spiritual forces of wickedness. He *"disarmed the rulers and authorities,"* those spirits that tempt and deceive the entire world. He broke the power of these spirits to accuse us by taking our sin and sentence of condemnation on Himself. On the cross, Jesus *"made a public display of them"* through His triumph on the cross and in the Resurrection. He rendered the devil powerless. As a result of what Jesus did through his death and resurrection, He has delivered His children from slavery to the fear of death. Guilt, condemnation, and dread of death need never captivate the believer's heart. We now know that death is simply the doorway into the fuller presence of Christ (see 2 Corinthians 5:8; Philippians 1:20–24). Jesus knows we still face temptation battles in their many forms. He faced the same battles to their fullest extent and came out as the victor. By His life and power and wisdom in us, we too can walk in His victory. Remember, He is also praying for each of us, each of His followers, each of the Father's children.

If we are to win the warfare in prayer, we must focus on the Lord—for He is the warrior who wins. How can we best focus on Him? We will begin to see in Day Two.

The Warfare in Prayer

DAY TWO

THE LORD EQUIPS US FOR PRAYING

We have battles. The earth is a war-torn planet, especially in the spiritual realm. How are we to fight? The Lord has given us some clear instructions for facing the battles and He has provided some excellent equipment for winning the battles. He wants us to know not only about Him as our warrior/commander but also about the armor He has provided and how that is used in prayer. We will see that in today's study.

Read Ephesians 6:10–20. What is of first importance? What do you find in verse 10?

____

____

____

____

According to verse 11–12, whose armor is this? Why is it necessary? What is the goal God has in mind for us in wearing this armor?

____

____

____

____

The focus of Paul in Ephesians 6:10 is not the strength of the devil or the size of the battle, but the strength of the Lord. If we are to win in the battles of life, we must be *"strong in the Lord."* Everything about victory revolves around our relationship with the Lord, the victor. We have seen that He is a warrior who wins all battles and if we are to win in life and in prayer, we must do so looking to Him. He wants us to be strong with *"the strength of His might,"* the kind of might that can overcome any lie, any temptation, or any sin. He knows how to face any and every kind of battle and has the strength to win. He gladly gives us that strength—He is our strength—as we turn to Him and trust in Him.

When we look at the armor with which He equips us, we find that it is *His* armor. It comes from Him. It has His nature. It must come from Him, because the battle is not a "flesh and blood" battle. Human armor is useless against spiritual foes and temptation strategies. Putting on the armor is really putting on Christ and His Word, appropriating all He has done and said to defeat sin, temptation, the devil, and all *"the spiritual forces of wickedness"* with their many lies and deceptions. In putting on *"the full armor of God,"* He intends for us *"to stand firm against the schemes of the devil."* That includes all the deceptions and lies, all the darts of discouragement and doubt, and all the plans to bring us down in defeat.

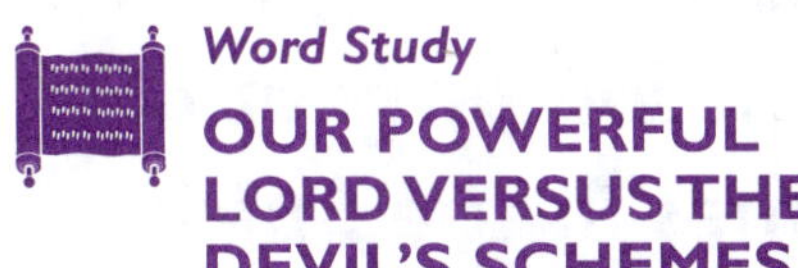

Word Study

OUR POWERFUL LORD VERSUS THE DEVIL'S SCHEMES

Ephesians 6:10 commands us to *"be strong in the Lord."* Paul uses three Greek words to convey the Lord's power. *"Be strong"* is a translation of *endunamóō*, which refers to implied ability, the power available to act. The word *"strength"* in this same verse is from *krátos*, which refers to the presence of force or power that is ready to be revealed when needed. The word *"Might"* is from the Greek word *ischús*, which indicates actual strength or power. It literally means "to have power." The Greek word for *"schemes"* or *"wiles"* in verse 11 is *methodeia*, which refers to methods or to systematic, orderly plans. We are commanded to look for the Lord's power and ability to be revealed as we depend on Him. The Lord has all the strength and power needed to overcome the schemes of the devil and all his orderly plans and methods of carrying out evil.

📖 How are we to wear this armor, and what does each part of the armor mean in our lives? Read Ephesians 6:14–17 and list the various aspects of the armor.

____

____

____

____

____

____

What insights do you glean in these verses about the Lord, about His armor, and about our wearing it?

____

____

____

____

With each piece of the armor there is a two-fold application, one concerning what the armor is and the other concerning how it applies. The armor begins with having on the belt of truth, not only believing the truth of God's Word, but living a truthful or honest life. That is the start. The breastplate of righteousness speaks of the gift of the righteousness of Christ received when we trusted Him for salvation, and of walking in the good works of righteousness as a result of our faith in Christ. The shoes of the *"preparation of the gospel of peace"* speak of our having experienced peace with God in receiving the gospel, of walking with a firm footing in the peace of God day by day, and of our readiness to share with others how they can know peace with God through Christ.

"With all prayer and petition pray at all times in the Spirit, and with this in view, be on the alert with all perseverance and petition for all the saints."

Ephesians 6:18

Praying God's Way

WATCH OUT FOR THE ACCUSER

The devil is the accuser of the brethren (Revelation 12:10) who often uses the weapon of accusation against us, especially in prayer. We must look to our advocate, the Lord Jesus, who defends us (1 John 2:1–2), and deals with our sin not by condemnation, but by the conviction of His Spirit. We need to know the difference between the Spirit's conviction and Satan's accusations. When the Spirit convicts us, He is always truthful in every detail. He is specific and pointed, noting the exact sin. Satan is often general and vague, condemning and cloudy, creating confusion rather than clear conviction. He deceives with half-truths and other kinds of lies. How do we know the difference? The more we know the Lord and His Word, the more alert and sensitive we will be to the Spirit's voice and to anytime we grieve or quench Him (Ephesians 3:20, 1 Thessalonians 5:19). The more we walk in oneness with the Lord and His Word, the more we will know the things that displease Him, even things that are seemingly insignificant to others. Ask the Lord to make you aware of His presence and His pleasure as well as His forgiveness and cleansing moment by moment in your daily walk (1 John 1:5–9).

Having the first three things in place (belt, breastplate, and shoes) we then can take up the final three items. In taking up the shield of faith we are affirming our knowledge of the truth Christ has spoken and our application of that truth—walking by faith in His Word. When the fiery darts come loaded with their lies, by faith we counter with the truth and stand on that truth. The helmet of salvation points to our personal knowledge of salvation and the hope or confidence we have in God to complete all He has promised. The sword of the Spirit is the sword of the word of God, the Spirit's pointed, sharp application of the Word that He gives us for any and every lie of the evil one.

📖 What do we do with the armor once we have it on, according to Ephesians 6:18?

____

____

____

____

The first word in the original Greek of verse 18 is translated *"praying,"* pointing to the connection between the armor and its use. The armor is given so we can pray God's way and see God's victorious answers. Paul focuses the application of the armor on prayer, all kinds of *"prayer and petition"* (*dĕēsis*—specific needs). This is continuous prayer—the phrase *"pray at all times . . ."* is literally *"praying at all times . . ."* pointing to daily, even moment-by-moment praying. That is to be done *"in the Spirit,"* with prayer linking us to our relationship with Christ. We are always dependent on the Spirit's strength, the Spirit's guidance, and the Spirit's sword—the word of God. We walk in agreement with Him and His Word.

In agreement with God and with the shield and sword in hand, we are prepared to pray. For what do we pray? We pray for all the saints, offering our petitions with perseverance, and we pray for the clear proclamation of the gospel message. Paul asked the Ephesian believers to pray specifically for him and his ministry, but the application is for any and every believer who has an opportunity to share that message. (We will see more about this in the lesson on "Praying for Others.")

Let's sum up. In winning battles God's way, we start with the fact that God is God—Jesus is Lord. Jesus is the victor who conquered all on the cross. We agree with those truths by humbling ourselves under His mighty hand (1 Peter 5:6), receiving and putting on His armor. He pours out grace on the humble heart and enables us to stand strong in Him, in His armor. That means receiving His Word and walking in His Spirit day by day, listening carefully, following closely, and resisting firmly. God's Word fortifies faith and enables us to quench fiery darts so they do not penetrate our thinking or affect our walking. The Word of God thus equips us with a firm faith; we stand with firm footing and can thereby wield the sword of the Spirit in prayer—always praying in the Spirit, depending on Him to guide us and to continually strengthen and establish us (1 Peter 5:6–11).

Think back to those times when Scripture pictures the Angel of the Lord standing with sword drawn, as we saw in Day One. Other examples are given in the chart at the end of this lesson. David saw the Angel of the Lord. So did Balaam (see Numbers 22:21–31). In Joshua 5:13–15, we read the account of Joshua seeing the Captain of the Host of the Lord, another appearance of the Angel of the Lord, standing with sword drawn. How fitting that the Lord, our Warrior King, would call us to stand firm, dressed in His armor with the Sword of the Spirit drawn, ready to win battles His way. What else does the Lord do to aid us in the battles we face? We will see in Day Three. But for now it is time to stop and pray.

In light of all you have seen in Days One and Two, pause and praise the Lord for being a mighty warrior, one who fights for us, who gives us victory. Thank Him for the armor with which He equips us and for the victories He gives day by day.

The Warfare in Prayer

DAY THREE

THE LORD ENCOURAGES US IN OUR PRAYING

Jesus is our commander in the battles we face. He understands all the details of all the battles since He faced the same kinds of battles while He lived on earth. He was *"tempted in all things as we are, yet* [He was] *without sin"* (Hebrews 4:15). Jesus knows how to train us, direct us, and encourage us. Christ trains us through the Scriptures. Today we will explore His words that we might be encouraged in our praying for all the battles we face.

One of the needs of any army is continued watchfulness and perseverance—staying in the battle when things look bleak and continually looking to the commander and trusting him when circumstances do not look encouraging. Watchfulness and perseverance are necessary for the army of Christ as we look to our commander, Jesus Christ, and faithfully trust Him.

📖 Ephesians 6:18 speaks about these things as we saw in Day Two. Read that verse again and record the encouragement Paul voiced, especially about "perseverance."

____

____

____

____

____

With the armor in place, the Christian is ready to pray with all kinds of prayer—praise, thanksgiving, petition for his or her needs, and intercession for others. The believer must pray under the Spirit's control, depending on the Spirit's strength and wisdom in prayer. Along with praying *"at all times,"* in all kinds of seasons and circumstances, comes the idea of being *"alert."* The Greek word translated "alert" in Ephesians 6:18 literally means, "without sleep," not dull and insensitive, but awake, alert, watchful. When we are spiritually and mentally alert, we can focus more fully in prayer and petition for the saints. We must pray with perseverance or endurance, remaining steadfast. How? By keeping our eyes focused on the Lord so we can follow Him and by keeping our ears open to hear His Word so we can pray His Word. In this way, we stay focused and stand firm.

Put Yourself in Their Shoes

WAKE UP!

Ephesians 6:18 exhorts us to *"be on the alert,"* or literally "be not sleeping" (Greek—*agrupnéō*, made of two words *a* [not] and *húpnos* [sleep]). Being awake and alert is essential for a soldier in a battle area. When Jesus found His disciples sleeping in Gethsemane, He urged them, *"keep watching and praying, that you may not enter into temptation; the spirit is willing, but the flesh is weak"* (Matthew 26:41). Proverbs 19:23 speaks of sleeping satisfied, showing that sleep is part of life on earth and essential. However, sleep can be a stumbling block, especially when it comes to prayer. Proverbs 6:10–11 and 24:33–34 talk of *"a little sleep, a little slumber"* leading to poverty and want. Proverbs 19:15 says *"laziness casts into a deep sleep,"* and Proverbs 20:13 says *"do not love sleep."* Sleep can rob us not only of food and material goods, but more importantly it can rob us of spiritual riches, especially the riches of time with God in prayer.

The Scriptures continually encourage us to persevere, especially in prayer. The word often translated "perseverance" in Scripture is *proskarteréō,* which means, "to endure toward" something. It can mean to stay close to or continue steadfastly with someone. Look at these verses that use this word and record your insights.

Acts 1:14 and 2:42

____

____

____

____

Acts 6:4

____

____

____

____

____

Romans 12:12

____

____

____

____

Colossians 4:2

____

____

____

____

____

The early disciples were men and women of prayer. They continued steadfastly in prayer after Jesus' ascension. Then in the days of the early church, they made prayer a priority along with focused attention on the Word of God taught by the apostles. They fought to keep the following priorities: spending time in prayer, growing in their understanding of the Word, and getting the message of Christ out to their neighborhoods and to the world. In ministry, devotion to prayer is essential, as Paul exhorted in Romans 12:12 and Colossians 4:2. As people are steadfast in prayer, believers will be encouraged in their walk, and doors will be open to share the Word with others. When believers persevere in prayer, they continue faithfully in the things that matter most—knowing Christ and His Word and making Him known. This is encouraging!

In the days of His ministry with the disciples, Jesus had some very important words about persevering. Read Luke 18:1–8. What was the reason Jesus gave this parable according to verse 1?

Word Study
PERSEVERANCE

In Ephesians 6:18, the Greek word *Proskartérēsis* is translated "perseverance." In other places in the New Testament, it is translated "endurance," "steadfastness," or "persistence." The verb form *proskartaréō,* which literally means "to endure toward," carries the idea of staying close, continuing faithfully with someone, or remaining steadfast. In Acts 1:14; 2:42; 6:4; Romans 12:12, and Colossians 4:2, *proskartaréō* is used to identify someone who is devoted to prayer. *Proskartaréō,* is also used in Mark 3:9, when Jesus requested that a boat *"should stand ready,"* in Acts 10:7 of a devout soldier *"in constant attendance"* to his commanding officer, and in Romans 13:6 of government officials *"devoting themselves"* to upholding the good and dealing with evil. We can learn something about being devoted to prayer from these pictures. We can be like a boat ready to carry someone, to bear a burden, like a soldier ready for service or battle, or like an official devoted to do what is right, to meet a need.

Jesus knew that giving up in prayer would be a real temptation for His followers. He was well aware that His disciples could get weary and want to drop out of the battle. He did not want them to lose heart, and so He gave them a parable to encourage them for those "want-to-quit" days.

According to Luke 18:3, what marked this widow's life? What marked her requests?

A certain widow faced some sort of legal problem, and she simply asked for protection from the judge. She had a legal adversary, an opponent who either meant her harm or would cause her harm by getting what he wanted. In her eyes, what he wanted was wrong, illegal, unjust. She kept coming and kept coming to the unjust judge, but he was unwilling to help. Yet, she kept coming.

What was the result of her persistence?

The widow kept coming, and finally the judge began to be bothered or troubled, the Greek word for *"bothered"* carrying the idea of weariness from toil. She was wearing him out, so much so that he finally granted her legal protection. Perhaps she went to him in the marketplace, or at his home, anywhere he might be found. If she kept coming, he saw that she would *"wear me out,"* a phrase literally rendered "hit under the eye." He was battered and frustrated by her persistent cries.

In Luke 18:7–8, what important prayer truths did Jesus reveal about us coming to His Father—in contrast to this widow and the unjust judge?

In verse 8, what does Jesus see at the heart of persistent praying?

Put Yourself in Their Shoes

THE WAR OF WAITING

Psalm 6 is the cry of David at a time of great distress. In a battle of waiting, he cried out, *"My soul is greatly dismayed; but Thou, O Lord—how long?"* Finally, he cried out with confidence, *"The Lord has heard my supplication, the Lord receives my prayer."* Psalm 90 is a prayer of Moses in which he utters the same words, *"O Lord; how long will it be?"* Often the people of God cry, "How long?" as they seek His will. In another cry, David declared with confidence and hope, *"Wait for the Lord; be strong, and let your heart take courage"* (Psalm 27:14). In the war of waiting, we too can take courage that the Lord will hear and answer.

WISE COUNSEL FOR END TIMES

The apostle Peter took to heart the words of Jesus about persevering in prayer. He told his readers, *"The end of all things is at hand; therefore, be of sound judgment and sober spirit for the purpose of prayer"* (1 Peter 4:8).

Put Yourself in Their Shoes

GRACE FOR THE MOMENT

God's grace was sufficient for Paul, for every weakness he faced. A modern-day example of God's grace being sufficient is found in the life of Oscar Thompson, a professor of evangelism at Southwestern Seminary in Fort Worth, Texas in the 1970s. While battling cancer he often counseled fellow sufferers with this phrase: "God gives 'dying grace' on dying days," at just the time one needs it. God takes care of each of his children for each step of the way. We can add to that truth the fact that God gives "trial grace" for each trial, "praying grace" for each point of need. As a matter of fact, He gives "living grace" for each day we live, "moment-by-moment grace" for each moment of our walk with Him.

By no means is Jesus saying that God is like the unjust judge of the parable. This judge was a mere man who neither feared God nor respected his fellow man. God is absolutely just, righteous in all His ways. He is ever compassionate and full of love and mercy toward His children; they are His chosen ones. When He hears their cries, He listens intently, carefully, with great love and concern. And, of course, Jesus is not saying that if we badger and bother God that He will eventually cave in to our every whim. God does not answer prayer based on the number of words, the number of times we say those words, or the number of people we get to repeat those words. He answers prayer based on His perfect love and unparalleled wisdom. However, Jesus is teaching through this parable that God will *"bring about justice"*—He knows what is best and does what is right. Also, Jesus is saying that God's children are right to *"cry to Him day and night."* They cry because they trust Him; that is at the heart of their cry. They cry in faith in this war of waiting, this battle of time. What will God do? He will answer and will do so *"speedily,"* though perhaps not immediately. When He acts, He will do so fully and suddenly. Therefore, keep praying, keep trusting, keep showing your faith by your praying all the way to the coming of the Son of Man.

Not only did Jesus encourage us in prayer, the Spirit continued to encourage believers throughout the days of the New Testament. We find an example in the life of the apostle Paul. God encouraged him in a most unusual turn of events in prayer (and in a battle).

Read 2 Corinthians 12:1–10. What was the battle Paul faced according to verses 7–8?

____

____

____

What did he do in prayer?

____

____

____

Paul experienced an indescribable journey into the third heaven, into paradise. To keep Paul from boasting in such an experience and exalting himself, God gave Paul "a thorn in the flesh," or a burden, something *"to buffet"* him as Paul said. He even called this "thorn" *"a messenger of Satan."* It was a battle point in his life that kept his pride in check. What was this "thorn"? We are not certain. Paul went to the Lord with the need—three times he *"entreated"* or *"pleaded"* with the Lord. He did not give up in prayer until he had an answer.

What was God's answer to Paul in verse 9?

____

____

How was Paul encouraged with this answer, according to verses 9–10?

____

____

____

The Lord pointed to His grace—His enabling power and presence—in Paul's life. This grace would be sufficient for Paul for any point of weakness, even for this "thorn in the flesh." The point of Paul's testimony is not what the problem or weakness may have been, but that God's grace was adequate for the problem. Paul actually boasted about his weaknesses, *"that the power of Christ"* might dwell in him as he depended on Christ for His enabling grace. He trusted in and surrendered to the ways of God in his life and ministry, and was even *"well content with weaknesses, with insults, with distresses, with persecutions, with difficulties, for Christ's sake."* He saw that though he was weak in himself, he was strong in Christ. That is victory in the midst of the battlefield.

We all face various kinds of battles, trials, different events and circumstances that could bring defeat. What more does our Lord want us to understand for those times of need? Read Hebrews 4:14–16 and record what you discover about Jesus in those verses?

____

____

____

____

____

____

____

What do you discover about the battles we face and the place of prayer in those battles?

____

____

____

____

____

____

Hebrews 4:14 speaks of Jesus as our *"great high priest who has passed through the heavens,"* pointing to His powerful victory over sin and death and the devil (see Hebrews 2:14–18). We can be confident in Him, never needing to waver in our confession of faith. Furthermore, He is a high priest marked not only by power, but also by compassion. He can "sympathize with our weaknesses" since He was *"tempted in all things as we are."* He understands the heat of the battles we face. Today He sits on a throne of grace to which we can come and receive His mercy and grace *"to help in time of need"*—well-placed grace, well-timed help. We can receive exact grace for the exact need at the exact time of need.

In light of all we have seen about the encouragement our Lord gives us, spend some time in prayer with Him.

What about when our prayers are not in line with God's heart and will, or when they are not prayed His way? We will examine this dilemma in Day Four.

"Therefore, He had to be made like His brethren in all things, that He might become a merciful and faithful high priest. . . . For since He Himself was tempted in that which He has suffered, He is able to come to the aid of those who are tempted."

Hebrews 2:17–18

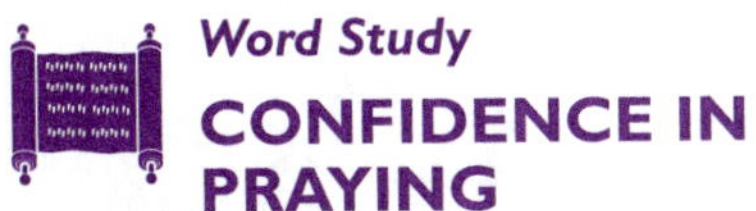

Word Study

CONFIDENCE IN PRAYING

The Greek word *parrēsía* is translated "confidence" or "boldness" in Hebrews 4:16. *Parrēsía* is made up of the words *pas* (all) and *rhēsis* (speaking), and literally means to speak all that one thinks or desires to speak. It points to the freedom to speak all that is on one's heart. What a promise for prayer! You can come before the Father at His throne of grace and speak all that is on your heart, confident that He is listening and willing to answer in your time of need.

The Warfare in Prayer

DAY FOUR

THE LORD SOMETIMES FIGHTS US IN PRAYER

You may question the title of today's lesson. What do you mean "the Lord sometimes fights us in prayer"? How could God fight His own children? That is a very good question and one that we must answer. What do we find in Scripture? How and when and where do we see God at war with His own? Battling God is one of the biggest battles, if not the biggest, that we face. Pride fights God's will to get its own will, to achieve self-agendas, and to gain self-glory. God fights pride and works to see His will, His agenda, and His glory come to pass. What do we learn about prayer battles in Scripture, battles with God Himself? We will see in today's study.

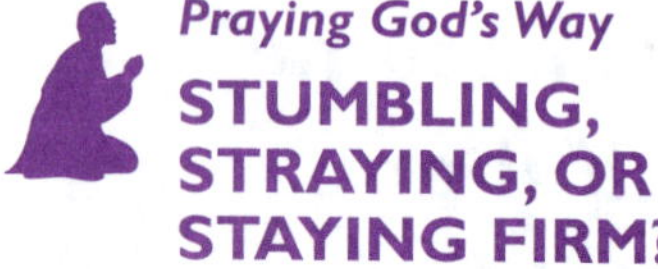

Praying God's Way

STUMBLING, STRAYING, OR STAYING FIRM?

How can we avoid stumbling or straying in our walk and in our praying? The Scriptures speak often about standing firm in the faith and by faith (Colossians 1:23; 2:6–7; 1 Corinthians 16:13; 2 Corinthians 1:24; Galatians 5:1; 1 Peter 5:9), as well as standing firm in the Lord (Ephesians 6:11, 13, 14; Philippians 4:1; 1 Thessalonians 3:8), in grace (1 Peter 5:12), in unity or oneness with other believers (Ephesians 4:1–3; Philippians 1:27), and in the Word (1 Corinthians 11:2; 2 Thessalonians 2:15). As we stand firm this way in our walk, we will stand firm in our praying.

Anywhere you find the heart of a man or woman; there you find a battlefield. It starts in the heart of everyone born on this earth. The battle is for control—who will be Lord of that person's life; what or who will rule that person's life; where will that person's dependence be? The answer to those questions also answers whether or not that person will be victorious in life **and in prayer.**

In the Old Testament, we have some examples of when God had to fight individuals who strayed away from His will. These examples can be instructive to us about how the Lord deals with us when we stand against Him in our praying and in our choices. One of those examples concerns a story many of us have heard. Numbers 22—24 records how the prophet Balaam was asked to go and prophesy against Israel and the Lord sought to stop him. The Angel of the LORD stood in the path with a sword drawn ready to slay Balaam, and Balaam's donkey stopped in her tracks (22:22–35). When Balaam objected, the donkey actually spoke, and Balaam's life was saved. God had to deal with Balaam for His actions. His story illustrates how the Lord will fight for His people to protect them, but also how He will fight against His people who go against Him and His purposes. Balaam was not right with God, and God had to correct him. In the life of King David, we see another example of God dealing with a prideful choice. We also see how it was answered with a return to right thinking and right praying.

📖 Look at the events in the life of King David in 2 Samuel 24. Look at verses 1–14 and record what David did and how God responded.

____

____

____

____

____

What was David's response according to verses 10 and 14?

____

____

____

____

David commanded a census of Israel, apparently with a proud heart, seeking to see his strength in troops rather than simply trusting in the Lord. After Joab (David's commanding officer) completed the census, *"David's heart troubled him."* He realized his folly and confessed his sin. God chose to discipline all Israel for this sin of pride. God sent Gad the prophet to David, giving him a choice of one of three punishments. All three proposed methods of punishment would be dreadful for David and the nation of Israel. One of the options was for David to be hotly pursued by enemy nations. David instead chose three days of pestilence, putting himself and the nation in the hands of God rather than in the hands of men, for he realized he could hope for the mercies of God.

In dealing with His children, the Lord is as forceful as He needs to be and as gentle and merciful as He can be.

📖 According to 2 Samuel 24:15–17, what did the Lord do, and what did David say when he saw the Angel of the Lord? What did David admit to the Lord, according to verse 17?

____

____

____

____

____

____

📖 What did the Lord command in verses 18–19? What do we learn about the Lord in dealing with His children?

____

____

____

____

The Lord chose to strike seventy thousand men with a pestilence and then stopped at that point. David saw the Angel of the Lord at Jerusalem and cried out, confessing his sin. In His mercy, the Lord spared Jerusalem and instructed David to build an altar there. This would be the sight of the future Temple David's son Solomon would build, a place for the people to meet God, pray to Him, and hopefully follow Him more fully. In dealing with His children, the Lord is as forceful as He needs to be and as gentle and merciful as He can be.

In the cases of Balaam and David, the Angel of the Lord fought to see His will accomplished among His people even when it meant fighting against someone as noble as David. He also fought battles **for** His people, as we saw in Day One where the Angel fought for the Israelites against the Egyptians at the Red Sea. [For more examples, see the chart "The Angel of the Lord—A Warrior Winning Battles" at the end of this lesson.] In both the Old and New Testaments, we see God as a warrior fighting for what is right and winning the battles to see His purposes fulfilled.

In the New Testament, we find the Lord at work to guide His people in praying and doing what is right. As we walk with the Lord, we discover that sometimes we stumble in our praying and that sometimes we are just plain stubborn, particularly in our asking from our Father. We miss what

God is doing in our lives, or we miss the truth He is seeking to reveal, or we simply miss God altogether.

What do you find in James 4:1–2? What is the problem we sometimes face according to verse 2?

____

____

____

____

____

What additional problem do we find in verses 3–4?

____

____

____

____

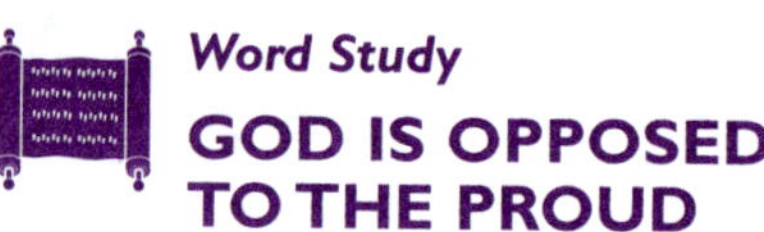

Word Study

GOD IS OPPOSED TO THE PROUD

James 4:6 says, *"God is opposed to the proud,"* (NASB) or *"God resists the proud"* (NKJV). The Greek word translated *"is opposed"* in this verse is *antitássō*, and it is made of the words *antí* (against) and *tássō* (to arrange). It is used of placing an army in battle array against someone. When God sees our pride or hears our proud, selfish praying, He fights us because He loves us. He is jealous for our loving devotion to Him and His will, because He knows that is always right and best.

What is the solution according to James 4:6–7?

____

____

____

____

There are times when we try to get what we want **without asking** God. We fight for our wants, and perhaps we even fight against God. We simply try to force our will, our way, and our desires into existence. Then there are times when **we do ask**—but with wrong or self-centered motives. When we want something, we usually want it now, and we ask God to give it to us. He does not, because He knows it will lead to further failure in our fellowship, more breakdowns in the quality of our relationship with Him and with others. When we do not get what we want, we can often be found fighting and quarrelling even more (with Him and with one another), revealing that we have been selfish and self-focused all along in this particular desire. We have not been concerned for the desire and delight of God, only with our own wrong desire and wrong delight. We have been trying the world's ways, wanting the world's delights, and so we find ourselves in a fight with God. A person who continually lives in this kind of lifestyle is showing the marks of an unbeliever, one who has never surrendered to the will of God. We as believers can stray into selfish praying, but the Holy Spirit will convict of us of that wrong and bring us back to surrender and a willing walk.

So how do we pray with right motives? How do we win the battle against self? The solution is simple—not always easy, but simple. We must turn from our sinful ways and sinful praying and submit ourselves to God, including our desires and our ways. He calls us to humble ourselves under His mighty hand and follow His wise ways. When we do, He pours out His grace. That means He gives us His power and ability so that we are able to carry out His will His way. The devil always tries to get us to go our own proud way (like he did), and to delight in the world's delights. In submitting to God, we take the first step in victory. As we stand submitted to God, we resist the devil, and as we stand against him, he flees. As we draw near to God in cleansing from sin and in fresh surrender and submission, we discover afresh the will and ways of God in our walk.

Surrender to God and His will are at the heart of our relationship with God and the foundation for every prayer He answers. Is there a desire or request where you see more fighting and quarrelling than quiet trusting and surrender? Are you resting, waiting on God to answer in His way and in His time, or are you fidgeting with impatience, wanting your way and your timing? Try this simple exercise. . .

"In Jesus' Name, I bring this request to You, Father" (Write your request in the blanks provided.)

____

____

____

____

____

____

"Father, what about this request agrees with Your heart, Your desires, Your nature, or Your will?"

____

____

____

____

____

"What does not agree?"

____

____

____

____

____

____

"I drop the request—**OR**—I change the request in this way…"

____

____

____

____

____

"I thank You that You are willing to teach me to pray, especially in how to ask for the right things in the right way! I surrender to You."

What about when we are seeking the will of the Lord, when we want to walk and pray God's way? Does that mean the battles cease? There are some battles that go hand in hand with our genuinely seeking the Lord. We will see some of those struggles in Day Five.

The Warfare in Prayer

DAY FIVE

FOR ME TO PRAY GOD'S WAY

Jesus gave His disciples "the Lord's Prayer" or "the Disciples' Prayer" as a pattern. As He guided them through that pattern, He covered the basics of what it means to follow God. He began with worship and surrender to the Father, the kind of surrender that hallows His name and desires to see others hallow Him. In addition, He focused them on the true kingdom and the prayer for that kingdom to come in individual hearts as well as in all the earth. Added to this focus, was the petition for the will of God to be done on earth as it is in heaven. Daily bread was not forgotten. This prayer pattern acknowledged that God was the supplier for each day's needs. It also acknowledged the need for personal forgiveness as well as a heart that forgives others. Jesus also knew they would face warfare—the temptations inherent in the world, along with the deceptions of the devil, as well as the ever-present war within, those desires of the "flesh." How can we apply that petition concerning the war we face, especially when it comes to praying God's way?

📖 Read Matthew 6:9–13. Write down your insights into the Lord's instructions in this prayer pattern, especially the petitions in verse 13.

____

____

____

____

____

____

Look at the second half of Matthew 6:13. What is the focus of Jesus in His instruction about this petition?

____

____

____

____

After instructing us to pray through our relationship with God, our personal needs, and our relationships with others, the Lord instructs us to focus on the danger points around us. *"And do not lead us into temptation"* brings us before the Father, acknowledging that we can be easily tempted. We need guidance away from any source of temptation, any snare that will trap us, any stumbling stone that will trip us up. This is not only an acknowledgement that we are weak and easily led astray, but it is also a point of surrender to the Lord's good guidance. When we pray like this, we are asking Him

Praying God's Way

DISTRACTIONS IN PRAYER

How do we handle the distractions that come when we spend time in prayer, things like wandering thoughts, false guilt, or even sleepiness? The first thing to do is to take care of the basics. Here is a good guideline: "Get up—Wake up—Look up—Listen up—Speak up." In the morning get up out of bed. It can be distracting fighting sleep. Wake up—wash your face or shower. Go to a quiet place, a "prayer closet" where you are less likely to be disturbed. "Look up" to the Lord. Start in His Word and "listen up." Concerning any guilt, know that His Spirit will bring up any sin that needs to be confessed and dealt with. Stand on the promises of His Word and thank Him for His forgiveness and cleansing. As you read His Word, "speak up." To help fight wandering thoughts, it may even help to write your prayers to help keep you focused and concentrating. For variety, take prayer walks or prayer drives, listen to worship music or read (or sing) hymns that help you concentrate on the Lord, His Word and His ways. From time to time, have a personal prayer retreat where you can have extended time, perhaps a Saturday or another day off. Times of prayer and fasting can help you focus also. How much time we spend is important, as in any relationship, but of greater importance is making sure you are spending **alert, awake** time in prayer.

to so superintend our walk that He makes us aware of any lures to sin, any bait along the way that would lead us into sin. He knows where each of us is weak, and He knows how to overcome any and every temptation. Overcoming sin starts with staying away from anything that could entice us to sin.

The Lord does not stop with a request for His watchcare over us. He tells us to pray *"deliver us from evil."* Some translate that *"deliver us from the evil one,"* the devil. The word *"deliver"* paints an instructive picture. The Greek word *rhúomai* means to deliver forcefully, even to drag away. There is an additional thought that we must see here. *Rhúomai*, "deliver," not only carries the idea of delivering forcefully, of snatching from danger, but also of bringing or drawing to oneself to the deliverer. This is a prayer for us to be delivered away from the evil one (Satan) and away from all the evil with which he is associated—the world system, the spiritual forces of wickedness, and even our own "flesh" that so easily and deceitfully seeks its own evil way. To be **delivered from** the evil one and the evil around us means to be **drawn to** our Lord and Savior, to His Word and His will. We look to Him when temptations are near. We call on Him. We depend on His armor and the sword of His Spirit.

The saying goes, "to be forewarned is to be forearmed." If we know what kinds of evil can trap us, we will know better how to avoid those things and recognize the ways the Lord is leading us in order to deliver us. How do we cooperate with the Lord in these matters? We must certainly pray, *"lead us not into temptation, but deliver us from the evil one."* After we have prayed, then what are we to do? Look at the following verses and record what kind of evil we must confront. Then, write a statement of personal application.

Romans 13:14 and Ephesians 4:22–24—Watch out for:

____

____

____

____

Here is how I cooperate:

____

____

____

____

____

1 John 2:15–17 and 1 Peter 2:11—Watch out for:

____

____

____

____

THE OVERCOMER

Jesus told His disciples not to be disturbed about the pressures of the world. He has overcome the world and knows how to deliver us day by day. He can give us peace in the midst of the pressures. John 16:33 says, *"These things I have spoken to you, that in Me you may have peace. In the world you have tribulation, but take courage; I have overcome the world."*

Word Study

THE DELIVERER

The one who delivers us from evil and from the evil one is the Lord Jesus. He is called "the Deliverer" (the *rhúomai*) in Romans 11:26, a quote of Isaiah 59:20, where the Septuagint (Greek translation of the Old Testament) uses *rhuomai* as well. In Exodus 2:19, the title, translated from the Hebrew word *natsal,* was used of Moses delivering Jethro's daughters from the shepherds at the well and then watering their flocks. Isaiah 48:17 and 20 use this title to speak of the Lord as the deliverer of Israel who took them and led them *"in the way you should go."* Our deliverer, Jesus rescues us from danger and draws us to Himself to follow closely and discover His provision and care.

Put Yourself in Their Shoes
FOCUSED DEVOTION

When the apostle Paul wrote to the Corinthian believers, he was very concerned that they not end up distracted from Christ and thus defeated by the devil. He expressed his concern with these words, *"But I am afraid, lest as the serpent deceived Eve by his craftiness, your minds should be led astray from the simplicity and purity of devotion to Christ"* (2 Corinthians 11:3). The more literal rendering is even more focused—lest you be *"led astray from the simplicity and purity in Christ."*

Here is how I cooperate:

____

____

____

____

1 Peter 5:5–9 and James 4:6–10—Watch out for:

____

____

____

____

Here is how I cooperate:

____

____

____

____

As we have seen in lesson after lesson, Scripture after Scripture, everything depends on our relationship with the Lord. We must ever keep Him as the focus of our walk. There are many substitute solutions in the world, everything from "self-help" books and seminars, to exotic adventures to help people "find themselves," to the latest spiritual fad that will guarantee spiritual victory in one or two easy steps. The answer is not found in any of these so-called solutions.

The answer to our warfare days is simple—not always easy to attain—but simple. We must put off the old self, die to self, and make no provision for the "flesh" and its lusts. We must call on God to deliver us. We must put on the Lord Jesus and His armor. We can now wear the new self, created by God *"in righteousness and holiness of the truth"* (Ephesians 4:24). As we walk with the Lord this way, He teaches us to depend more and more on Him, to surrender at new levels of faith. Such an inner dependence upon God involves a continual walk of humbling ourselves before the Lord and before one another—clothing ourselves with humility day after day. As we continually humble ourselves, we recognize more of the subtle ways of the world, more of its *"boastful pride,"* its *"lust of the flesh,"* and its *"lust of the eyes"* (1 John 2:16). As God continues to reveal what the "flesh" is really like, what kind of world we live in, and how deceptive the devil is, we recognize how needy we are, how dependent we must be on the Lord Jesus to walk and pray God's way.

With this understanding and with daily dependence on the Lord, we can stand on His truth—trusting His Word while we resist the devil. We resist, remaining firm in our faith by remaining consistent in His Word, continually being taught by Him. Scripture does not call us to rebuke and bind, but to stand firm in our relationship with the Lord—looking to Him to deliver us and resisting anywhere we see the devil tempting. We stand against him by our standing **in the Lord** and by believing **His Word.** We resist lies and rebuke temptations with the sword of the Spirit, the Word of God. The

Doctrine
WE ARE SAFE

Not only are we saved by our Lord and Savior Jesus Christ, we are also safe. Speaking of the coming of Jesus Christ, 1 John 5:18b says, *"He who was born of God keeps him and the evil one does not touch him."* The word "touch" in this verse (Greek—*háptō*) signifies more than a surface touch. It can carry the idea of touching or grasping to harm. The Lord Jesus **keeps** all those born of God, all those born from above in the new birth. That means He guards us so that while the evil one (Satan) can tempt us, test us, accuse us, or incite others to persecute us, he cannot touch us to ultimately harm us. The Lord is sovereign. The devil can only go as far as the Lord allows (Job 1—2; 42; John 10:28–30; 17:11–15; 1 John 2:13; 2 Timothy 4:17–18).

devil continually seeks to get us away from the Lord and His Word. That is what he did in the Garden of Eden. That is what he tried to do with Jesus in the wilderness temptations. That is what he tries to do with us every day. We must draw near to God, deal with any sin He shows us, and obey what He says to us. That is a walk of victory.

Father, I thank You that You win battles, that You are a warrior who fights to see all Your purposes accomplished. I am grateful that surrender to You is at the heart of winning the battles I face. Thank You that Your armor is adequate for any attack, any deception, any scheme of wickedness. Since You give grace to the humble, I want to humble myself before You, submitting to You and Your will. I ask You to continually lead me away from temptation and to deliver me away from the evil one. Lead me to Your Word as my sword for my every temptation, for every weakness I have, every wrong desire that comes up. Lead me to Yourself, to focus on You, to love You, to listen and learn from You, to be clothed in You. Thank You for the encouragement You give in Your Word. May I too be an encouragement to fellow believers as they face their various battles. May You be exalted above all as the mighty and victorious Warrior and King who is indeed the Overcomer of the world, the flesh and the devil, of sin, death, and hell. In Jesus' Name. Amen.

Write your prayer to the Lord or make a journal entry.

Doctrine

ALL EYES ON JESUS

Our focus is not on our power or any certain knowledge, nor on our enemies or our battles, but on the Lord Jesus. As we resist the devil and pray for the Lord to deliver us from all evil, including the evil one (Satan), we look to the Lord to deal with the devil, to rebuke him as He chooses. Michael the archangel understood this truth. Jude 9 says, *"When he* [Michael] *disputed with the devil and argued about the body of Moses, did not dare pronounce against him a railing judgment, but said, "THE LORD REBUKE YOU."* Michael the archangel depended on Jesus Christ the warrior, The Angel of the LORD, to win the battle against the devil.

The Angel of the LORD

A WARRIOR WINNING BATTLES

The Angel of the Lord is considered a Christophany, an appearance of Christ in the Old Testament

SCRIPTURE	EVENT	PLACE
Genesis 16:1–15, note verses 7–13	The Angel of the LORD found Hagar and Ishmael in the wilderness, running from Sarai's harsh treatment. He delivered them.	Wilderness near Shur
Genesis 18:1–33	The LORD came to the home of Abraham in the form of a man with two angels who were also in the form of men. He spoke to Abraham and Sarah about their coming son Isaac and to Abraham about the coming judgment of Sodom.	By the oaks of Mamre near Hebron
Genesis 21:8–21 note verses 17–18	The Angel of God met Hagar and Ishmael in the desert and provided water for them	Wilderness of Beersheba
Genesis 22:1–19 note verses 11–19	As Abraham was offering up Isaac on Mount Moriah, the Angel of the LORD stopped him, spoke to him, and gave him many promises.	Mount Moriah (modern Jerusalem)
Genesis 28:10–22; 31:11, 13	The LORD appeared to Jacob in a dream at Bethel, promising him the land, many descendants, and a seed through whom the earth would be blessed. This same LORD appeared to Jacob as the Angel of God twenty years later.	Bethel
Genesis 31:10–13	The Angel of God spoke to Jacob in a dream instructing him to leave Haran and return to Canaan.	Haran
Genesis 32:22–32; Hosea 12:4–5	The Angel of the LORD wrestled all night with Jacob and blessed him at the Jabbok River.	Jabbok River
Exodus 3:1–6 note verse 2; Deuteronomy 33:16; Acts 7:30–34; Mark 12:26; Luke 20:37	The Angel of the LORD appeared to Moses in a flame of fire in the midst of a bush in the desert of Midian	Mount Horeb (also known as Mount Sinai)
Exodus 4:24–26	The Lord met Moses and sought to kill him for failing to circumcise his son. This was possibly the Angel of the LORD.	On the way to Egypt
Exodus 14:19–20; Isaiah 63:9	The Angel of God appeared in the Pillar of Cloud and of Fire, guiding and protecting the children of Israel from Pharaoh's army.	At the Red Sea
Exodus 23:20–23	Moses received God's promise that He would send the Angel of the LORD to guide Israel into Canaan. (*"My name is in Him." "My Angel will go before you."* [NKJV])	At Mount Sinai
Exodus 32:34 33:1–6, 12–16	The Lord told Moses that He would send a representative angel before the people, not the Angel of the LORD, for He Himself would not go with them because of their sin. Moses interceded and God promised, "My presence shall go with you."	At Mount Sinai
Numbers 22–24 note 22:22–39	The Angel of the LORD met Balaam and his donkey on the journey with the princes of Moab to meet Balak.	The Plains of Moab
Joshua 5:13–15; 6:1–5	A "man," the Commander of the Army of the LORD, met Joshua near Jericho and instructed him in how to conquer the city.	Near Jericho in the land of Canaan
Judges 2:1–6	The Angel of the LORD rebuked Israel for disobeying Him in not dealing with the Canaanites as He had commanded.	Bochim (means "weeping")
Judges 5:23	The Angel of the LORD cursed the people of the town of Meroz for not fighting with the people of God against the Lord's enemies in northern Israel.	Meroz
Judges 6:11–24, 25–27	The Angel of the LORD appeared to Gideon calling him to lead Israel against the Midianites	Ophrah
Judges 13:1–24	The Angel of the LORD appeared to Manoah and his wife, promising them a son and then ascended in the flame where they were offering a burnt offering.	Zorah
2 Samuel 24:10–25, note verses 15–17; 1 Chronicles 21:1–30 note verses 12–20, 27, 30	The Angel of the LORD was involved in judging David's sin of numbering the people (probably to enhance his military might or perhaps out of pride in his military potential).	Israel and Jerusalem

SCRIPTURE	EVENT	PLACE
Psalm 34:7 (with 1 Samuel 21:10–15)	David celebrated the protection of the Angel of the LORD in the danger he faced from Achish, king of Gath.	Gath, city of the Philistines
Psalm 35:5, 6	David prayed for the help of the Angel of the LORD against an enemy who was against him without cause.	Israel
1 Kings 19:7	The Angel of the LORD touched Elijah and instructed him to eat in preparation for the journey ahead.	Wilderness south of Beersheba
2 Kings 1:2–17 note verses 3, 15, 16	The Angel of the LORD instructed Elijah to go and deliver a message to Israel's King Ahaziah.	Samaria
2 Kings 19:35–36; Isaiah 37:36	The Angel of the LORD struck 185,000 Assyrian troops, bringing Sennacherib's threats to naught and delivering Hezekiah and the people of Jerusalem.	Near Jerusalem
Daniel 3:19–30	God *"sent His Angel"* and delivered Shadrach, Meshach, and Abed-nego from the fiery furnace. To Nebuchadnezzar, this fourth "man" in the furnace appeared *"like the Son of God"* (or "a son of the gods") (3:25, 28 NKJV).	The Plain of Dura in the province of Babylon
Zechariah 1:7–17 note verses 11, 12	The Angel of the LORD appeared in Zechariah's first vision as the Commander-in-Chief of the angelic hosts, riding on a red horse of judgment seeking to bring mercy and restoration to Israel.	Israel and the Earth
Zechariah 3:1–10 note verses 1–2, 3–4, 6	The Angel of the LORD appeared in Zechariah's fourth vision, rebuking Satan and declaring Jerusalem and the nation (represented by Joshua the High Priest) as the cleansed and restored people and priesthood of God. With this declaration, comes the promise of the coming Messiah (Servant, Branch, Stone) and His kingdom.	Israel
Zechariah 12:8	Zechariah prophesied about the future of Israel when the nation will be strong like David or like a nation with the Angel of the LORD leading them.	Jerusalem and the area surrounding it

Notes

10

PRAYING FOR OTHERS

DISCOVERING AND PRAYING THE HEART OF GOD FOR SAINTS AND SINNERS

We saw in our last lesson that the Christian encounters many skirmishes with the world, the flesh, and the devil in the course of life; skirmishes that are lost or won on the battlefields of the mind within and of encounters with others. Every battle won produces a **victor** who is rejoicing; every battle lost produces a **victim** who is discouraged. When we have a victory, we should praise and exalt our Lord, the Victor, for it is always by His strength, wisdom, and skill that we experience victory. We should encourage others in their battles, knowing that when we face defeat or discouragement we need to be encouraged by others. **Praying for others** is one very important way to bring encouragement to others and is one of the most crucial and vital ministries for this day. Millions are lost, not knowing or following Jesus Christ as Lord and Savior. We need to pray for them. There are millions of Christians following Christ, but many are faltering along the way. We must pray for them also. What does the Scripture say about praying for others—for the unredeemed sinner and the saved-by-grace saint? That is the focus of this week's lesson.

Millions are lost, not knowing or following Jesus Christ as Lord and Savior. We need to pray for them. There are millions of Christians following Christ, but many are faltering along the way. We must pray for them also.

How are we to pray for fellow believers? What guidelines does God give us? What is most important in His eyes for each of His children and each of His churches? He has shown us how to pray for fellow saints in several passages and in actual prayers in Scripture. We will look at many of those examples in this lesson. What about those who do not know Jesus Christ? How do we pray for them? Are there passages in the Bible that show us what to pray for the lost? We will explore those as well.

Praying for Others

DAY ONE

"My House: A House of Prayer for All the Nations"

To understand what it means to pray for others, we must understand the heart of God toward those "others." What do we find in Scripture about the ways of God with His people and with those invited to become His people? We start with the heart of our Lord Jesus. His actions and words reveal the heart of the Father and show us what it means to do the will of the Father, especially when it comes to praying for others.

Read Mark 11:15–18. What upset Jesus according to verses 15–16?

___

___

___

According to verse 17, what reason did He give for what He did?

___

___

___

Did You Know?

THE TEMPLE AREA

The Temple area consisted of more than the Temple itself (the Outer Court for sacrifice, the Holy Place, and the Holy of Holies). In New Testament days, Herod's Temple complex (the Temple remodeled by Herod) encompassed the Temple itself, plus a court for women, and an area immediately around the Temple where any Jew could worship. A wall surrounded that area beyond which no Gentile could go. The area outside that wall was known as the Court of the Gentiles, an expanded platform built to house the many pilgrims who came to Jerusalem during the feast times. The entire Temple area encompassed an area about 900 feet by 900 feet. The trade in sacrifices and money changing must have been considerable. Jesus addressed the greedy transactions taking place here by clearing out the sellers and their goods, as well as the buyers.

At the Temple in Jerusalem, Jesus cast out those buying and selling sacrificial animals and doves and overturned the tables of the moneychangers. He also stopped people from carrying various vessels and goods through the Temple area. They were regarding the Temple and the God of the Temple with great disrespect, turning God's house into nothing more than a marketplace, even a den of thieves. Jesus saw no atmosphere of prayer, no focused attention on God—and no true worship.

If we understand the historical background of this event, it will help us see the full picture. The time was the week of preparation for the Passover and just a few days before Jesus was crucified. At the beginning of the week, He made His triumphal entry as the crowds shouted *"Hosanna! BLESSED IS HE WHO COMES IN THE NAME OF THE LORD; blessed is the coming of the kingdom of our father David"* (Mark 11:9). The people were looking to Jesus as their Messiah, the fulfillment of all the Old Testament prophecies. The day after the triumphal entry, Jesus entered the Temple and began casting out those buying and selling the various animals and birds to be offered in sacrifice. Pilgrims in Jerusalem for the Passover chose to buy their sacrificial animals at the Temple rather than bring them from their home places. All the animals and birds had to pass a rigorous inspection by the priests. The animals at the Temple would have been officially declared clean. These selected animals were most likely sold at an inflated price. They brought a nice profit to the sellers, possibly part of the family of the High Priest or sellers who paid the priests for the opportunity to sell in the Temple.

In addition, those from other lands would need to exchange their Roman or Greek currency for Jewish or Tyrian currency to pay the half-shekel Temple tax (Exodus 30:11–16). Moneychangers were in place to make the exchange and charged a ten to twelve percent fee. All of this market activity took place in the Court of the Gentiles, the only place set aside for a Gentile to worship. Only the Jews could go into the nearer Temple courts. The Jews had built a wall around those courts and posted signs warning Gentiles to stay in their area and not come into the Jewish courts on penalty of death. Jesus saw the sellers and moneychangers crowding out the Gentile area, putting up a barrier to their worship and prayer. He forcefully "cleaned house."

What was at the heart of all this? When Jesus saw the well-organized trading going on and saw the prices and methods of the leaders there, He recognized their wrong motives. This was religious business, and He saw them as robbers in the Temple, stealing not only money, but of greater concern, stealing attention away from God and from the true worship He desired. The Temple was designed to be a place where all nations, all people-groups, could come to worship, pray, and petition God. Religious business, even greed (which is idolatry) had gotten in the way of a loving relationship with the one true God.

📖 Jesus quoted from Isaiah 56:7 and Jeremiah 7:11. Read Isaiah 56:6–8 and note what you discover about the Lord's "house of prayer." Describe the worshipers found in verse 6.

____

____

____

____

____

____

In what activity are they involved, according to verse 7?

____

____

____

Who does God want coming to this "house of prayer" according to verses 7–8?

____

____

In Isaiah 59, we see the Lord's desire to gather Israel to Himself that they might be His faithful worshipers. He also desires to see "foreigners," Gentiles from the nations, join themselves to Him in order *"to minister to Him, . . . to love the name of the LORD,"* and to walk with Him, obeying His Word. He wants to *"make them joyful in His house of prayer."* This is not simply a call to come to a "house of prayer" located in Jerusalem, but to come into the household of faith, to enter into a personal relationship with the Lord.

Being a house of prayer for all the nations is not just an application to the Temple of Isaiah's day or Jesus' day. It applies to our day, to the people of God today. God wants every gathering to be a place where **anyone** from **any**

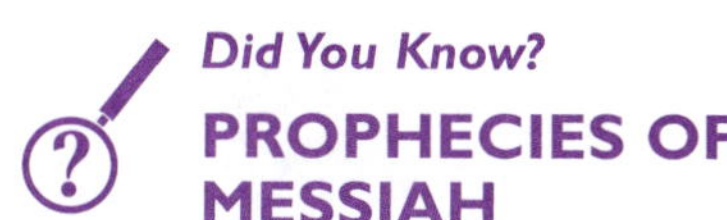

Isaiah prophesied about Jesus the Messiah, *"And now says the Lord, who formed Me from the womb to be His Servant, . . . in order that Israel might be gathered to Him. . . . I will also make You a light of the nations so that My salvation may reach to the end of the earth"* (Isaiah 49:5–6).

nation can call on the Lord. Being a house of prayer also involves gathering together to pray for other people of all nations to come to the Lord and call on Him as their Lord and Savior. Just as the worshipers of long ago could offer to God acceptable sacrifices, so God wants people from all nations to offer those spiritual sacrifices of prayer, praise, and petition from a heart of surrender and love. The Lord still seeks those who will call on Him in prayer and walk with Him, loving and honoring His name. He also desires that we join Him in seeking as we pray for all nations.

What does God want? What is His goal in these days and how do we overcome the obstacles to that goal? We have seen the importance of the armor of God enabling us to stand firm against the schemes of the devil, to live and walk firm in our faith. Then we are ready for the activity that brings the armor into fullest use, "praying at all times with all prayer and petition" (Ephesians 6:18). Specifically, God want us praying first "for all the saints" and then for the proclamation of the gospel. This matches God's goal of a family in the image of Christ. To reach that goal, there are some obstacles to overcome. As the "Best" Shepherd, Jesus came to destroy the works of the devil, to redeem the lost out of darkness and defeat, and to bring His people from every nation "safely to His heavenly kingdom" (2 Timothy 4:18; John 10:1-30). He is committed to reaching that goal, and has mysteriously chosen to use praying as part of the process—praying in line with His goal.

The discussion in Isaiah 56 is rooted in what the Lord revealed in Isaiah 49 about gathering Israel to Himself like a shepherd gathering His flock. Not only will He gather Israel, but also those from the nations (see Isaiah 49:5–6). How does that relate to the New Testament? Jesus spoke of Himself as the Good Shepherd.

📖 What do you find in John 10:14–18 that adds light to what is found in Mark 11, Isaiah 56, and Isaiah 49?

____

____

____

____

____

What is the goal of Jesus? Why did He come according to John 10:14–18?

____

____

____

____

Jesus wants to gather His sheep, not only the sheep of the house of Israel, but "others" from the nations of the world and make them one flock with one Shepherd. To fulfill His desires for His sheep, He came to lay down His life for them, to die to redeem them. Any obstacles to coming to Him He wants removed. That is why He cleansed the Temple, removing the obstacles both to Jews and Gentiles, those from many nations, many peoples. As Isaiah 59:7 states, the Lord wants *"all the peoples,"* people-groups from all the nations, to come before Him in prayer, calling on His name and loving His name. John 10 points to Jesus as the Shepherd whose voice many will hear and begin to follow, acknowledging Him as Lord and Savior and following Him joyfully and wholeheartedly.

Just as Jesus wanted the Temple to be a place to pray, a place to call on the Lord, so He wants every gathering of believers to be a place where access to the Lord in prayer is free of obstacles. He also wants every believer to be a temple, a place of worship and witness through which any person from any nation can come to God, calling on Him in repentance and faith and starting a life of calling on Him (as we saw in Lesson 1). Pause and pray about **1)** any obstacles that are hindering your worship or your praying for others, **2)** any obstacles in your life that would hinder someone coming to Christ and **3)** any obstacles in your church that are hindering prayer or an effective witness to the lost.

Today we have seen the heart of God concerning the nations of the world in both the Old and New Testaments. Today and in previous lessons, we have seen the Lord Jesus clearing the way for people to come to Him, removing the obstacles in the Temple then and ultimately removing the obstacle of our sins on the Cross. There are still some obstacles in the way in the minds and hearts of many. Those obstacles begin to be removed as we pray and speak the truth of God's Word. How are we to pray for those who have not yet come to Christ or for Christians that are in need of prayer in some area of their lives? What obstacles stand in the way? We will begin to see in Day Two.

Praying for the "Nations"— The Lost Throughout the Earth

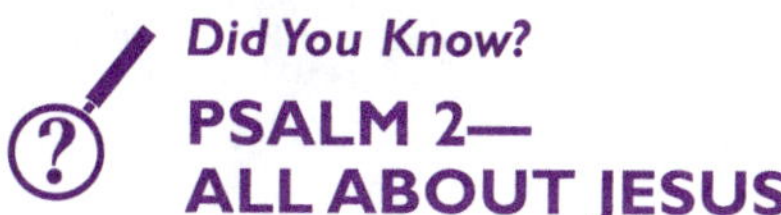

Scripture speaks in many places about the nations of the earth either acknowledging the Lord or failing to acknowledge Him. As early as Genesis 12, we find the Lord promising that all the families of the earth would be blessed through Abraham. That blessing would ultimately come through the Seed of Abraham, the Messiah Jesus. Jesus is the one who can bless the families of the earth with forgiveness of sins, the presence of His Spirit, and eternal life. How is God blessing today, and where does prayer fit in? Let's explore the Scriptures for answers to this question.

Psalm 2 is a prophecy about the Messiah. Read Psalm 2:1–12. What does the Father promise concerning the nations in verse 8?

____

____

____

How does one become a part of this kingdom and receive the blessing of God according to verses 11–12?

____

____

____

The Father is sovereign Lord who has installed His Son as King, regardless of those who oppose the Son's reign or the Father's choice of Christ as King. The Father has settled the issue of who rules. Because that is true, He commands the Son, *"Ask of Me, and I will surely give the nations as Thine inheritance, and the very ends of the earth as Thy possession."* This is both a command and a promise that the Messiah, Jesus, will reign as King of kings and Lord of lords. The Father wants the people of all nations on earth to acknowledge who Jesus is and, in so doing, acknowledge who the Father is in His power, wisdom, love, mercy, and even His judgment. Jesus is worthy of worship and is to be greatly honored and feared. God calls all to *"do homage"* or literally, *"kiss"* the Son, a Middle Eastern picture of showing utmost respect and submission. The one who places faith in Christ, who takes refuge in Him, will be blessed. The one who does not will *"perish in the way."*

Did You Know?

PSALM 2— ALL ABOUT JESUS

In the New Testament, we find Psalm 2 quoted five times in reference to Jesus Christ. In the prayer meeting found in Acts 4:24–31, we hear the early Church quoting from Psalm 2:1–2. Paul quoted Psalm 2:7 in his message in Pisidian Antioch recorded in Acts 13:33–34. We find it quoted again in Hebrews 1:5–6 and 5:5 and then in Revelation 2:26–27.

Doctrine

PSALM 2

When the Father said to His Son, *"Ask of Me, and I will surely give the nations as Thine inheritance,"* we can know that Christ's request would be answered to the fullest. Revelation 5:9 speaks of people *"from every tribe and tongue and people and nation"* being in the kingdom of God. Revelation 11:15–17 speaks of Christ reigning over all—*"the kingdom of the world has become the kingdom of our Lord, and of His Christ."*

Word Study
REFUGE

Psalm 2:12 says the one *"who takes refuge"* in the Son will be blessed. According to *The Complete Word Study Old Testament* (© 1994, AMG Publishers, p. 2317), the word translated "refuge" in this verse is *chacah*, a Hebrew word meaning "to flee (for protection), to seek refuge, . . . to trust in (someone)." *Chacah* is used of literal protection in the rocks of the Judean wilderness (Psalm 104:18) and of the Lord as a spiritual protection (Psalm 46:1). Isaiah 4:6 and 25:4 also speak of the Lord being a protection and refuge.

Word Study
THE GENTILES

The word "nations" or "Gentiles" is a translation of the Greek word *éthnē*, which is the plural form of *éthnos* (nation), the root of our English word "ethnic." It refers to a nation or people group. In Acts 17:26, Paul speaks of all the family of mankind as *éthnos*, "one nation," including both Jews and Gentiles. *Éthnē* often signifies the "Gentiles" or the "nations" apart from the Jews. The word *laós* (people) is often used to refer to Israel as the people of God.

In Revelation 5:9, we find a fulfillment of this promise and prophecy. In John's revelation of heaven and the scene around the Throne of the Lamb, he saw and heard the twenty-four elders sing about the Lamb's redemption of people *"from every tribe and tongue and people and nation,"* every people-group on earth. They have been purchased by the blood of the Lamb and have become part of the kingdom of God and *"will reign upon the earth."*

What do these promises and prophecies have to do with praying for others? If we know the mind and heart of God, we can call on Him, agreeing with Him in prayer. As we depend on the Lord to guide us in prayer, we can know that we will see people *"do homage to the Son"* and to know Jesus as Lord and Savior. Is there someone or some family or group of people for whom God has placed on your mind and heart to pray? Pause and pray for that person or persons.

In the New Testament, we find that God chose Saul of Tarsus to become Paul the Apostle. (An apostle is "one sent with a message.") Paul was sent to both Jews and Gentiles, but especially to "the Gentiles" or "the nations." He told the Romans, *"I am eager to preach the gospel to you . . . in Rome."* Then, in Romans 1:16, he expressed his heart, *"For I am not ashamed of the gospel, for it is the power of God for salvation to everyone who believes, to the Jew first and also to the Greek."*

What was Paul's burden and prayer for the lost? Read Romans 9:1–3 and 10:1 and record your findings.

____

____

____

____

____

____

When Paul saw the negative response of so many of his fellow Jews to the message of Christ as their Messiah, Lord, and Savior, it caused him *"great sorrow and unceasing grief."* He was willing to do anything, even be condemned himself, if that would change their hearts and minds, but that was not possible. Instead, Paul continued to speak the message and pray the longing of his heart. The Greek word translated "prayer" in Romans 10:1 is *dḗesis*, referring to a specific request backed by a strong desire or sense of need. Paul prayed specifically for those to whom he spoke, calling on God for their salvation.

Paul saw that a **wrong understanding** of how a person gains a **right standing** with God was an obstacle that had to be removed. For a person to experience the salvation Christ gives, he or she would have to do things God's way. This obstacle would be a matter for prayer for Paul. In Romans 10:2–4, Paul spoke of his Jewish brethren as zealous for God, but zealous to establish their own human righteousness before God. They would not submit to God's way of making a person right with Himself. The only way to know God's way of righteousness is to believe in Christ, to trust His righteous death as payment for one's sin, and to receive that payment and His eternal life as a gift from God. But how does one do that?

Romans 10:4, 8–13 spells out what a person must do to be saved, to know the salvation God alone can give. A person must understand that self-righteous works never merit anything in God's eyes, especially salvation from sin. Such redemption comes only through Christ. Christ has put an end to the Judaic Law as a way to salvation. Repentance of sin and faith in Christ and His work—His life, His death, His resurrection—will bring the gift of God's righteousness to a person's life. Repentance literally is turning away from sin and a self-directed life to a life of trusting God and trusting that the Word God has spoken is true and trustworthy. When a person repents and believes in his or her heart that Jesus is raised from the dead, that person will sincerely confess Jesus as Lord and will surrender to Jesus as God and Savior. What is in the heart is revealed through the mouth. When one honestly calls on the Lord to save him or her, God answers that prayer. What an awesome God we serve who provides an awesome salvation in such a simple way!

In Romans 10:14–17, Paul spoke of how this process of repentance would necessarily take place. For a person to repent, that person must first hear the message. In order for a person to hear the message, a messenger of Christ must first be sent to that person to proclaim the message of Christ. Once that message about Christ is heard, then that person can place faith in Christ and call on Him for salvation. The process is simple. First, one is **sent** with the **word**. Then there is **hearing**; then **believing**; then **calling**; then **salvation** is received.

How does prayer relate to all of this? Paul said his prayer for his Jewish brethren was for their salvation (Romans 10:1). Implied in his desire for their salvation is prayer for every part of the process—the **sending** with authority, the **message** spoken with confidence and clarity, the **hearing** with understanding, the **believing** from the heart, and the genuine, heartfelt **calling on the Lord**. What else can we learn about praying for others? What do we learn about those speaking the message and those hearing the message?

📖 What did Jesus pray in John 17:20–21? What do you see in these verses about the speakers and the hearers?

____

____

____

____

Jesus prayed for all those who would believe in Him through the word of the apostles. That implies, first of all, that the apostles would be faithful to communicate the message clearly, fully, accurately, and truthfully. Those who would hear and believe include both Jews and Gentiles, people from all the nations. The word of the apostles includes the Scriptures written by them (what we know today as the New Testament) and by those who were taught by them. Jesus prayed that those who believe would be one with other believers and one with the Father and the Son so that others would believe that God the Father sent Jesus the Son to earth. That means Jesus was praying that the lost would have a change of heart, that their very nature would be changed from the inside out as a result of the positive witness of Christian people. In essence, Jesus prayed for **the work** of the Spirit and **the Word** of God and **the witness** of believers to come together to see unregenerate sinners become born-again worshipers and live a life of calling on the Lord.

Put Yourself in Their Shoes

PAUL'S TESTIMONY

In Paul's testimony before Agrippa, he revealed his past life without Christ (Acts 26:4–11); how he met Christ (26:12–15); his change of heart and mind upon meeting Christ and coming to faith in Him (26:19–23); his commission to share the message of Christ with others (26:16–18); and his prayer for all who would listen to that message, that they too would come to Christ (26:29). Acts 26 gives the full account, and in Acts 26:29, Paul expresses his prayer burden: *"I would to God that whether in a short or long time not only you, but also all who hear me this day, might become such as I am, except for these chains."* The phrase *"I would to God"* can be translated "I would pray to God." It reveals the heart and the activity of Paul in prayer for others.

Doctrine
THE NEW COVENANT

In Jeremiah 31:31–34, God promises a New Covenant in which the law will be written on the heart and all sin will be remembered no more. Hebrews 10:15–17 quotes Jeremiah, applying that promise to the work of Christ on the cross and in the heart of everyone who trusts Him for salvation. Ezekiel 36:25–27 pictures this redemption for Israel and promises cleansing from sin, removal and replacement of the stubborn heart of stone with a tender, pliable, new heart and a new Spirit. Added to this new heart is the presence of God's Spirit within, causing them to walk in obedience to God's Word—all marks of the salvation both Jews and Gentiles can enjoy today by grace through faith in Christ.

Did You Know?
WRONG PRAYING FOR OTHERS

Not all requests in Scripture are according to God's will. We find one such example coming from the lips of two of Jesus' disciples. We read in Luke 9:51–56, that after a Samaritan village refused to receive Jesus and His disciples, James and John said, *"Lord, do You want us to command fire to come down from heaven and consume them?"* (9:54). While Elijah in 2 Kings 1:9–16 did call down fire on certain idolatrous Israelites who refused to hear his words, Jesus told James and John that sudden wrath was not what He wanted in this village. It is interesting to note that later, in Acts 8:25, we find Peter and John preaching in Samaria and in *"many villages of the Samaritans,"* perhaps even in the village that had once rejected Jesus. Jesus *"did not come to destroy men's lives, but to save them"* (9:56).

We can understand what we need to pray for the lost if we can grasp what Paul understood about **the condition of man**, the condition or attitude that would have to change. What was Paul's understanding of the condition of man? What had the Lord revealed to Him? When Paul prayed for the salvation of men and women, what would be some of the things he would pray? What do the Scriptures say about praying for a lost person? We find the answers in the writings of the New Testament.

📖 First, let's look at the characteristics, the condition of a lost person's heart? Look at the following verses and record these characteristics. (Note, Paul wrote or spoke all of these verses except those in John.)

John 3:18–20, 36

Acts 26:18

Romans 3:9–18, 23

2 Corinthians 4:3–4

Ephesians 2:1–3

Before a person comes to Christ, he or she is dead in sin, walking in the darkness of spiritual blindness and disobedient to the Word and will of God. Such a person is in rebellion against God, blinded by the god of this world (Satan), enslaved in the kingdom of darkness, in fact, loving that darkness rather than loving the light of God. In that condition, such a person is condemned, the wrath of God abiding on that person because he or she walks in unbelief, not trusting in Jesus Christ as Lord and Savior and so not surrendering to Him as God. Such an individual does not seek God, nor fears Him, but ever falls short of the standard and the glory of God. This person is destined for hell and the wrath of God forever unless there is a change of heart, mind, and will.

When we see the condition of the lost person, we realize we are helpless in ourselves to change one part of one heart. We can't even change our own hearts. This recognition is a call for us to humble ourselves before God and acknowledge that He alone can change a person's heart. It is a call to depend on His Spirit and His Word to work in hearts. We can and must speak His powerful Word, but we must also call on Him to make that Word effective in turning hearts and minds, bringing people to repentance over their sin and unbelief.

In light of what we have read in the Scriptures, we can ask God that, through His Word and by His Spirit, He will **raise up** dead hearts, **open** blind eyes, **bring light** to darkened hearts, **plant** the seed of faith in unbelieving, stony hearts, **call** them to give up on their self-righteousness (their own "good works"), **bring** them to a point of surrender to Jesus as Lord and Savior, and trust Him and His gift of righteousness alone for salvation and eternal life. Pray these things for someone God has placed on your heart.

📖 What else does the Scripture show us about who to pray for and how to pray? Paul wrote some guidelines for how a church should function and sent those to Timothy in the city of Ephesus. We have those in the letter of First Timothy. What do you discover about praying for others in 1 Timothy 2:1–4, and what kinds of prayer does Paul mention?

____

____

____

____

____

____

____

Paul sees the matter of prayer for others as a priority in the life of the Church—*"First of all, then, I urge. . . ."* This was a priority for Paul, and, by the Holy Spirit, he instructed Timothy (and us) to make it a priority, too. He spoke of four aspects or dimensions of prayer *"on behalf of all men."* *"Entreaties"* or "supplications" (Greek–*déēsis*) refers to specific petitions prayed with a strong sense of need. The Greek word translated *"prayers"* (*proseuchḗ*) is the general word for prayer, but it focuses on the aspect of surrender to the will and ways of God, of bowing to His will. We must pray God's will for the people for whom we pray. The word translated *"petitions"* or "intercessions" (*énteuxis*) speaks of meeting with someone to make a request on behalf of someone else. It was often used of coming before a king and usually referred to a request before a superior. "Thanksgivings" (*eucharistía*) refers to all the ways we can give thanks for others. All of these Greek words for prayer describe the ministry of praying for others, the kind of praying we do *"on behalf of all men."*

Put Yourself in Their Shoes

PAUL'S BOAST

Paul knew that the fruit of his ministry—the people who placed faith in Christ, the churches that were started, the pastors and missionaries sent out to proclaim the message of Christ, and the believers strengthened and growing in their faith—all came as a result of the work of God. Because Paul knew that God had to touch hearts and overcome obstacles, he regularly prayed for the lost and for believers, and he asked others to pray for him. When considering the fruit of his ministry he told the Romans, *"Therefore in Christ Jesus I have found reason for boasting in things pertaining to God. For I will not presume to speak of anything except what Christ has accomplished through me, resulting in the obedience of the Gentiles* [the nations] *by word and deed"* (Romans 15:17–18). To the Corinthians he wrote, *"I labored even more than all of* [the other apostles], *yet not I, but the grace of God with me"* (1 Corinthians 15:10).

On whom does Paul specifically focus? For whom should we pray?

Paul speaks of praying *"on behalf of all men,"* or as that could be translated "on behalf of each and every man." The secondary translation makes it much more personal; in other words, when we are able, we pray for people by name. Paul specifically mentions that we are to pray for *"kings and all who are in authority"*—those in government, civil service, military, education, law enforcement, fire and rescue, and others placed in position to guide some aspect of the community. Each person has needs for which we can pray, the most important of which is the need for a right relationship with God through Jesus Christ.

In verse 2, what reason does Paul give for praying in this manner?

Word Study

A QUIET LIFE

In I Timothy 2:2, the word "tranquil" (Greek—*ēremos*) emphasizes a placid life, the outward circumstances of life remaining calm, while the word "quiet" or "peaceable" (*hēsúchios*) points to not disturbing others as well as being undisturbed, in other words, quiet and peaceful conditions. In the Greek Old Testament (Septuagint) in Judges 3:11, 30, *hēsuchía* is used to speak of the peace Israel enjoyed, the years when they were undisturbed by foreign enemies. In those conditions, there is more opportunity and time to focus on the priority of growing in one's relationship with God and of helping others come to know Him. Paul adds the desire for a *"life in all godliness and dignity."* "Godliness" (*eusébeia*) refers to one's devotion to God, an inner reverence, while "dignity" or "reverence" (*semnótēs*) refers to respect for God, which results in a life that is attractive and inviting to others. The outer testimony is one of "dignity." Godliness (inner reverence) and dignity (outer testimony) are a good foundation on which to share the truth of Jesus Christ.

What difference do you think Paul's reasoning would make in effectively communicating the message of salvation in Christ?

Paul prays for those in authority that they might govern and administrate well so that believers could *"lead a tranquil and quiet life in all godliness and dignity."* Paul knew the importance of a peaceful and orderly personal life and community life, and he knew that God desires order for each community and country. Think, for example of Noah's day. God took no pleasure in the corruption and confusion that occurred in that society, the lack of a tranquil and quiet life. Where a society or community or even a country is in turmoil, whether the unrest is due to economic, political, or military concerns, or even the tragic consequences of natural disasters, the time and energies of people are taken up with the turmoil. While some look to God for answers, most are only concerned with surviving and coping. Where there is an undisturbed life, the gospel has a clearer path on which to run, and Christians can devote more time and energy to getting that message out to others.

What is the goal of praying for all people, according to verses 4–6?

Paul knew the importance of prayer for various matters and for the men and women in the various communities. They need to be saved and to come to the knowledge of the truth, especially the truth that there is only one way of salvation; there is only one mediator between God and man, *"the Man Christ Jesus."* Christ's death on the cross provided *"a ransom for all,"* redemption from sin. The message of Christ's redemption must be communicated prayerfully, clearly, and without disturbance so that people can come to Christ. Paul's conclusion to the matter of praying for *"all men"* is found in 1 Timothy 2:8, *"Therefore, I want the men in every place to pray, lifting up holy hands, without wrath and dissension."* Now is a good time to stop and pray.

Considering all we have seen about praying for the lost throughout the earth, especially in 1 Timothy 2:1–8, for whom can you pray? Pray for a person **by name**, one of those *"all men"* on whom Paul focused. Pray in light of the Scriptures we have seen today.

The concept of praying for the lost throughout the earth is not all the Scripture reveals about praying for others. We are also called to pray for laborers in the fields and leaders among the flocks. We will look at how we are to pray for laborers in Day Three.

Praying for Laborers and Leaders

Praying for Others

DAY THREE

Praying for the lost is only part of the ministry to which God has called us in learning to pray God's way. There are many aspects of God's redemptive work, with many people—laborers and leaders—involved in reaching men and women with the message of salvation in Christ. Today we will see what the Scriptures say about praying for laborers in the fields and leaders among the flocks.

In Matthew 9:35–38, what did Jesus say about the lost, about reaching them, and about prayer for others?

____

____

____

____

____

____

Jesus came ministering to the many needs of the people in Israel, but His greatest concern was for their spiritual needs. When He looked at the crowds of people, Jesus felt deep compassion for them. He understood the problems sin had brought, the personal sin of the people as well as the sin of the religious leaders leading them astray from the truth of Scripture. He saw them as distressed and downcast sheep without a shepherd to care for them, feed them, or protect them from their many enemies. They were helpless and vulnerable, wide open to the ravages of the wolves, those false teachers and inept leaders. What did Jesus propose as the solution? He told His disciples to pray to the Lord of the Harvest to send out or thrust out workers into the fields. He saw a plentiful harvest of people ready to receive and believe the message of grace through Christ. People were starving for a word of hope. God was providing a gracious way to be part of a kingdom

Praying God's Way

PRAYING WITH COMPASSION

Jesus had compassion on the people who were like sheep without a shepherd. He prayed with compassion and tears, for example, over Jerusalem (see Luke 19:41–44). As we grow in Christlikeness, we will also grow in compassion for the lost and for Christians in need. One of the Old Testament pictures of care and compassion is found in Psalm 126, a psalm about the captives returning from Babylon to Israel and beginning to sow once again. As they sowed in tears of repentance for the sin that brought the captivity, they would reap the blessing of the Lord in His abundant harvest. This also pictures the process of the people of God sowing the Word of God. As we sow His Word with dependence on Him and with His tears of compassion for the lost, so we will see God's harvest with great rejoicing.

marked by all that Christ could give. This plan of grace includes forgiveness, freedom from guilt, eternal life that produces freedom from the fear of death, and a relationship with God the Father in an eternal family that produces real freedom from the emptiness of not belonging.

It is worthy of note that immediately after Jesus said these things, the disciples became part of the answer to this prayer for laborers. Jesus sent the Twelve out with the message He had been teaching them. What else do we see in Scripture about praying for laborers and leaders?

📖 Look at Hebrews 13:18–19. What do you see about praying for laborers and leaders?

____

____

____

____

The writer of Hebrews clearly acknowledged the need for prayer on the part of himself and his ministry companions. His request for prayer is strong. It is in the present imperative and could be translated. "I urge you to keep on praying for us." Every Christian leader senses the need for the prayers of others, sometimes more intensely than at other times. The writer wanted the people to know that his request came from a clear conscience and a will to always walk with integrity and honesty. In this letter, he had spoken some weighty words, including some stern warnings, but all was in an effort to bring them to the fullness of what God wanted for them in their walk of faith. His final request to be *"restored to you"* appears to come from a great sense of need. It could refer to restoration from prison or from some sickness, but we are not sure. Regardless, one of the main points of verse 19 is that as a leader, he made a second strong request for prayer—*"I urge you. . . ."* Leaders need prayer, and we have the privilege of praying for laborers and leaders throughout the kingdom of God.

PRAY Is there a leader for whom you need to pray? Pause now and pray for a pastor, a deacon or elder, a missionary, a Bible teacher, or some other leader perhaps in your church or in another location. Trust the Spirit of God to bring someone to mind and to guide you in prayer.

📖 According to Ephesians 6:19–20, on what prayer point did Paul focus for his ministry?

____

____

____

📖 What additional request do you find in Colossians 4:2–4?

____

____

____

____

Paul asked the Ephesian believers to continually pray that when he had the opportunity, he would be given the right words and speak with boldness or confidence, as he ought to speak. The Greek word translated "boldness" is *parrēsía*, which refers to the freedom to speak all that is on one's heart and mind. Paul wanted the freedom to speak so that the gospel was clearly understood. To the Colossian believers he voiced a similar request. Paul asked them to pray for an open door for the word and for the ability to speak that word with clarity. The word *phaneróō,* translated *"make it clear,"* means to show fully or make a revelation. The root idea is to shine as a light. Paul wanted to speak in such a way that the message of the gospel would shine clearly as it should. Paul wanted the message to be a revelation to his hearers.

What were Paul's requests in 2 Thessalonians 3:1–3?

____

____

____

____

What was his concern, according to verse 2?

____

____

____

____

Of what was Paul confident for himself and for the Thessalonians in verse 3?

____

____

____

When Paul wrote to the Thessalonian believers, he requested prayer for himself and those with him. He desired that their message, *"the word of the Lord,"* would *"spread rapidly and be glorified."* The Greek word for *"spread rapidly"* is *tréchō*, which the New King James Version translates *"run swiftly."* It is a word picture taken from the Greek games. In addition, Paul asked others to pray that the word of the Lord *"be glorified."* Recall that "to glorify" (*doxázō*) means to form a good opinion about. Paul wanted the word of God to be seen in its true light, to be honored as it should be. Just as a runner runs swiftly to the finish line and is honored or glorified by the crowds of people, so Paul asks believers to pray *"that the word of the Lord may run swiftly and be glorified"* and honored in the hearts and lives of his hearers. So may it be in our lives and in our witness.

With that request, Paul added another request and a concern. He asked that he and his companions be *"delivered from perverse and evil men."* The idea of "perverse" or "unreasonable" (Greek—*átopos*) refers to those who are "out of place" or "out of line." They are also "evil" or "wicked," pointing to a malicious bent that is ready to inflict harm. These were men in opposition to Paul and to the gospel. Writing from the city of Corinth, Paul used these words to describe those without faith, unbelievers who would gladly disrupt the ministry he was seeking to carry out there (see Acts 18:1–17, especially verses 9–17). Understanding that he would have to contend with those with-

Put Yourself in Their Shoes

"PRAY FOR ME!"

Paul often asked believers to pray for him. We find his requests for himself in Romans 15:30–33; Ephesians 6:19–20; and Philemon 22. He requested prayer for himself and his ministry companions in 2 Corinthians 1:11; Colossians 4:3–4; 1 Thessalonians 5:25; and 2 Thessalonians 3:1–2.

Word Study

THE LORD'S PROTECTION

We learn from the Lord's Prayer that we must ask God the Father to *"deliver us from the evil one"* (Matt. 6:13 NKJV). The fact that we are to pray this prayer is indicative that God can and will offer us protection. Paul was quite confident in the Lord's protection. In 2 Thessalonians 3:3, he assures the Thessalonians that the Lord would *"protect"* or *"guard"* (NKJV) them *"from the evil one."* In Matthew 6:13 and in 2 Thessalonians 3:3, *"from the evil one"* is identically translated from the Greek. Jesus asked His Father to *"keep"* His disciples *"from the evil one"* (John 17:15). Three different Greek words in these three verses speak of the ways of God's protection:

- "**deliver**" (*rhúomai,* Matthew 6:13), to rescue
- "**protect**" and "**guard**" (*phulássō,* 2 Thessalonians 3:3), to guard or keep watch like a sentinel
- "**keep**" (*tēréō,* John 17:15), keeping the eye on someone so as to protect from harm.

out faith, Paul rested on the fact that God is faithful. He was confident in the faithfulness of the Lord for himself, his ministry companions, and the Thessalonians. He knew the Lord would "strengthen" or "establish" them as well as guard and protect them from "the evil one" (Satan).

What a privilege to pray! God has chosen to work through our praying to make a difference in how the Word of God impacts others. In prayer, we can touch others; we can ask God to make an impact on their hearts, minds, and wills. Are you or is someone you know seeking to share *"the Word of the Lord"* with a friend or with others in a ministry situation? Follow Paul's counsel in 2 Thessalonians 3:1.

Immediately after Paul requested prayer for himself and his ministry companions and after giving the Thessalonians a word of encouragement, he expressed his prayer for them, *"And may the Lord direct your hearts into the love of God and into the steadfastness of Christ"* (2 Thessalonians 3:5). Paul knew not only that the lost need prayers said on their behalf, not only that laborers and leaders need prayers said on their behalf for the ministries God gives, but that all the people of God, each and every Christian, needs the prayers of others. That is the focus of our Scripture exploration in Day Four.

Extra Mile

PRAYING FOR OTHERS IN GENESIS

Several examples of praying for others are found in Genesis. For a wonderful journey, explore Abraham's prayer for Lot and the city of Sodom (Genesis 18:17–33), the prayer of Abraham's servant Eliezer as he sought God's direction in finding a bride for Isaac (24:1–67), Isaac's prayer for his barren wife Rebekah (25:20–21), and Jacob's prayer for his sons' mission back to Egypt (43:11–15, note verse 14).

Praying for the People of God

Throughout the Old and New Testaments we find God's people praying on behalf of one another, reflecting the care of the Father for those in the family. Today, we will see numerous examples of God's people praying for others, each of which can guide us in praying for other believers in their walk of following God.

One of the most well known examples of praying for others occurred between Moses and the Lord on Mount Sinai. Read Exodus 32. According to versus 1–10, what did the people of Israel do, and what was God's response?

____

____

____

____

____

How did Moses respond in prayer for the children of Israel according to Exodus 32:11–12?

____

____

____

____

____

Look at Exodus 32:13. What was the basis of Moses' prayer? Why did he request what he did, and how did God respond?

____

____

____

____

____

____

While Moses was receiving the Law on Mount Sinai, the people at the foot of the mountain grew impatient. They wanted a god they could see, and they desired worship that they could control. They convinced Aaron to make them an Egyptian-like golden calf, and they began to feast and "rose up to play." The Hebrew verb translated play (*sahaq*) indicates that their activities centered around drunkenness and immorality. God saw the fruit of their stubborn, corrupt hearts and told Moses of His anger, even of His plan to destroy them and start over with Moses, a new line through which to work. Moses responded in earnest, intercessory prayer for them. In spite of their gross immorality, they were God's people. Moses was concerned for the reputation and honor of God. He wanted no Egyptians maligning God or His work. Then Moses made his request for God to turn from His anger based on His covenant promises to Abraham, Isaac, and Israel. Long ago, God had promised to multiply the descendents of Abraham and give them the land of Canaan forever. Upon hearing this prayer, God honored Moses' pleas, and Moses went down the mountain to deal with the people of God. We too can pray for God's people based on our knowledge of the promises noted in His Word, seeking His will for these promises to be filled and desiring His honor in and through their lives.

Moses prayed more than once for the people of God as he led them toward the Promised Land. For example, in Numbers 14, we find another intense encounter between the people and the Lord over their unbelief and mistrust of Him and their grumbling over the leadership of Moses and Aaron. There again, Moses interceded for the people. Later, we find others interceding—Joshua over the defeat at Ai, many of the judges of Israel over the needs of the people, Samuel the prophet over Israel begging for a king, and, through the ages, a host of other prophets crying out to God over the wayward tendencies or the heartfelt needs of the people of God. All of them sought the Lord, sometimes for deliverance or the withholding of judgment and at other times for guidance or blessing in some way. At times they sought the Lord with prayer and fasting, as in the case of Ezra in Ezra 8. In Lesson Eleven, we will see how Joshua, Ezra, Nehemiah, and others came to God in prayer. You will find several examples and Scriptures regarding fasting and prayer in the section, "Guidelines for Prayer and Fasting" at the end of this lesson. Today, we continue with an exploration in the New Testament Scriptures.

What examples of praying for others do we find in the New Testament? One of the joys of praying for others is found in prayers of thanksgiving. Paul shows us this many times. Read the following verses and list the people to whom Paul is talking and note the things for which he is thankful.

MOSES' "PRAYER CLOSET"

When Moses prayed for the people of God, he would often go to a place outside the camp, *"a good distance from the camp,"* and set up the Tent of Meeting, a place where he could meet with God and talk to Him *"just as a man speaks to his friend"* (Exodus 33:11). He did this in interceding for the Lord's presence to go with them into Canaan after the Lord had said He would send an angel rather than going with them Himself (Exodus 33:1–3, 12–17). Moses had a place to go where he could meet with the Lord to offer requests for himself and to pray for the needs of others. Moses' example is a good example for us to follow—we, too, need a place for prayer. In this place, we should offer up prayers for others.

MOSES' INTERCESSORY PRAYER

Moses prayed again for the people of God when He was ready to destroy them. In Numbers 13—14, we find God's people crying out against God at Kadesh Barnea. They declared that He did not love them and had brought them to Canaan to kill them. At that point, God was ready to destroy them and start over with Moses. Moses interceded, again praying for the honor and reputation of God. The Lord listened and dealt with the people, sending them back into the wilderness to wander forty years there. Then He brought them back to Canaan under the leadership of Joshua.

Romans 1:8

Put Yourself in Their Shoes

GIVE THANKS

Paul gave thanks in several of his letters. We find words of gratitude in Romans 1:8; 1 Corinthians 1:4; Ephesians 1:15–16; Philippians 1:3; Colossians 1:3; 1 Thessalonians 1:2; 2:13; 2 Thessalonians 1:3; 2 Timothy 1:3; and Philemon 4.

1 Corinthians 1:4–6

Philippians 1:3–5

1 Thessalonians 1:2–4

Did You Know?

PAUL'S PRAYERS

We find the prayers of Paul in almost all his letters, including the following: Romans 1:8–10; 15:30–33; 1 Corinthians 1:4–5; 2 Corinthians 13:7; Ephesians 1:15–21; 3:14–21; Philippians 1:3–5, 9–11; Colossians 1:3–5, 9–12; 1 Thessalonians 1:2–4; 2:13; 3:9–10, 11–13; 5:23–24; 2 Thessalonians 1:3, 11–12; 2:13, 16–17; 3:5, 16; 1 Timothy 1:12, 17; 2 Timothy 1:3, 16, 18; 4:22; Philemon 4–6.

Paul told the Roman believers that he thanked God for their faith and their testimony that had spread far and wide. Paul thanked God for the evident grace He had given to those in Corinth, grace that had enriched them immeasurably. The Philippians' participation in the gospel caused Paul to joyfully thank God every time he thought of them. The work of faith, the labor of love, and the steadfast hope of the Thessalonian believers were at the heart of Paul's prayer of thanksgiving for them. In these and in several other letters, Paul's heart and his writing overflowed with thanksgiving to God for the change He had made in heart after heart, life after life. God is worthy of great praise and abundant thanksgiving for the difference He makes in giving His gracious gift of eternal life in Christ.

Ephesians 1:16–21 is an example of how Paul prayed for others and reveals what was at the heart of Paul's prayers. What do you discover in Ephesians 1:16–21?

In the prayer recorded in Ephesians 1:16–21, we see Paul asking the Father of Glory to give the believers at Ephesus *"a spirit of wisdom and revelation in the knowledge of Him."* Paul is praying for them to really know the Father to the fullest. In other words, he is asking the Father that their hearts would be given the wisdom to see who God the Father is and what He has done in their lives. He asks the Father to unveil the truth so that they grasp the awesome work He has done for them—that they see what the Father is up to through Jesus Christ. Specifically, he prays that their hearts be enlightened to really see and know *"the hope of His calling,"* that is, the confident expectation we have because He has called us to Himself. Then, Paul prays they would know *"the riches of the glory of His inheritance in the saints"* and *"the surpassing greatness of His power toward us who believe"*—the very resurrection power of Christ. Just like the Ephesians, the more we know and understand Jesus, the more we will know and understand the Father. Paul prayed this for the Ephesian believers, and we can pray it for believers today.

Read Paul's prayer for the Ephesian believers in Ephesians 3:14–21. Note his desire that they know all the dimensions of the love and power of God. Use this prayer to pray for others (and yourself).

📖 Read Colossians 4:12 and record what you discover about Epaphras and his prayers for the Colossian believers. For what did he pray?

____

____

____

____

____

In all likelihood, Epaphras founded the churches in Colosse, Hierapolis, and Laodicea. He was deeply concerned for the believers in that region known as the Lycus Valley in Phrygia (western Turkey). Paul testified that Epaphras continually labored earnestly for these believers in his prayers. The words *"laboring earnestly"* in this verse are a translation of the Greek word *agōnízomai,* rooted in *agṓn*, a contest or struggle, with the word *agōnízo,* referring to the act of contending in the Greek games. Epaphras was like a wrestler, continually laboring in prayer that the Colossian believers would stand mature and full of assurance in knowing and doing the will of God. We too can continually labor for believers, and we can be encouraged by the example of Epaphras.

We see much in Scripture about the priority of praying for the spiritual needs of both the lost and the saved. Does that mean we should not pray for people with sickness or facing surgery? No! Evident in Jesus' ministry was a concern for all the needs of people, the spiritual, physical, and emotional needs. This was also evident in the ministries He gave the apostles. Peter, John, Paul—all of them saw God heal people with various illnesses. What should we do? We should pray for all the needs of people. In personal prayer times, through phone prayer chains, in intercessory prayer rooms, in prayer meetings at church and in homes, wherever the Lord makes us aware of a need and guides us in praying, we should pray faithfully and biblically. In our praying, we must make sure the physical condition is not all we pray for. The priority remains the spiritual well being of people—salvation for the lost and growth and fruitfulness for the saved. The Apostle John prayed, *"Beloved, I pray that in all respects you may prosper and be in good health, just as your soul prospers"* (3 John 2).

Let's look at one more example of praying for others and apply that to our daily praying. Paul prayed for many different individuals and many different churches, desiring the will of God for their lives. One of those prayers is recorded in Colossians.

📖 Read Colossians 1:9–12. (It may be helpful to read these verses in several translations to gain fuller insight and understanding.)

____

____

____

____

____

____

____

Put Yourself in Their Shoes

GROWING IN KNOWING

When Paul and others expressed their prayers for other believers; they often spoke of growing in the knowledge of Christ and His will. The words "knowledge," "know," and "understanding" are often used. Prayers for an increase in knowing and experiencing God's "love," "power," and "peace" are also evident.

When Paul prayed, he focused on the Colossian believers being *"filled with the knowledge of His will,"* being more and more under the influence of God's mind and heart, truly knowing God's desires and will. Such knowledge would involve having *"spiritual wisdom"* (like the *"wisdom from above"* mentioned in James 3:17). Having spiritual wisdom is more than possessing intellectual data. Spiritual knowledge and understanding changes the way a person thinks, chooses, and acts. A person that possesses this knowledge begins to walk pleasing to the Lord and begins to bear fruit in the good works in which God guides him or her. As a result of that interaction with God, this person grows or increases in the true, personal knowledge of God, experiencing His strength and power and might. This results in one having a steadfast walk and being patient with others. Along with this patience is the ability to endure a variety of circumstances and to do so with joy. Experiencing patience also produces much thanksgiving to the Father for His work in the present and for His promises for the future, even into eternity when the *"inheritance of the saints in light"* will be fully realized.

PRAY Here is another example of the way to pray for others. Take the prayer in Colossians 1:9–12 and pray it for someone on your heart (and for yourself). Let this passage of Scripture frame and form your prayer. Remember, praying the Scripture is not about saying certain words that have some magical power. It is about praying the heart of God, learning to line up your heart with His heart and pray accordingly. You may want to write your prayer or some insights or meditations from that prayer in the space below.

____

____

____

____

____

____

How can we begin to apply all we have seen about praying for others? We will see in Day Five.

Praying for Others

DAY FIVE

FOR ME TO PRAY GOD'S WAY

We have seen much about praying for others. It has been part of the activity of God's people since the beginning. Praying for others means discovering and praying the heart of God for others—for saints (God's people) and for sinners (not yet born into the family of God). God has revealed His heart in many ways. Today we want to see how this applies in our daily walk.

First, look at the following prayer points to **pray for a fellow Christian** and then pray these requests for someone who is involved in sharing the message of Christ with another. Pray for the person witnessing . . .

- to seek God in prayer for His empowering to accomplish His work in the fields (Acts 4:24–31)
- to be sent by the Father into His appointed fields for His divine appointments (Matthew 9:37–38; Acts 17:17)
- to go in the adequacy and power of the Spirit of God (2 Corinthians 2:14–17; 3:3–6)
- to go through the open doors the Father gives (Colossians 4:3)
- to be protected from opposing people (Romans 15:30–31; 2 Thessalonians 3:2)
- to be protected from the evil one (John 17:15; 2 Thessalonians 3:3)
- to speak clearly the right words at the right time (Colossians 4:4)
- to speak boldly all that is needed (Ephesians 6:19–20)

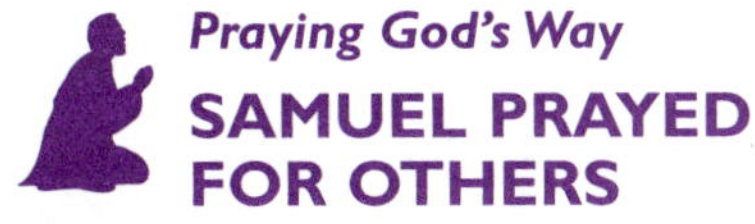

Praying God's Way

SAMUEL PRAYED FOR OTHERS

"Moreover, as for me, far be it from me that I should sin against the Lord by ceasing to pray for you; but I will instruct you in the good and right way." (1 Samuel 12:23)

Look at the following prayer points to pray **for a lost person** and then pray these truths for someone you know who needs to come to Christ as Lord and Savior. They are given with the acrostic R.I.G.H.T. H.E.A.R.T.

Pray for the person by name—"all men" each and every one (1 Timothy 2:1–8).

"Lord, I pray for ________________________, that he/she would . . .

R **recognize** Jesus as Lord and the only Savior (John 14:6; Acts 4:12)

I have **insight** into his/her condition—dead in disobedience and the darkness of sin, bound and blind (Ephesians 2:1–2, Titus 3:3, 2 Corinthians 4:4)

G be **guarded** and protected from the distractions of the world, the deceptions of temptations, and the devil stealing the seed of the Word (Luke 8:11–14).

H **heed** the call to give up on his/her own "good works" and **hope** in Christ alone (Ephesians 2:8–9, 12, Titus 3:5)

T **take seriously** the promises of God's Word and the mercy of God's heart (Romans 10:17; Titus 3:5)

H **hear** the Father's invitation to come to Christ and call on Him (Matthew 11:28–30; Romans 10:13)

E **expect** Christ to forgive, save, and change his/her heart by grace through faith (Romans 10:4, 9–13, Ephesians 2:8, Hebrews 11:6)

A **acknowledge** and repent of sin and self-righteousness (Romans 3:23, 10:3–4)

R **receive** Christ as Lord and Savior by faith (John 1:12, Galatians 3:26)

T **turn** to Christ quickly, **trust** Christ wholly, and **take** Him fully at His Word (John 6:37; Romans 10:4; 1 Corinthians 6:2; Galatians 3:2).

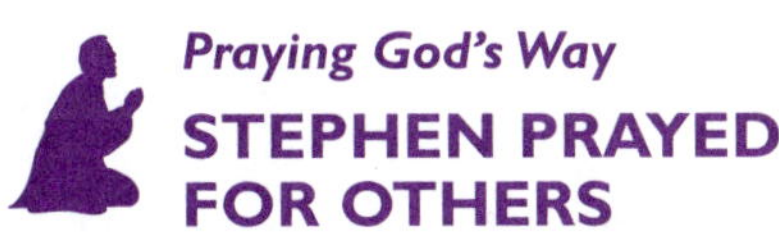

Praying God's Way

STEPHEN PRAYED FOR OTHERS

When Stephen was being stoned for giving his testimony concerning Christ, he prayed for others—for those who were stoning him as it says in Acts 7:60, *"And falling on his knees, he cried out with a loud voice, 'Lord, do not hold this sin against them!'"* Among those for whom he prayed was Saul of Tarsus, who would later meet Jesus on the road to Damascus, become a Christian, and be called by the Lord to become the apostle Paul. Stephen had a part in Saul's redemption through his prayer while being stoned. God answered Stephen's prayer and touched and changed Saul's life forever. What an impact God makes through Spirit-led prayer!

Continue to pray for the person to come to Christ, to have a **RIGHT HEART** with Him, knowing that salvation that comes with a **RIGHT HEART** lasts forever. Ask the Lord for further insight in how to pray for this person, trusting Him to guide you in prayer.

The Holy Spirit has given us some of the prayers Paul prayed for believers, prayers placed in Scripture that are clearly the will of God for a Christian. These prayers/blessings speak of others growing in their faith and in their walk with God. Read each one of the prayers given below and then pray that same prayer for someone. These prayers have an added space, so you can fill in the name of a particular person.

"Now . . . may the Lord cause you [______________________] to increase and abound in love for one another, and for all men, just as we also do for you; so that He may establish your hearts unblamable in holiness before our God and Father at the coming of our Lord Jesus with all His saints." (1 Thessalonians 3:11, 12–13)

"Now may our Lord Jesus Christ Himself and God our Father, who has loved us and given us eternal comfort and good hope by grace, comfort and strengthen [______________________] your hearts in every good work and word. . . . Now may the Lord of peace Himself continually grant you [______________] peace in every circumstance. The Lord be with you all!" (2 Thessalonians 2:16–17 and 3:16)

"I pray that you [______________________] may be active in sharing your faith, so that you [______________] will have a full understanding of every good thing we have in Christ." (Philemon 6 NIV)

We have seen in this week's lesson that there are many ways we can pray for others. The important thing now is not what we know but what we do with what we know, specifically, that we walk a walk of truly praying for others.

Father, thank You for the opportunity and blessing of praying for others. Thank You that others have prayed for me throughout my life—and continue to pray for me. What a blessing! I pray that I will become more sensitive to the spiritual needs of others as well as the physical or material needs. I also pray that You will continue to show me how to pray the Scriptures for others—for those who already know You and for those who have not yet come to You. May I know all it means to pray in dependence on the Spirit with all kinds of prayer for all the saints and for effective witnesses. May I be wise in praying with the armor fully on, the shield of faith ever ready, and the sword of the Spirit—that Word of God—steady in my hand and in my heart. In my praying, may I join You as You touch the "nations" and bring them into Your kingdom. I pray that others will come to hallow Your name as You deserve, that they will bow to Your Son's rule as King and to Your will as supreme. May I mature in Christlikeness, honoring You and growing in my capacity to pray for others as You did . . . and as You still do. In Jesus' name. Amen.

"Cease striving and know that I am God; I will be exalted among the nations, I will be exalted in the earth."

Psalm 46:10

Write your prayer or a journal entry in the space below.

GUIDELINES FOR FASTING AND PRAYER

THE PURPOSE OF FASTING

Why fast? The Scriptures clearly reveal the purpose of fasting through several examples in the life of the nation Israel, in the life of Jesus, and in the early church. In a Survey of the Scriptures there are at least three summary reasons given for fasting.

1) One is **a humble admission of need**. The need may be forgiveness of sin, comfort over some grief or sorrow, concern over the situation of an individual, a city, or a nation, or the need for guidance and direction from the Lord. For example, when Nehemiah heard about the condition of Jerusalem, he immediately began to mourn and seek the Lord in fasting and prayer (Nehemiah 1:4–11). He readily admitted the need of the people of God. In Daniel 9:3, Daniel writes, *"I gave my attention to the Lord God."* Literally the verse says, "I set my face to the Lord God." The verse pictures one who has focused concentration on the Lord, ready to admit the needs of the moment. (For other examples see 1 Samuel 7:6; 31:13; 1 Kings 21:27–29; Nehemiah 9:1; Esther 4:1–3; Psalms 35:13; 69:10; 109:24; Isaiah 58:5–6.)

2) The second summary reason is **a humble request for help**. This is closely linked to the first reason. Before we will ask for help we have to admit we have a need—a need we know we cannot meet. God alone can give the needed help. Our requests can include seeking the Lord's guidance for a decision (Judges 20:26), for healing (2 Samuel 12:16–23), or for safety and protection (Ezra 8:21–23). Esther 4:16 records Esther's plea for the people to fast for her for three days concerning the deliverance of the Jewish people. In Jonah 3:3–10, the entire city of Nineveh entered into a fast to repent of their wickedness and to seek deliverance from certain judgment. Another example of a national plea for deliverance is found in 2 Chronicles 20:3–4. Other examples of asking for a need are found in Daniel 9:3; Isaiah 58:7–12; and Jeremiah 36:1–9.

In the New Testament, we find examples of those who sought the Lord with a whole heart at a time of great need or as an expression of humble dependence on the Lord to guide or provide in some way. In Matthew 4:2, Jesus revealed His dependence on His Father during the wilderness temptations. The forty days of prayer and fasting were a time of intense focus on the Father and submission to all of His will and His Word. When Jesus taught on fasting, He clearly showed that it was a matter of a heart–to–heart focus on the Father, a submission to His will, and an act of trusting in His supply for the need (Matthew 6:16–18).

In Luke 2:37, Anna's life of *"fastings and prayers"* reveals a lifetime of focused service and dependence on the Lord. In Acts 13:1–3 and 14:23, we see clear evidence of a step-by-step dependence on the Lord in the early Church. Whether determining the Lord's will in the direction of ministry or in appointing the right leadership, these church leaders sought the Lord wholeheartedly in prayer and in fasting.

3) A third summary reason used by some for fasting can be stated as **a haughty attempt to get one's own way**. Isaiah 58:1–4 is one of the clearest rebukes to a proud heart full of selfish motives. This type of fasting is of no benefit. In Zechariah 7:5, we find a people who have performed a regular fast but for selfish reasons and with no sensitivity to the Lord and His ways (see 7:1–12). In Luke 18:12, a ritualistic Pharisee found no response from God. God was not impressed with his self-righteous fasting.

God looks at the heart not the outer man. He is concerned that we are walking humbly before Him with a desire only to do His will. He delights in us seeking Him with a whole heart, and sometimes a whole heart requires a time of fasting. This thought brings us to **the practice of fasting.** How do we go about a time of prayer and fasting? What are the procedures?

THE PRACTICE OF FASTING

There are several kinds of "fasts" that we can practice. Many times the intensity of the need will determine this. Let's answer some basic questions about the practice of fasting.

What kind of fast? There is **1)** **a limited fast**—A person limits their diet for a time as a part of seeking to do the will of God. An example is found in Daniel 1:8–13, where Daniel and his three friends asked for a limited diet in order to follow God's Law and God's will.

There is **2)** **a standard fast**—A person eats no food but does drink liquids. This is the most common fast in the Scriptures.

There is **3)** **an absolute fast**—A person does not eat or drink for a period of time. Esther called for a three-day fast of this kind (4:1–17). (A person normally cannot go without liquids for more than three days. Moses experienced two supernatural fasts of forty days each in which he neither ate nor drank anything in the presence of the Lord on Mount Sinai (Exodus 34:1–2, 27–28; Deuteronomy 9:9–29; 10:1–5, Note verses 9:9 and 9:18)).

Who should fast? A fast can be by one person—**a personal fast**. It can be **a partner fast** in which two or more enter in. This would be true of a husband and wife, a small group such as a class or leadership team (Acts 13:1–3), or a congregation coming together in a heart-to-heart seeking of the Lord (Ezra 8:21–23). There are also **community fasts** (city, tribe, or nation) in which all are called to fast as in Jonah 3 or 2 Chronicles 20:3.

When should a person or group fast? The Scriptures command one **regular fast** for those under the Old Covenant. In Leviticus 16:29–31 the nation of Israel was told to humble their souls (implying fasting) on the Day of Atonement. There are no regular fast days commanded in the New Testament. Any *regular* fast day practiced among church members today is the product of man-made regulations and is usually marked by a generous helping of man-centered pride (Luke 18:12; Colossians 2:16–23). Under the New Covenant, fasts were to be conducted occasionally according to the need of the moment.

The final question in regard to fasting is **"How is a fast to be done?"**

First of all, the heart attitude and motive must be right. Fasting is directed to the Lord not to people (Matthew 6:16–18).

Secondly, let the Lord lead you as to the timing and length of a fast. Remember, it is the heart attitude. We cannot go on a "holy hunger strike" and expect the Lord to "give in" to our desires.

Thirdly, there are some **practical guidelines**:

- Keep your focus on the Lord, trusting Him in the situation and need (Hebrews 11:6).
- Stay in an attitude of prayer throughout the day. Set aside segments of time for specific prayer. Pray often.
- Read Scripture much during your time of prayer and fasting. Praying is as much listening as talking. Record any insights you gain. You may want to write down some of your specific requests in a journal or notebook.
- Concerning meals missed, skipping one, two, or three consecutive meals is a normal fast. Some may chose one, two, or three days. Others may fast several days. Drink plenty of juices and/or water as you fast. (For those who go on an extended fast, it would be helpful to read one of the books that gives information and guidelines on an extended fast.)
- For those on medication or who have been ill, be cautious and get an OK from your doctor.
- Some are not able to fast because of a physical condition. They must have regular meals. The Lord may lead you to "fast" from certain foods, etc. Remember, the important thing is the heart attitude not the calorie count.
- Sometimes, there may be a little dizziness, headache, or nausea from not eating. Do not be alarmed. Remember to drink extra liquids.
- At the end of your fast it is helpful to eat fruit or soup, etc. Do not eat a big meal. Your eyes may be bigger than your stomach so watch out for gluttony. *("The fruit of the Spirit is . . . self-control"*—Galatians 5:22–23.)

When all is said and done, may we have the testimony of Daniel, *"So I gave my attention to the Lord God to seek Him by prayer and supplications, with fasting"* (Daniel 9:3).

Notes

11

PRAYING TOGETHER

DISCOVERING THE ADVENTURE OF PRAYING WITH LIKE-HEARTED BELIEVERS

We have seen what God says about calling on Him, coming to Him with our needs and with the needs of others. We have looked at the essential attitude of humility, recognizing our place as God's children and as our King's subjects. At the same time we gladly honor and praise our Father and King. One of the things that greatly pleases our Father is the unity of His family, when brothers and sisters walk together with one heart, especially in prayer.

One of the things that greatly pleases our Father is the unity of His family, when brothers and sisters walk together with one heart, especially in prayer.

We know the Lord works in the hearts of individuals—calling to salvation, calling to repentance and faith, calling people to follow and obey Him, and calling men and women to do His will. We also find Him calling people to walk together following Him, which involves praying together along with proclaiming His Word together and growing as His Family together.

When Jesus taught us to pray, He emphasized two aspects of a balanced prayer life—periods of prayer alone with God and periods of prayer with fellow believers. We recall that Jesus taught His disciples to avoid the trap of "show-off" praying—to be seen and rewarded by public applause. That is why He said in Matthew 6:6, *"But you when you pray, go into your inner room, and when you have shut your door, pray to your Father who is in secret, and your Father who sees in secret will repay you."* But even there, He did not say to think only of ourselves. He said to pray *"Our Father. . . ,"* recognizing that we are part of a family. In this lesson, we will look in the Old Testament and the New Testament to see some clear examples of praying together, examples that can lead us to more effective praying together with like-hearted believers.

Praying Together

DAY ONE

THE PEOPLE OF GOD CRY OUT TOGETHER

We have seen how God called out Abram and how Abram and many others called on the name of the Lord. Through the providence of God, the people of God were led to Egypt during a great famine. There, under the leadership of Joseph, the people grew and prospered (see Genesis 39–50). Then a Pharaoh arose who did not know nor honor Joseph or his people. Instead, he enslaved them for his work projects. The people had a hard life (Exodus 1). How did they respond, and what did God do in their midst?

📖 Read Exodus 1:8–14 and 2:23. What was the plight of the people of God?

____

____

____

____

What was their response to the bondage under which they labored?

____

____

____

____

What was God's response according to Exodus 2:24–25 and 3:7–9?

____

____

____

____

____

____

The people of God, once favored under the leadership of Joseph and those who knew him, now faced a new regime and with it taskmasters who imposed hard labor on them. The Israelites were in bondage; an enslavement marked by grief and toil, a life *"made bitter with hard labor."* In response, the people cried out for help from God, and He heard their cry. He remembered His covenant with Abraham, Isaac, and Jacob. He told Moses that He had seen their affliction, that He was fully aware of their sufferings, and that He was at work to deliver them from that bondage. He promised to bring them out of Egypt in order to bring them in to *"a good and spacious land, to a land flowing with milk and honey,"* the land of Canaan.

The Lord raised up Moses to guide the people out of Egypt. After God struck Egypt with ten plagues, Pharaoh released the children of Israel. God's chosen people then began their journey to the promised land of Canaan. Led by the Lord in the Pillar of Fire, they came to the Red Sea and found themselves caught between the sea and Pharaoh's approaching army. What could they do?

Put Yourself In Their Shoes

A TESTIMONY FROM THE PSALMS

Psalm 107:6 says, *"Then they cried out to the LORD in their trouble; He delivered them out of their distresses."* Those words are repeated almost word for word in verses 13, 19, and 28. The final verse exhorts us, *"Who is wise? Let him give heed to these things; and consider the lovingkindness of the LORD."*

📖 In Joshua 24, Joshua recounted the works of God on behalf of the people of God. Read Joshua 24:5–7. What is the testimony of God's people in verse 7? (You may want to read the full account in Exodus 14.)

____

____

____

____

____

____

____

When God brought them to the Red Sea, facing the sea in front of them and Pharaoh's army behind them, they cried out to the Lord. God moved the fiery pillar between the Israelites and the Egyptians, protecting them, placing darkness between them and the Egyptians and giving light to His people. Exodus records the details of how God then parted the waters of the Red Sea and led them through on dry ground. Pharaoh's army, on the other hand, drowned as the walls of water came over them.

These events in the early years of God's earthly kingdom are not typical "prayer meetings." They were times when the people joined together to cry out in desperation, sometimes in fear, calling on the Lord that something might be done. God wants His people in every generation to call on Him, not only individually, but also together with others. Let's look at one pattern He gave His people in Exodus.

📖 Read Exodus 23:14–17 and 34:23–24 along with Deuteronomy 16:13–17. What was God's plan for His people?

____

____

____

____

God commanded that all the men of Israel gather *"before the LORD"* to celebrate a feast to Him. This command not only applied to the men but also to the women and children, servants and strangers—all coming to the place where the Tabernacle rested to join together in a special time of feasting, rejoicing, and offering gifts and sacrifices to the Lord. It was a public time of seeking Him together. Scripture shows us that the Tabernacle was eventually moved to Jerusalem, God's chosen place of worship (2 Samuel 6–7). There the Temple was built as the permanent place to which they could come. God desired that all His people come and even assured them of His protection of their lands and possessions while they left their home to gather in the place He chose.

📖 In Deuteronomy, we find another piece of the puzzle concerning God's heart for His people coming together. Read Deuteronomy 31:10–13 and record your findings.

____

____

____

____

____

"Assemble the people . . . in order that they may hear and learn and fear the LORD your God, and be careful to observe all the words of this law."

Deuteronomy 31:12

Every seventh year at the time of the Feast of Booths (also called the Feast of Tabernacles or Feast of Ingathering), the people were to gather not only for the sacrifices and offerings, but also to hear the Word of God. There at the place chosen by God, the leaders were to read the law to them (the Law of Moses consisting of the books of Genesis, Exodus, Leviticus, Numbers, and Deuteronomy). Why? So that all Israel—men, women, children, and foreigners—could *"hear and learn and fear the LORD your God,"* being careful to obey all His Word. By hearing the Word of God, each generation would learn to fear the Lord and walk with Him in the wisdom He would give. They would also know His will for them. He would guide them in knowing what it meant to follow Him with a whole heart, to call on Him and worship Him individually and together as the people of God.

How did the people of God respond once they were in the land of Canaan? We will see in Day Two.

FOLLOWING, FORGETTING, AND FAILING TOGETHER

Joshua led the people of God into the land of Canaan, and over a seven-year period of time they conquered most—but not all of the land. There were still some Canaanites left, still some vestiges of Canaanite religion influencing the Israelites' thinking and their worship. What would happen to the Canaanite peoples?

Did You Know?

CANAANITE WAYS

Leviticus 20 catalogues many of the practices of the Canannites, practices of horrendous immorality and hideous religious rituals, even offering their children in sacrifice to their false gods. God wanted people to come together in holiness to call on His name.

📖 Read Judges 2:8–15 and 3:5–8. What problems do you see? List the things the Israelites did wrong.

____

____

____

____

How did the Lord deal with His people?

____

____

____

A generation arose that did not know the Lord nor His work among Israel. Instead of worshiping the Lord, calling on Him for their needs, they forgot and forsook the Lord and looked to the Baals, the false gods of Canaan. In their idolatry they bowed down to these gods, intermarrying with the people of the land and adopting their pagan ways. The hand of the Lord was against them, bringing judgment through "plunderers" and other enemies, thus bringing great distress and affliction on the people.

📖 When the people came under bondage to Cushan-rishathaim of Mesopotamia, what was their response to the Lord, according to Judges 3:9?

____

____

____

____

📖 What did God do when Israel cried to Him, according to Judges 3:9–11?

____

____

____

The people served Cushan-rishathaim for eight years, and at some point in their servitude they cried out to the Lord. In their distress, they recognized that He alone could deliver them. Then the Lord raised up Othniel as a deliverer for His people, giving him skill and success in the war against Cushan-rishathaim. Israel was set free, and the land had rest under Othniel for forty years.

📖 Read Nehemiah 9:27–29 and summarize what you find about the people of God during the early era of the Israelite nation living in the promised land of Canaan. Note what they did in verses 27 and 28.

____

____

____

____

____

____

In recounting the history of Israel, Nehemiah wrote of how often Israel rebelled against the Lord. These rebellions happened not only during the times of the judges, but also during the reigns of the various kings. They repeated a pattern of disobedience—oppression—crying to God—deliverance—rest—disobedience. The testimony of prayer is this—*"when they cried to Thee in the time of their distress, Thou didst hear from heaven, and according to Thy great compassion Thou didst give them deliverers."* Then, *"when they cried again"* God heard and answered. Why? Nehemiah answers, *"many times Thou didst rescue them according to Thy compassion."* What an awesome God, who listens when His people call on Him, even when they have been stubborn and rebellious!

"And the sons of Israel did what was evil in the sight of the LORD, and forgot the LORD their God, and served the Baals. . . . Then the anger of the LORD was kindled against Israel. . . . And when the sons of Israel cried to the LORD, the LORD raised up a deliverer."

Judges 3:7, 9

THE COST OF IDOLATRY

Think of the cost of idolatry. Judges 2:14 speaks of being in the *"hands of plunderers,"* those who took what they wanted when they wanted it—the economic cost. Families practiced pagan ways. Some even sacrificed their children to false gods, and then the hand of the Lord was against them so that they were *"severely distressed"*—the emotional and relational cost. Judges 2:18 says the foreign conquerors *"oppressed and afflicted"* the Israelites so that they groaned under the burden—the physical and mental cost. The greatest cost was their relationship with God—the spiritual cost. God became angry with His people for their disobedience and wayward ways and placed them in difficult circumstances to convict them and bring them back to Himself. He sent prophets to call them back to following God. Often, but not always, they recognized the costs of idolatry and cried out to the Lord.

What is God saying to you? Have you had some "stiff-necked" days lately, or do you know someone walking in the stubbornness of his or her heart? Stop and pray. Call on the Lord who is *"a gracious and compassionate God"* (Nehemiah 9:31). We know He hears prayer, and we have seen how He listens to His people when they pray together. Gather with some other believers and pray for one another. Pray for those who are straying from the Lord and failing to following Him.

Praying Together

DAY THREE

COMING BACK TO FOLLOWING GOD TOGETHER

The story of the people of God has its ups and downs. There have always been those who faithfully followed, Him and there have always been those who forgot, forsook, and failed to follow. Yet the story does not always end with failures. Our Heavenly Father is the God who hears "again"—*"when they cried again to Thee, Thou didst hear from heaven"* (Nehemiah 9:28). We can come back to following God as individuals and as a people following together. Today, we will see that God continues to work in the lives of His people as they seek Him together.

"When they cried again to Thee, Thou didst hear from heaven, and many times Thou didst rescue them according to Thy compassion."

Nehemiah 9:28

God's chosen people were sent into captivity in Babylon because of their idolatry and rebellion against the Lord. In 722 B.C., Israel (the Northern Kingdom) was destroyed and scattered by the Assyrians. In 605 B.C., the Babylonians conquered Judah (the Southern Kingdom) and took several into what is often called the "Babylonian Captivity." There were three phases of restoration and return from captivity—the first phase led by Zerubbabel (536 B.C.), the second led by Ezra (458 B.C.), and the third led by Nehemiah (445 B.C.).

In the return led by Ezra, we see the people of God praying together. Read Ezra 8:21. Why did Ezra proclaim a fast?

____

____

____

As they joined together, what did they seek from the Lord?

____

____

____

____

Doctrine

FASTING WITH PRAYER

There are at least two reasons for prayer with fasting. First, fasting can express a humble admission of need coupled with a humble request for help. Fasting and humility go hand in hand because one who walks in humility admits that he cannot meet the need and that God alone can truly meet the need. Therefore, the humble man or woman seeks God's answer to the need.

Ezra and the people who were preparing to return to the land of Israel first began fasting, an act of humbling themselves before the Lord. They were willing to admit they could not meet the need set before them and that they needed God to work on their behalf. God's intervention included protection and safety for those returning from captivity. These people wanted to be free from hindrances such as enemies, robbers, wild animals, or any sort of opposition on the journey. God's people sought the Lord together on behalf of each person, for their children, and for their possessions. This was a classic example of all-encompassing prayer being offered up for all-encompassing needs.

According to Ezra 8:22–23, what was the testimony of the people before the king?

____

____

____

____

What difference did this testimony make in their prayers?

____

____

____

The people, including Ezra, had boasted of the power of the Lord to protect those who seek Him. Only those who would forsake the Lord would face His anger and His power against them. For Ezra and the people, this meant there was no need for the king's troops and horsemen to help defend against any enemies. The Lord would defend them. Because of this testimony before the king, Ezra was *"ashamed,"* embarrassed, to ask for the king's troops. This meant the people were even more intense in seeking the Lord in prayer and fasting *"concerning this matter."* They joined together and sought the Lord.

How did God respond to their cry to Him, according to Ezra 8:23?

____

____

____

God *"listened to"* or "was entreated by" their cry. The Hebrew word *athar,* means "to entreat" and pictures an intensity and focus in prayer. It is used of one who prays in simplicity, imploring and beseeching God, knowing that He is listening and ready to answer. Note how the whole group was involved in prayer. Scripture records that God *"listened to* **our** *entreaty"* [emphasis added].

What was Ezra's testimony of how God worked? Read Ezra 8:31 and record what you discover. [Note the wealth the Israelites carried with them as recorded in Ezra 8:25–30.]

____

____

____

____

____

The journey from Babylon to Jerusalem was over a thousand miles and could take around three to four months. Ezra rejoiced that on the journey *"the hand of our God was over us,"* and protected them from some very real dangers. There were enemies and robbers who would have gladly taken advantage of this caravan of families if they could. God's people had much wealth in silver and gold, including many utensils for the Temple (Ezra

Word Study

"SAFE JOURNEY"

When Ezra prayed for a "safe journey," he was asking God literally for "a straight way." The Hebrew word *yashar,* translated "safe," literally means "level" or "straight." In other words, Ezra prayed for a way or a journey without obstacles in the way.

8:25–30). However, God protected them from enemies and many potential ambushes, which doubtless would have meant loss of life and possessions for some. Ezra testified that God *"delivered"* them, another picture of the power of God's hand. The Hebrew word *natsal* translated "delivered" means "to snatch away" or to be snatched or drawn out—thus being delivered from harm, to escape any harm or danger. The hand of God was over them, covering them, snatching them from danger—in answer to their prayers.

Praying God's Way

PRAYING IN NEHEMIAH'S DAY

When one reads the account of Nehemiah and the rebuilding of the wall of Jerusalem in an amazing fifty-two days, one is struck with three obvious facts. First, Nehemiah and the people of Jerusalem were devoted to God and showed it in their active praying and through their actions while building the wall. Secondly, they faced many distractions, from the enemy outside the wall and from certain problems within. With every distraction, we find these faithful servants going to God in prayer, and we see God giving His direction—practical, well-timed, and fitting in every detail. When they faced opposition, the people led by Nehemiah experienced the honor of praying for God's provision and protection in order to fulfill the purposes of God in Jerusalem. God wanted the wall built and Jerusalem functioning again as His chosen city. We have the same privilege—we can pray for the provision and protection of God to fulfill the purpose of God in our lives and in our churches. Whatever the distraction, we can call on the Lord out of our devotion to Him and find His direction for the next step.

In Nehemiah's day, the people of God *prayed together* and *worked together.* The results were clearly the work of God in and through them—even the nations *"perceived that this work was done by our God"* (Nehemiah 6:16 NKJV).

A few years later, Nehemiah led the third return from Babylon to Israel (445 B.C.) and prepared to rebuild the walls of Jerusalem. As he began, he and the people of Jerusalem were not without opposition. What did they do when others opposed them?

📖 Read Nehemiah 4: 1–15 and answer the questions below.

Look at Nehemiah 4:1–3. What was the reaction to the progress being made on the wall in Jerusalem?

____

____

____

____

____

How did Nehemiah and the Jews in Jerusalem respond to these enemies, according to 4:4?

____

____

____

____

The enemies intensified their opposition. Describe what you find in Nehemiah 4:7–8.

____

____

____

____

What response do you find in Nehemiah 4:9? How did God respond according to 4:15?

____

____

____

____

____

The enemies of Israel, Sanballat, the Samaritans, Tobiah and others, mocked the Jews and their efforts to rebuild the wall. Nehemiah and the people responded by turning to the Lord, *"Hear, O our God"* and prayed for

God to deal with these enemies. The work continued, and the enemies intensified their opposition. The enemy's next step was not just to talk against the Jews, but to plan some way to confuse and disrupt the building process. However, the testimony of Nehemiah and the people remained focused, *"but we prayed to our God. . . ."* God's people prayed together, and they worked together. As a result, God continued to give them direction, and He *"frustrated"* the plans of the enemy. The Hebrew word translated "frustrated" literally means to crush or crumble or to break in pieces. God answered the prayers of the people, crushing the enemy plans and strengthening the plans of His people.

About one month after the wall was finished, Ezra and Nehemiah gathered the people together for the Fall Feast of Trumpets (first day of the seventh month) and led them in worship of the Lord. Read Nehemiah 8:1–12 and record what you find. What activities were included in this time of gathering together?

____

____

____

____

____

____

____

____

____

A host of people—including men, women, and children—gathered to listen to the law of God read and explained. As Ezra led the people in praising the Lord, all the people joined in with refrains of "Amen, Amen!" with lifted hands and then with faces bowed before the Lord in worship. As they heard the law read, they began to weep, convicted by their need of forgiveness. Nehemiah, Ezra, and the Levites sought to explain to the people that this was to be a day of joy—the Feast of Trumpets being the prelude to the Day of Atonement and the Feast of Booths. It was a time of great celebration for the Lord's goodness. As they understood what they were told and what they were taught, they began to rejoice and celebrate in all the Lord had done for them and to anticipate the joy of the Lord for the days ahead. This gathering for seeking God truly became a meeting **with** God for all the people as they spent time in His Word and in prayer.

Twenty-four days later, on the day after the Feast of Booths, the people gathered for a time of fasting and prayer before the Lord. There they called on Him, reading from the book of the law, confessing sin and worshiping Him. They cried out to the Lord together and blessed Him for who He is and all He had done in the history of Israel up to the present time. They came back to following God. Read Nehemiah 9:1–38 and reflect on this awesome time of meeting God together. You may want to spend some time in prayer alone or gather with some other believers for a time of Scripture reading and prayer.

Put Yourself In Their Shoes

SPIRITUAL AWAKENING

The events that occurred in Ezra's return to Israel from captivity in 458 B.C. and then the events in Jerusalem under Nehemiah's and Ezra's leadership (445 B.C.) are examples of Old Testament spiritual awakening, times when the people of God came back to faithfully following their Lord and God with renewed love for Him and fresh obedience to His Word. We see this particular awakening evidenced in the events recorded in Ezra and Nehemiah. God worked in some amazing ways to bring His people back to spiritual vitality. He has done such restoration work throughout history. One common thread we find in every spiritual awakening, both those recorded in the Scriptures and throughout Church history, is the practice of believers **intensely praying together** with other like-hearted believers. Another common thread is a powerful movement of the Holy Spirit of God impacting vast numbers of people—in a city, region, or even a country. In such "awakenings," multitudes come to Christ and begin faithfully following Him. We would do well to come together in prayer, asking God for a spiritual awakening among the believers in our city, region, or nation, and for multitudes in our day to come to know and follow Jesus Christ as their Lord and Savior.

The New Testament Church—A New Day of Praying Together

W hen Jesus taught the disciples to pray, He emphasized **two** aspects—a walk of **prayer alone** with God and a **together-with-others prayer life**. Before Jesus ascended to heaven, He told His disciples to wait together in Jerusalem for the promise of the Spirit sent from the Father. They began to wait and pray. What can we learn about praying together from these first disciples?

Word Study

DEVOTION TO PRAYER

The Greek word *proskartaréō,* translated "continually devoting" or "in constant attendance," is made up of two Greek words: *pros* meaning "toward" and *kartaréō,* meaning, "to endure." Therefore, we have the fuller meaning to endure toward something, to keep at a task, or to stay with a person or job to fulfill the need. *Proskartaréō* is used of prayer in Acts 1:14; 2:42; 6:4; Romans 12:12; and Colossians 4:2. God calls us to endure in prayer, especially with other believers. The Father wants us to endure in seeking Him together with other believers as well as alone in the "prayer closet."

📖 Read Acts 1:12–14. Describe what the disciples did.

____

____

____

____

What was the distinguishing mark of this time in prayer?

____

____

____

The eleven disciples gathered together in the "Upper Room," and with them were the women who had followed Jesus, including Jesus' mother Mary. Christ's brothers were also in this room. Others were there also, up to 120 believers total. These were *"continually devoting themselves to prayer."* They spent much time praying together. The Greek word translated "devoting" (*proskartaréō*) speaks of something or someone continually standing ready or remaining active—as a lifeguard ready to dive into the water to rescue a struggling swimmer at a split second's notice, as a soldier standing at attention available to serve, or as a ruling official continually serving the community (see Mark 3:9; Acts 10:7; Romans 13:6). *Proskartaréō* is in the present tense, meaning continual attention and action. This was the focus of their time together in the "Upper Room." This time in prayer was characterized by being *"with one mind,"* a translation of the Greek word *homothumadón,* which means to have the "same burning" or the same burden and desire in prayer. What were they praying? Doubtless, they were seeking the Father with some of the same questions they had asked Jesus just days before. They probably wanted to know His will about the days ahead—what were they to do, how were they to carry on in ministry.

This first thing we read about in this ten day period was the replacement of Judas as one of the apostles, a matter that most likely grew out of their time in prayer. Peter led them in dealing with the issue of replacing Judas, and again we see them praying together seeking the Lord's guidance as to who should fulfill this role (Acts 1:24–26). The Lord led them to Matthias. This pattern of praying together did not end with these initial ten days between the ascension of the Lord and Pentecost Sunday. This was the beginning of praying together. Let's see how they did this.

On Pentecost Sunday, the Holy Spirit came to indwell the 120 believers and then birthed 3,000 more into the family of God. What marked these first believers? What do you discover in Acts 2:41–42?

Three thousand people *"received"* the word proclaimed by Peter, repented of their sins, and received spiritual life with the coming of the Holy Spirit into their lives. They were baptized as a testimony of the new life they had received in Christ.

What did this "new life" look like? There were four elements that occupied the lives of these new believers. First, they were *"continually devoting themselves"* (*proskartaréō*) to the teaching of the apostles (both Old Testament Scriptures and New Testament revelation as the Spirit gave it). This was later written in the books of the New Testament we have today). They also spent time in fellowship (*koinōnía)* with other believers. In other words, these believers continually shared with each other the common experiences found in their new life and new walk in Christ. They were involved in *"the breaking of bread,"* a reference not only to meals together, but more specifically to times of worship centered around the Lord's Supper and its focus on the death of Christ, their life in Christ, and their anticipation of the return of Christ. Finally, we read that they were devoting themselves *"to prayer"* (literally *"to the prayers"*). This mention of prayer was most likely a reference to the public times of prayer at the Temple at 9:00 in the morning and 3:00 in the afternoon. Worship and prayer had now become essential to their daily existence and to their daily walk as new believers. The purposes of God continued to be fulfilled in these believer's lives as the Church continued to touch the lives of scores of people.

The church in Jerusalem continued to grow, and Jewish officials were by no means pleased. In Acts 3 and 4, we read about Peter and John being arrested for spreading the teaching about the Messiah Jesus. After they were released, they returned to a gathering of the believers.

Read Acts 4:23–24. What was the first response of the people to all Peter and John had told them?

Look at their prayer in Acts 4:24–31 Where was their focus? For what did they pray?

Word Study

PRAYING WITH ONE MIND

The phrase "with one mind" in Acts 1:14 is a translation of *homothumadón*, a Greek word made up of two Greek words, *homós,* meaning "the same" and *thumós,* literally meaning "to burn." This word, often translated "same mind" or "same purpose," paints a beautiful picture of praying together. *Thumós* is from *thúō*, which means "to rush along or on, to be in a heat, to breathe violently" (from *A Greek-English Lexicon of the New Testament* by Joseph Henry Thayer, Grand Rapids: Zondervan Publishing House, 1962, p. 293). *Thumós* carries the idea of burning and can speak of any strong emotion. That is why *thumós* is often translated anger or wrath. In the context of Acts 1:14, referring to prayer, *homothumadon* carries the idea of having the "same burning"—the idea of praying with the same heart burden or the same passion. The application to praying together is obvious. God intends for us to pray with united hearts, burning with the desire to know and do God's will, the burden of His heart for us.

Did You Know?

PRAYER TIMES

The early Church prayer times in Jerusalem coincided with the times of the burnt offering and the offering of incense on the golden altar in the Temple, which occurred every day at 9:00 A.M. and 3:00 P.M. The offering of incense was considered a symbol of prayer, intercession, and worship to the Lord (see Psalm 141:2; Revelation 5:8). Luke 1:10 speaks of the Jewish practice of gathering together at the Temple for one of these hours of prayer. The early Christians continued this practice as they called on their heavenly Father.

How did God respond to their prayer, according to Acts 4:31?

____

____

____

When the people heard all that Peter and John revealed, they immediately joined together in prayer, again, praying *"with one accord"* or *"with one mind"* (*homothumadón*). They were lifting their voices with a common heart burden. Their focus was on the sovereign Lord, the Creator of heaven, the earth, the sea, and *"all that is in them."* They acknowledged the events around them as fulfilling what the Lord had spoken concerning the coming and the crucifixion of the Messiah, events that fulfilled the purposes of God. In prayer, they acknowledged the response of the "Gentiles" and the "peoples" to Jesus and then the current "threats" of the officials in Jerusalem. Note that they did not pray against these officials. They simply brought the matter to the Lord to deal with. They asked Him for His power to be the witnesses they needed to be. God answered, even shaking the building where they were gathered. They were filled with the Holy Spirit and began declaring the word of God with boldness.

As the Jerusalem church continued to grow, it faced growing pains. Acts 6 tells us about a conflict that arose over the care of the widows among them. This was no small matter since the church at this juncture could have numbered over twenty thousand. The apostles instructed the congregation to select seven men to oversee this task while they focused on two main areas. Acts 6:4 says, *"But we will devote ourselves to prayer, and to the ministry of the word."* There is a very important word about praying together in this verse. The phrase *"to prayer"* can be literally translated *"to the prayer,"* pointing to specific times of praying together led by the apostles among the congregation. This phrase suggests that a high priority was placed upon the act of praying together in the early Church. This suggestion is made even clearer when we look at the words, *"the ministry of the word"* in Acts 6:4. These words point to the public proclamation of the Word of God—the Greek word used here for "ministry" is *diakonía*, the same word used for serving tables in Acts 6:3. Serving tables was a necessary part of taking care of the widows. It was a public ministry. Serving the Word to those who had not heard (evangelism) and to those who had received that Word (discipleship) was the task of the apostles, one of the two priorities given them by the Lord. This was what it meant to *"make disciples of all the nations"* (Matthew 28:18–20). Acts 6:7 points to the result, *"And the word of God kept on spreading. . . ."*

Did You Know?

THE CHURCH AS A FAMILY

Church imagery in Scripture points to the reality of believers belonging together, needing one another, caring for one another, loving one another, and growing together as a result. Think about what the Church is called—a family of many "children," a body of many "members," a household of many "servants," a temple of many "stones," an army of many "soldiers," a flock of many "sheep." All of these pictures reveal that we are interdependent. We need one another. You need others, and others need you. As a matter of fact, God gives us about forty "one another" commands to show us how to live with and minister with and grow with one another. God continues to lead us to pray and to lead us to reach out to others to bring them in to the circle of "one another" in the Family of God. He wants the "picture" to be complete.

Acts 12 brings us to another example of the Jerusalem church in prayer together. Herod arrested some belonging to the church. He put James, the brother of John, to death. Then, Peter was arrested and placed in jail, most likely awaiting an execution by Herod. What did the church do in response?

Read Acts 12:1–17 and answer the questions below.

According to Acts 12:1–5, what did the believers do?

____

____

____

____

What did God do according to Acts 12:6–11?

____

____

____

____

What do you discover in Acts 12:12–17?

____

____

____

____

____

When the church heard that Peter had been arrested they began praying "fervently," or "without ceasing," the Greek word for fervently being *ektenēs,* meaning "to stretch out." It carries the idea of something going on continually and intensely. The church at Jerusalem was intense in its praying for Peter. God sent an angel to miraculously release him. When Peter realized what had happened, he went to the home of Mary (not the same Mary who is the mother of Jesus) and her son John Mark. Verse 12 notes that this home was a place *"where many were gathered together"* and seems to imply that it was only one of several locations where people were praying. Most likely, there were other homes where believers were interceding on behalf of Peter. At this home we see a very human response, a look at actual people being stretched in their faith as they prayed together. The result is given for us in a summary verse, Acts 12:24—*"The word of the Lord continued to grow and to be multiplied."* As with all the other references to praying together, we see the purposes of God being fulfilled and the kingdom of God continuing to grow. That is what God is doing in our present day as we come together to **pray His way**.

"But prayer for him was being made fervently by the church to God."

Acts 12:5

Acts 13:1–3 shows us that these gatherings were not just occurring at Jerusalem. The leaders in Antioch, in the midst of a time of prayer, fasting, and worship, heard the call of the Spirit of God to set apart Barnabas and Saul to a new work, a work of declaring the Word in several regions of Asia Minor. What is known as "the first missionary journey" grew out of a time of prayer together. Again, we see the purposes of God being fulfilled and the kingdom continuing to grow.

What does God want to do through you and other believers gathered together in prayer? You may be the one that God wants to lead such a group, or He may want you to be a support and encouragement to some other leader. Such leadership is not limited to formal, scheduled meetings for prayer. God is calling people to prayer in new ways and new days. You may want to get together with some of the leaders of your church to see what God may be calling you and them to do in praying together. Encourage others, perhaps in your Sunday school class or home group or discipleship group. Spend some time praying with other believers, seeking the Lord for how He wants to fulfill His purposes and grow His kingdom where you are. [You may want to look at the guidelines for praying together given in the **"S.A.M.E. H.E.A.R.T."** outline at the end of this lesson.]

Praying Together

DAY FIVE

FOR ME TO PRAY GOD'S WAY

How are you to pray together? What does it mean to join with others in prayer? There are three more examples of praying together at which we need to look. With those examples we will ask three application questions: **1)** Where is your focus? **2)** Where is your fight? and **3)** Where is your fellowship? Let's see how these three examples help focus our attention more firmly on the Lord to see His will done more fully in our lives and in the lives of the body of believers with whom we worship.

"O our God . . . we have no power against this great multitude that is coming against us; nor do we know what to do, but our eyes are upon You."

2 Chronicles 20:12 (NKJV)

In 2 Chronicles 20:1–13, we read the story of Jehoshaphat and Judah and the attack from the three armies—the armies of the Moabites, the Ammonites, and those of Mount Seir (Edom). They were coming against Judah. What would the people of Judah do?

Read 2 Chronicles 20:1–13 and answer the following questions.

What was Jehoshaphat's response in 2 Chronicles 20:3? How did the people respond in verse 4?

____

____

____

____

____

____

What are the main elements of Jehoshaphat's prayer in verses 5–13?

____

____

____

____

____

Where is the focus of Jehoshaphat and the people according to verse 13?

____

____

____

____

Jehoshaphat and the people turned to the Lord in prayer with fasting. Many "gathered together" in Jerusalem to seek the Lord. Jehoshaphat began by praising God as God in the heavens and ruler over all nations. He affirmed that no one can stand against God. As Jehoshaphat prayed, he rehearsed the faithfulness of God in bringing the children of Israel out of Egypt and planting them in the land of Israel. In coming into the land of Canaan, the people obeyed God in not interfering with the nations who were now coming against Israel. Jehoshaphat recalled the promise that if Israel faced such a day, they were to pray, to call on the Lord. While admitting that they did not have the power to withstand their enemies nor did they know what to do, Jehoshaphat declared that his focus and the focus of the people was on the Lord—*"our eyes are on Thee."* That focus made all the difference and in 2 Chronicles 20:14–30, we read of the great victory God gave them.

APPLY WHERE IS YOUR FOCUS? Check all that apply to your life and situation.

- ❒ My problems
- ❒ My finances
- ❒ My plans/opinions
- ❒ My friends
- ❒ Others' opinions
- ❒ The Lord/His Word
- ❒ God's will
- ❒ God's kingdom

PRAY Look again at what Jehoshaphat prayed in 2 Chronicles 20:13. That verse could be paraphrased "Lord, we are powerless facing this problem. . . . We have never experienced anything like this before, and we don't know what to do—but our eyes are on You." Does this prayer apply to you in some issue you are facing right now? Or is there a situation in the life of someone you know where this proverb applies? Pause and pray. Perhaps you may want to gather with some other believers and pray together.

The year was A.D. 57. Paul was writing to the Romans from the city of Corinth, planning to go to Jerusalem with an offering to help the famine-worn believers there. He knew there were those opposed to him in Jerusalem, and He asked the Roman believers to join in prayer together with him. Read what Paul says in Romans 15:22–33.

📖 What are the specific prayer requests Paul made in verses 31–33?

____

____

____

____

Paul asked the believers to pray first that he be protected from those who opposed him and the ministry Christ had given him. He also desired that the believers in Jerusalem would receive the offering he was bringing and that he would be able to come to Rome *"in joy by the will of God"* and have refreshing rest and ministry among the believers there.

What part were the Roman believers to play in Paul's desires, according to verse 30?

____

____

____

When Paul asked the Roman believers to *"strive together with me in your prayers to God for me,"* he used the Greek word *sunagōnízomai,* meaning to "agonize" together, the idea being to make a strenuous effort together. He

Put Yourself In Their Shoes

ALL ABOUT FOCUS

It's all about focus, not about numbers or resources (our power) or strategies (our wisdom). Jehoshaphat and the armies of Judah were outnumbered, but their focus was on God. In another Old Testament example, we read about Elijah on Mount Carmel—one man focused on the Lord God opposing 850 prophets focused on Baal (see I Kings 18). Elijah's testimony emphasizes that God is not interested in numbers, but in one's focus. Without the right focus, there is no passion for the fight, no willingness to stand alone. With the right focus, we can stand, joining God in what He is doing.

Word Study

STRIVE TOGETHER

In Romans 15:30, "strive together with me" is a translation of the Greek word *sunagōnízomai,* a word made up of *sún* (together) and *agōnizomai,* translated "strive together," "fight together," or "agonize together." *Sunagōnízomai* pictures people joining together in *agōnizomai,* the word used of contending in the Greek games. An *agōn* was a place of assembly, often used to refer to the Greek games where runners and others "agonized" or exerted great strength to win a race or a contest (as in wrestling, one "agonizes" with his opponent). *Agōnia* refers to severe mental struggles and emotions, and the word *agōnizomai* literally means "to enter a contest" or "contend in the gymnastic games," or can mean "to contend with enemies," "to struggle with difficulties or dangers" or "to make an effort with great zeal." The Spirit here pictures the Roman believers joining Paul in prayer, agonizing, striving with all their strength, calling on the Lord to answer the requests Paul had made.

wanted them to join in praying for him. He knew the Lord had designed the Body of Christ to work together in fulfilling the purposes of God—to work with God first and then for God's work to become real in the lives of other believers. Through this passage, Paul paints a long-distance picture of Roman believers joining him in prayer, agonizing, striving with all their strength, calling on the Lord to answer the requests Paul has made. The result—when we read Acts 20–28, we see how God answered those prayers. Paul had the opportunity to proclaim the message of salvation in Christ to hundreds, even to thousands of people, eventually getting to Rome and having a very fruitful ministry there.

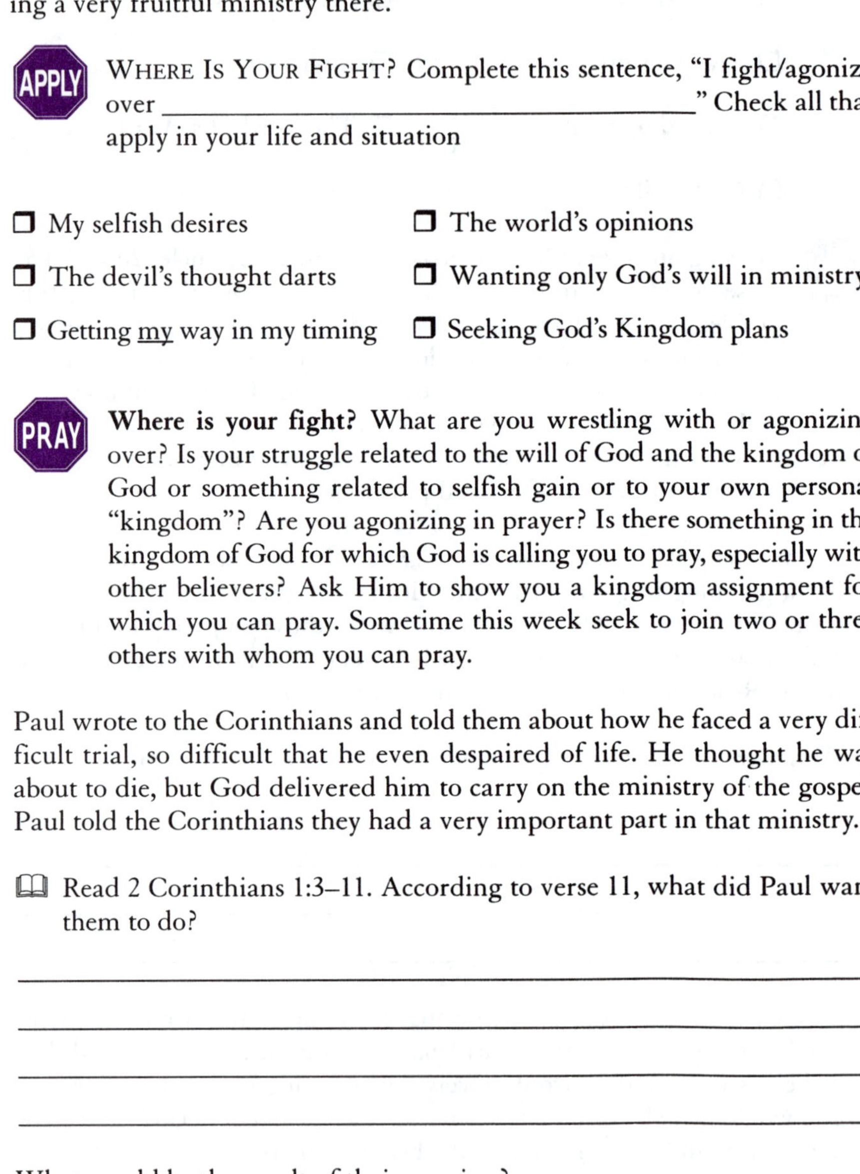

APPLY WHERE IS YOUR FIGHT? Complete this sentence, "I fight/agonize over ______________________________________" Check all that apply in your life and situation

❒ My selfish desires ❒ The world's opinions

❒ The devil's thought darts ❒ Wanting only God's will in ministry

❒ Getting my way in my timing ❒ Seeking God's Kingdom plans

PRAY **Where is your fight?** What are you wrestling with or agonizing over? Is your struggle related to the will of God and the kingdom of God or something related to selfish gain or to your own personal "kingdom"? Are you agonizing in prayer? Is there something in the kingdom of God for which God is calling you to pray, especially with other believers? Ask Him to show you a kingdom assignment for which you can pray. Sometime this week seek to join two or three others with whom you can pray.

Word Study

"JOINING IN HELPING"

The Greek word *sunupourgéō* translated "joining in helping" in 2 Corinthians 1:11 is made up of three words—*sún* + *hupó* + *érgon*—literally meaning "together + under + work." The idea is thus: to give service together with another or to help together. Paul assured the Corinthians that they were serving together with Paul, helping in the work of getting the message of the grace of God to more and more people.

Paul wrote to the Corinthians and told them about how he faced a very difficult trial, so difficult that he even despaired of life. He thought he was about to die, but God delivered him to carry on the ministry of the gospel. Paul told the Corinthians they had a very important part in that ministry.

📖 Read 2 Corinthians 1:3–11. According to verse 11, what did Paul want them to do?

____

____

____

____

What would be the result of their praying?

____

____

____

Paul desired that the Corinthian believers join together in helping through prayer for him and his ministry companions. In 2 Corinthians 1:11, "joining in helping" is a translation of the Greek word *sunupourgéō,* which is made up of three Greek words meaning "to work under together." Paul saw the Corinthians as partners in ministry, working under the load **through** prayer and helping carry the load **in** prayer. They were part of a fellowship of service, of sharing the load. They were being a genuine help to Paul, his companions, and the ministries in which they were involved. The result—many hearts giving thanks for God's grace given to Paul and his companions and for God's grace given to those who heard the message of Christ through them.

APPLY

WHERE IS YOUR "FELLOWSHIP" OF PRAYER?—Where are you spending time with others or where are you joining with others in prayer? Check all that apply.

- ❐ Church worship service
- ❐ Sunday school class
- ❐ Home fellowship group/small group
- ❐ Sporting events/watching TV
- ❐ Dining out with others
- ❐ Concerts/movies

Where is your fellowship, your place of sharing your life and energies with others? Are you spending time with others in prayer? Do you have a place to give your time in prayer for others, for matters in the kingdom of God? Ask God to show you a place where you can join in praying for someone or some ministry.

Think about it: Where is your FOCUS? Where is your FIGHT? Where is your FELLOWSHIP? Look at your walk with the Lord *with others* and look for open doors to *pray together* with others. Focusing and agonizing in prayer with others are all part of praying God's way.

Lord, thank You for placing me in Your Family, in the Body of Christ, in Your Flock. Thank You for making me a living stone in Your Temple, for using me in the building of others alongside me. There are so many things I do not know or understand about praying together with others. I ask You to guide me and teach me in the days ahead. May I be a part of the Body of Christ that fulfills the purpose for which You placed me in the Body. Empower me to be the family member I should be, one who comes alongside my brothers and sisters in prayer—to pray with them and to pray for them. Father, may I keep the right focus on You through prayer, fight the right fight in prayer, and fellowship in the right way by serving others through prayer. Teach me both to pray alone and together with others. I need my fellow believers, and they need me. Thank You for making me part of Your kingdom. I love You. Thank you for loving me. May I show Your love to others as I pray for them and with them. In Jesus' name, Amen.

Father, may I keep the right focus on You through prayer, fight the right fight in prayer, and fellowship in the right way by serving others through prayer. Teach me both to pray alone and together with others.

Record your prayer to the Father in the space provided.

____

____

____

____

____

____

____

____

S.A.M.E. H.E.A.R.T.

S.A.M.E. H.E.A.R.T. is a guide to praying together designed for the small group or for a church prayer meeting in which time in prayer is the main purpose. Read over these guidelines. The first four guidelines in the acrostic "S.A.M.E." help center attention on the Lord both in preparation time and in prayer time. The final five guidelines in the acrostic H.E.A.R.T. give tracks for the activity of prayer. Attention set and active prayer carried out—that is the goal of S.A.M.E. H.E.A.R.T. (Rick, please make this last sentence clearer.

S.A.M.E.—Four Actions That Help You Pray with One Heart/One Accord

S— **Set or Center Attention on God**, not on your needs. As you gather together, you need His mind and heart about the burdens you have. We must be God-centered, not needs-centered.

First, Prepare for Prayer—Spend some time in the Word together as you prepare to pray together. To center your attention, use Scripture, testimonies of answered prayer, and/or hymns and songs of worship (quoted or sung). As you come together for prayer, call to mind who God is, how God thinks, what God likes or dislikes, what God is up to now, and how important it is to join Him.

[As a leader, remember that as you spend time in the Word and in prayer together, you are investing time in that which touches, trains, and warms the heart to see God and His mission of bringing many into His kingdom and then bringing those *"many sons to glory"* (Hebrews 2:10).]

A—**All Agendas Surrendered . . . All Hearts Involved and In Tune.** As you lay aside personal "agendas" you can more readily pray the Will of God and involve all the hearts gathered together. If you are to pray with one heart/one accord, you must build hearts together. That takes time **in Scripture** and **in prayer together**. As you walk in a common relationship, you will grow a common heart. Spend time together. You can be assured that the Spirit of God will build unity (or oneness) and "one-accord" praying, and He will also encourage and build up believers. He will convict people of sin and uncover "fleshly" agendas so that you can walk with a cleansed heart in oneness with Him and one another and pray with the confidence of an uncondemned heart. First John 3:21–22 reminds us, *"Beloved, if our heart does not condemn us, we have confidence before God; and whatever we ask we receive from Him, because we keep His commandments and do the things that are pleasing in His sight."* Note: Surrendering our agendas does not mean you cannot pray personal heart burdens. You can certainly do that as well as pray for one another, as long as you are following the Lord's direction.

M—**Magnify the Lord. Make Much of Who God Is.** To help keep the focus on God, spend time blessing the Lord and magnifying His Name. Speak His names—Lord, King, Savior, Friend, Holy One, Lord of Hosts, God of Heaven, Provider, Healer. Ask those gathered to tell who God is . . . ."God is ______," "______," "_____." Quote Scripture. This builds faith and helps place your heart where it should be, in humble dependence on the Lord.

E—**Expect to Meet God—to Hear God—to See God Answer**. This is the essence of faith in Hebrews 11:6—When you believe God is who the Scriptures say He is, you come expecting to meet Him, you diligently seek Him expecting to find Him, to hear Him and expecting to be rewarded and given answers by Him. Look for the working of the Spirit of God as you pray. . . . Then . . .

H.E.A.R.T.—Five Heart Attitudes/Actions That Help You Pray the Will of God

H—**Heart Burdens Lifted Before the Lord.** As you pray, the Lord directs and joins hearts in line with His Will and His Word. As you are gathered together, the prayer leader can begin in a number of ways such as by sharing a particular need, or event. He or she can make a connection of prayer to some need in the life of an individual, family, church, city, or nation. He or she can point to an action needed for which prayer is essential. These may be kingdom needs, church needs, or personal needs that you lift before the Lord.

As the prayer time continues, remember the Spirit of God directs or redirects hearts about a particular burden. This also means you must learn how to hear God and how to respond to Him. Remember, He guides into Truth, gives insights from Scripture, and focuses your hearts on God's interests. He may intensify the burden or give a simple release from that burden. This is all part of the relationship you have with the Lord and with one another. Look for the Spirit's working. Pour out your heart burdens, the things weighing on you. Bring your burning desires to the Lord. Unveil your deepest longings. And never forget, **God responds to the heart,** not formulas or outlines.

E— **Eager to Discover His Will, His Burdens, the Things Burning in His Heart**. First John 5:14 promises, *"And this is the confidence which we have before Him, that, if we ask anything according to His will, He hears us."* Asking according to God's will means continually magnifying the Lord, continually surrendering any "agenda" to the Lord, or yielding our will to know His will. This also implies remaining ever sensitive to uncover the Spirit's burdens, to join together in all seeking the will of God. As you pray, you can encounter God together—God will guide hearts and minds in the direction of His Will. Use the Scriptures much—God speaks through the Scriptures, revealing truth, reminding of His promises, and keeping your focus on the person, character, and will of God.

You must be sensitive to His Spirit in your prayer times together. As He speaks, you should adjust your praying, spending longer or shorter times on the burdens He gives you. You may often find that the burden you intended to spend much time over is quickly lifted and a new burden is placed on your hearts. You must ever be in prayer with a child's heart responding to the Father's voice, eager to follow your loving Master with a servant's heart.

A—**Asking, Humbly Acknowledging the Needs You See**. God has chosen to train us and grow us and provide for us as His children through the relationship of a child asking a Father. Ask Him concerning the needs you face individually and as a Family/Body/Building/Army/Flock. Ask humbly, never arrogantly. Walk in the fear of the Lord, honoring Him as Lord and remembering He understands your needs—He is the Perfect Father, worthy of honor, wanting a trusting heart in each of His children and deserving the deepest respect.

R—**Rejoicing Before the Lord for Receiving Direction from the Lord**. Spend time thanking the Lord for His presence, His guidance, and His specific care for the needs you have brought to Him. Thank Him for His abundant mercy and grace. Allow those with whom you are praying time to give thanks to the Lord for His ways and His work, for His timing and for the ways He will answer what you have prayed.

T—**Time Spent in Prayer**. How much time you spend in prayer as you meet together will vary according to the **intensity** of the burden, the **unity** of the group, the **purity** of the hearts in prayer, and the **sensitivity** of the believers to God and His directions. You may pray for minutes, hours, days, weeks, months, even years, lifting the burdens before the Lord. He will answer, sometimes quickly, sometimes slowly, according to His perfect timing. His timing will determine your time in Prayer. Whatever the case, learn to pray together with the **S.A.M.E. H.E.A.R.T.**

Notes

JESUS PRAYED

THE PRAYER LIFE OF JESUS THEN AND NOW

When we turn the pages of Scripture to the life of Jesus, we discover one who considered prayer essential in everything He did. Jesus came as the God-Man, marked by the character, nature, and power of His Father, yet He was always dependent on His Father in prayer. This is one of the most amazing aspects of Jesus' life. Jesus prayed frequently and fervently. He prayed as no other man has ever prayed. We are often amazed that Jesus spent so much time in prayer, but that is because we often misunderstand the full meaning of prayer as well as the full ministry of prayer. Jesus understood both.

We are often amazed that Jesus spent so much time in prayer, but that is because we often misunderstand the full meaning of prayer as well as the full ministry of prayer.

When we look at the lifestyle of our Lord, we find many ways in which He instructs us by example. We have already seen the ways He instructs us by His teaching and the commands of His Word. As we look at His life from boyhood through manhood, we will see a life saturated in prayer. When we look at His "growing up" years, we will see the central place prayer played in His life. Then we will look at how prayer played a crucial role as He began His ministry and how prayer continued to be His lifeline to the Father in those all-important ministry years. Jesus never tried to minister without time spent in prayer with His Father. His prayer life in the last days of His ministry will show us how He prayed facing the greatest trial anyone has ever faced. Seeing His ongoing prayer life—His intercession for us will encourage us as we seek to follow Him.

As we look at our own prayer lives, we need to allow Jesus' example to encourage and challenge us. We need to let His walk with the Father instruct us. While Jesus had a very unique relationship to His Father, we can let His walk with the Father help us picture the kind of relationship the Father wants with each of His children. Jesus knew what it meant to live **praying God's way**. He will guide us to do the same.

Jesus Prayed

DAY ONE

THE PRAYER LIFE OF JESUS IN THE "PRIVATE YEARS"

What kind of daily life did Jesus have? What would we expect to find on His schedule each day, especially in those first thirty years, those "private years" of which we know so little? As we look at the Scriptures, we find some clues as to what a day in the life of Jesus would look like. As we look at His lifestyle, we can see some of the struggles He may have faced. We can also see the pattern in which Christ was led by the Father down the dusty roads of Israel some two thousand years ago and discover some of the ways the Father leads in our own lives.

📖 The first glimpse of Jesus' life is found when He was twelve years of age. Read Luke 2:41–52. Describe the events in Jesus' life at this point. What stands out about Jesus?

____

____

____

____

____

____

____

Read Luke 2:49 again. What insights do you glean from Jesus' question to Joseph and Mary? Does this say anything about His prayer life?

____

____

____

____

____

____

____

____

In Luke 2, we get a glimpse of the life of Jesus as a twelve-year old boy, celebrating the Passover feast with His family and others in Jerusalem. In the festive and crowded atmosphere of the Temple, we find Jesus talking to the teachers of the Law, those men learned in all the Old Testament Scriptures. Jesus was there listening, asking questions, and answering questions—and all were *"amazed at His understanding and His answers."* While He was doing this, His family was journeying back to Nazareth. When Mary and Joseph realized that Jesus was not on the return caravan, they traveled back a day's journey to Jerusalem. Then they searched diligently for Him for at least another day. Finally finding Him in the Temple was a relief and a surprise, but Jesus was surprised at their surprise. His question to them is literally, "Did you not know that I had to be in the things of My Father?"—a testimony that Jesus understood the things of His Father and that His Father had revealed those things to Him. Those two facts reveal that the prayer life of this twelve-year-old boy was very real and vibrant.

What further insights do you find in Luke 2:52? What clues can you glean about Jesus' lifestyle? What would this say about His prayer life?

____

____

____

____

____

____

From age twelve on, Jesus grew *"in favor with God,"* meaning His relationship with God the Father stayed healthy and growing. It would also seem from that statement that the prayer life of Jesus continued to grow, remaining ever vibrant and strong. This is a testimony that He stayed in close fellowship with His Father, always walking in the light. Nothing ever marred that fellowship. Concerning His relationship with His Father, His family, and His fellow man, Jesus never had a mark or stain of wrongdoing in His life. The way remained continually open for Jesus to talk to His Father—any time, any place, and any circumstance. In addition, His relationship with others continued to grow strong.

"The Lord God has given Me the tongue of disciples, that I may know how to sustain the weary one with a word. He awakens me morning by morning, He awakens My ear to listen as a disciple."

Isaiah 50:4

📖 We have looked at an informative verse in an earlier lesson, but it would be good to review it at this point. Look at Isaiah 50:4, a prophecy about the coming Messiah. What do you see that would apply to Jesus' lifestyle, especially to His prayer life?

____

____

____

____

From what Jesus said to Mary and Joseph, it is evident the Father had already been teaching Him many things, waking Him *"morning by morning . . . to listen as a disciple."* The teachers of the Law and all who heard Him in those days at the Temple were astounded at His understanding and ability to answer questions about the Scriptures. Jesus proved to be a good disciple of His Father, a good listener in prayer, and a scholar when it came to searching and learning the Scriptures. Think of what it must have been like for the boy Jesus to be in prayer to His Father, always eager to hear Him. Jesus, ever the obedient learner, wanted to know His Word and was ever-attentive in prayer, having the heart of a disciple to His Father. The Father wants us to know a similar delight as we listen to His Word and learn to pray God's way.

Is there a way to know the delight of praying God's way more fully? How do we know for sure what went on in Christ's earthly life, say from age 12 to age 30? We again find a clue in the Scriptures. Luke 3:23 says, *"And when He began His ministry, Jesus Himself was about thirty years of age."* That statement comes immediately following His baptism and before the account of His temptation in the wilderness. What can we learn from the events surrounding Jesus' baptism by John in the Jordan River? These precursor events give us another look into this Man, our Lord, and they reveal some wonderful truths about His lifestyle and His prayer life.

📖 Read the account of Jesus' baptism in Luke 3:21–22. What does Luke note about Jesus when John baptized Him?

____

____

____

____

What part did the Holy Spirit play in this event? (You may want to look at the testimony of John the Baptist in John 1:29–34 as well.)

____

____

____

____

As He was being baptized, Jesus was praying, revealing both His dependence on and His love for His Father.

Jesus came to be baptized by John and begin the ministry the Father sent Him to fulfill. As He was being baptized, **Jesus was praying**, revealing both His dependence on and His love for His Father. After Christ was baptized and while He was **still praying**, the Holy Spirit descended upon Jesus in bodily form as a dove. John the Baptist recounts that the Father had revealed this as the sign to look for to signal the Messiah.

What did the Father declare at Jesus' baptism? What thoughts do you gather from that statement?

____

____

____

____

____

____

The Father spoke from heaven, *"Thou art My beloved Son, in Thee I am well-pleased."* The Father dearly loved His Son. What a delight it must have been for the Father to walk and talk with His Son in perfect fellowship and flawless communion. What a joy—how well-pleasing it must have been to experience every day that oneness of heart and mind with Jesus, always receiving from His Son the love that flowed from all His heart, soul, mind, and strength, a love of complete and unwavering trust. Jesus was well-pleasing to His Father.

At this point, we must ask some questions: What does it mean to be well pleasing to God? Is there something special we must do, or some secret we must know, or something we must own? How can we be well pleasing to the Father? How does this relate to praying God's way? What pleases God about our praying? We will see this in Day Two.

The Prayer Life of Jesus and the Beginning of His Ministry

Jesus Prayed

Day Two

We have seen at the very outset of Jesus' ministry that the Father declared He was well pleased with His Beloved Son. This was before He preached any messages, gave any parables, taught any lessons, or performed any miracles. What was the foundation of this well-pleasing life of the Lord Jesus, and where does prayer fit in?

To see the truth of a well-pleasing life we need to look at two testimonies from Scripture. These will help us see how we can be well pleasing to God and how prayer relates to that aim. The first Scripture is from the pen of the apostle Paul.

📖 Read 2 Corinthians 5:6–9. What does Paul highlight about his walk (and the walk of those who truly know the Lord)?

____

____

____

____

There is a connection between what Paul says in verse 7 with what he says in verse 9 concerning our earthly walk and life in our heavenly home. What does Paul emphasize in verse 9?

____

____

____

____

As Paul reflected on his ministry and his earthly walk in 2 Corinthians 4 and 5, he came to a summary statement in verse 7 of chapter 5. There, he speaks about walking by faith, not by sight, trusting that what God has said is true. He knew that one day his life on earth would end—his body or "earthly tent" would be "torn down"—and that one day, every believer in Jesus Christ would walk in the fullness of eternal life, with new bodies in a new home (5:1–5). The common element in our earthly walk and in our heavenly home is the desire to be pleasing to God. On earth, that comes

Doctrine
PLEASING TO GOD

At Jesus' baptism, the Father said He was well pleased with the Son (Luke 3:22). Over two years later, the Father made the same declaration about His Son on the Mount of Transfiguration (Matthew 17:5). Second Corinthians 5:7–9 and Hebrews 11:6 point to the necessity of faith to please God, while Romans 12:1 focuses on surrender to God as *"a living and holy sacrifice, well-pleasing to God."* That is an act of faith. Romans 14:8 speaks of being well-pleasing to God as members of the family of God who do not condemn one another, but rather love and build up one another. Paul taught the Thessalonians how to please God through a holy walk (1 Thessalonians 4:1–8), and he prayed for the Colossians believers to walk pleasing to the Lord *"in all respects"* (Colossians 1:10). As with Paul and his companions, may *"we have as our ambition ... to be pleasing to Him"* (2 Corinthians 5:9).

"Enoch . . . had this testimony, that he pleased God. But without faith it is impossible to please Him, for he who comes to God must believe that He is, and that He is a rewarder of those who diligently seek Him.

Hebrews 11:5b–6 (NKJV)

through our walk by faith. Faith or confident trust in God pleases God. A walk in faith says to our Father, "We love You and trust You. We believe what You have promised." That is what Jesus did in His earthly walk, and what Paul did as well.

Walking by faith is essential to pleasing God as we walk on earth. In heaven, our faith will be complete, and all we do will be pleasing to Him. Revelation 22:3 says that we, His bondservants, *"shall serve Him"* unhindered by any distractions, any deceptions, or any darkness. The Lord Himself will "*illumine*" us, and we will walk in the light with Him—reigning with Him forever.

There is another verse that gives us insight into what marks one who is walking in faith and thus pleasing God? Read Hebrews 11:6. What action is true of one walking in faith according to Hebrews 11:6?

____

____

____

____

The one who believes that God is God, who believes He is who the Scriptures say, will keep coming (present tense) to God, diligently seeking Him in prayer and desiring a walk of fellowship. The one coming to God in faith expects God to hear him and to answer him. Such faith pleases God. That was the mark of those who walked by faith, people like Enoch in Hebrews 11:5. That was the mark of Jesus throughout His life.

Think back to Jesus' baptism and what the Father said about Jesus' life. Luke 3:22 makes it clear that the Father was *"well pleased"* in His Son. Therefore, what characteristic can we conclude marked Jesus' life in those growing up years and into manhood?

____

____

____

____

____

Even as a child, Jesus pleased His Father because Jesus walked in faith, believing that He was who the Scripture says He is. Jesus was (and still is) God the Son, and, while on earth, He daily came to God His Father. (Don't lose the significance of this in the mystery of it all.) Jesus' practice of continually coming to the Father in prayer did not stop in childhood. All His days on earth, Jesus pleased His Father as He diligently sought the Father in prayer. After more than two years of ministry as He was on what became known as the Mount of Transfiguration, the Father declared again, *"My Beloved Son, with whom I am well pleased"* (Matthew 17:5). As He walked and ministered and prayed, Jesus knew His Father was a rewarder to those who would come to God, earnestly seeking Him day by day. Day in and day out, Jesus desired only to be *"in the things of* [His] *Father."* Jesus knew His Father's will as the Father revealed it. Everything the Father revealed, Jesus wanted to obey . . . and did obey. He wanted to join His Father in the work He was doing. Jesus desired to accomplish all the Father sent Him to do.

That faith walk, that walk of diligently seeking His Father, greatly pleased the Father.

How about you? Are you walking, pleasing the Father by diligently seeking Him? Perhaps now would be a good time to pause and talk to the Father about the work He is doing, about the assignments He has for you, and about how you can walk pleasing Him. Remember, by the Holy Spirit in you, the life of Jesus can be real to you. His Spirit can fill you with His life and teach you to pray and walk in such a way that the pleasing life of the Son is experienced and seen in you. Daily seeking the Father is well pleasing to Him.

As we look at Jesus in the days of ministry, we can learn much from His lifestyle. The first thing we need to look at is how He sought His Father in those days in the wilderness. How He walked through those forty days and how He began His ministry will help guide us in how we face trials and temptations—even when we are doing the will of God.

What do you learn from Luke 4:1–2?

____

____

____

____

Luke tells us that Jesus returned from the Jordan River after His baptism *"full of the Holy Spirit."* The leadership of the Spirit marked Jesus moment by moment. The Spirit of God led Jesus about the wilderness for forty days as He fasted. Fasting in the Old Testament was always considered a time to humble oneself and seek the Lord. Jesus walked in humility, always depending on the Spirit and the Father to accomplish what the Father wanted. During those days, the devil tempted Jesus in a variety of ways. When the forty days ended, Jesus became hungry. Because He was under the guidance of the Spirit, Jesus responded to the devil's temptation in the power of the Spirit. What can we learn from Jesus about how to respond to temptation (even during a time of intense prayer)?

Read Matthew 4:3–11. How did Jesus respond to the tempter? What common factor is true in each response? In Luke 4:14, what does Luke highlight immediately after this encounter?

____

____

____

____

____

____

____

____

The tempter questioned whether or not Jesus was the Son of God and offered Him an opportunity to prove it while at the same time satisfying His physical

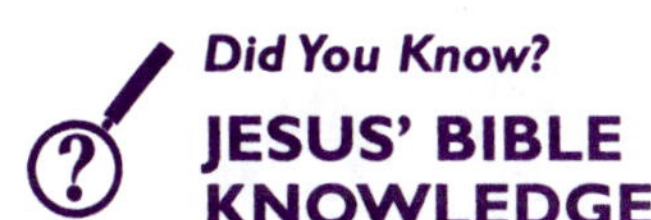

Did You Know?

JESUS' BIBLE KNOWLEDGE

Jesus countered each temptation from the devil with Scripture, first noting the God's words as the true bread needed by man. Jesus was quoting from Deuteronomy 8:3. In the other two temptations, Jesus responded from this very same book (Deuteronomy 6:13, 16). Jesus was well versed in God's laws for His people and followed these commandments in His heart. He had read and heard and meditated on God's Word, and it became His bread, His inner strength, and His sword, His outer weapon, at the moment of temptation.

need for food. Jesus responded with the Word of God, *"It is written. . . ."* and pointed out that it is more important to follow what God says than to follow one's physical desires, even the basic desire for simple bread. Following God and His Word will provide the true nourishment for the true life man needs. Satan then used the Word of God to try and lead Jesus astray from following the leadership of His Father. Jesus countered with the Scriptures that command never to put God to the test or to presume upon Him. Jesus was always more concerned about His relationship with the Father than with any external reality, be it bread or miraculous physical protection. When Satan offered the kingdoms of the world with all their glory, Jesus again focused on His Father's will and His Father's Word. Nothing is more important than worshiping Him, not even *"all the kingdoms of the world."*

Jesus stood firm because He stood faithful to His Father and His Word.

Jesus stood firm because He stood faithful to His Father and His Word. In constant humility, Jesus depended on the Spirit of God, the Word of God, and the guiding hand of His Father. The result was victory at every point, never defeat in any point. Immediately after this, when Jesus came into Galilee, He came *"in the power of the Spirit."* Here is another picture of His absolute dependence on the Spirit and His continued focus on His Father.

How then did Jesus live day to day? What marked His schedule? We will see in Day Three.

Jesus Prayed

DAY THREE

PRAYER IN THE DAYS OF JESUS' MINISTRY

It is vital to see how Jesus walked day in and day out after those forty days in the wilderness. How would His daily pattern differ with all the demands and needs of people all around Him? How would He deal with those needs as well as the needs of those not-quite-mature disciples, those men who failed to "get it" time after time? We will see in today's lesson.

📖 We have looked at Mark 1:35–38 in an earlier lesson. Look again and summarize what you see there. (Recall what we have seen in Isaiah 50:4.)

____

____

____

____

Early in the morning while it was still dark, Jesus got up and went to a solitary place to pray to His Father, an example of the *"morning by morning,"* mentioned by Isaiah. There, the Father gave Jesus His directions for the day, the wisdom He would need for the many ministry encounters He would face.

📖 Luke gives us another glimpse at Jesus in prayer. Read Luke 5:16 and write what you discover in that verse?

____

____

____

Jesus would *"often slip away"* to a deserted place, a place to be alone with His Father. There, He would spend time in prayer. *Proseúchomai,* the Greek word translated "pray" in Luke 5:16, is the general word for prayer, indicating both the heart attitude of bowing to the Father about all kinds of needs, but also offering to the Father praise and thanksgiving. A heart attitude of prayer, praise, and thanksgiving was certainly true of Jesus' earthly walk and is an excellent example for us to follow. We too often need to "slip away" to spend time with our Father.

"But He Himself would often slip away to the wilderness and pray."

Luke 5:16

Another aspect of Jesus' walk in prayer is the attention He gave to major decisions and turning points in His life. We have already noted that Jesus was praying at His baptism and that He spent forty days in fasting and prayer before He began His ministry.

📖 What do you find in Luke 6:12–16?

____

____

____

____

Sometime around the summer of A.D. 28, after about eighteen months of ministry, Jesus went up to a mountain to pray and spent the whole night in prayer. The next day He called twelve of His disciples to be His apostles, His "sent ones." They would live in a special relationship to Him, being trained as the leaders of the early Church. The implication in this passage is that Jesus chose the Twelve based on what the Father revealed in His prayer time. Most likely, this was not the only time Jesus spent the night in prayer. John 7:53 and 8:1–2 note that Jesus went to the Mount of Olives and spent the entire night there and came from there back into Jerusalem the next morning. The Mount of Olives was the location of the Garden of Gethsemane, where Jesus and His disciples often met together. It is likely that Jesus and His disciples often met here for times of prayer.

📖 What part did prayer play in His ministry in Matthew 14:13–21? Also read what Jesus did in John 6:11 (note also 6:23). Record what you find from these two eyewitnesses.

____

____

____

____

____

____

The crowds wanted to be where Jesus was. Many came to be cured of their sicknesses. Others wanted to hear His teaching or simply see and experience His power and His miracles. Evening came, and the disciples suggested that the crowds disperse and go to the nearest village to find food—but Jesus had another idea. He asked the disciples to provide food, and they responded pointing to a mere five loaves and two fish. Jesus asked them to bring those, and then He took them, looked up toward heaven, thanked the Father, blessed the food, and began breaking it and giving it to the disciples to distribute. Miraculously, they kept distributing food until all had enough to eat, more than enough for the crowd of *"about five thousand men"* plus many women and children. (Recall it was a lad or small boy there who had the five loaves and two fish.)

📖 We find another very instructive look into Jesus' life immediately after this incident of the feeding of the five thousand. What do you discover in Matthew 14:22–23? What happened then in Matthew 14:24–33?

____

____

____

____

____

____

Immediately after the miracle of the loaves and the fish, Jesus sent His disciples into a boat to go to the other side of the Sea of Galilee. The crowds went their way, and Jesus stayed behind and went up to a mountain to pray. When evening came, He was there on the mountain praying alone while His disciples were on the Sea struggling with the winds and the waves. Jesus stayed on the mountain for quite some time. He did not come walking on the water to where the disciples were until "the fourth watch" which was between 3:00 and 6:00 A.M. That means Jesus stayed on the mountain praying from around 6:00 P.M. to at least 3:00 A.M., a period of more than nine hours. After that, a series of miracles occurred. First, Christ walked on the water to where the disciples were struggling. Then He called Peter to come to him, and Peter walked on the water for a few moments. Then Jesus entered the boat, and the winds and waves stopped—and according to John 6:21, the boat was immediately at the shores of the land they were trying to reach. This was a night of prayer and miracles, revealing to the disciples that Jesus was indeed God's Son.

"I do nothing on My own initiative, but I speak these things as the Father taught Me. And He who sent Me is with Me; He has not left Me alone, for I always do the things that are pleasing to Him."

John 8:28–29

📖 What was Jesus' own testimony about how He knew what to do and what to say? Read John 8:25–29 and 12:49–50 and record your findings.

____

____

____

____

____

Jesus made it clear that His Father set His agenda. Jesus did nothing on His own initiative. What He did and what He said came out of His time with the Father—listening and learning and then carrying out what the Father gave Him to do in the power of the Spirit. Jesus continually practiced the presence of the Father, confident that the Father was with Him and that He Himself only desired to please His Father. We can do the same as we learn to pray God's way.

Jesus was a child of prayer, then a man of prayer, then a man of prayer in ministry. He was a man who walked in that closest of relationships with His Father. That life of prayer did not end with His ministry days. His last days on earth would prove to be His greatest days of prayer, revealing the greatest agony any man has ever endured in prayer as well as the greatest triumph anyone has ever experienced.

Prayer in Jesus' Last Days

The most significant days in the life of our Lord Jesus were the last days before His death on the cross. In those days we see the fervency and fire of His praying more than any other time in His life. We see His compassion and agony at their greatest intensity. We also see the wonder and the expectation of an awesome future and a glorious eternity. We can learn much as we walk through the events of Christ's final days on earth, so pay close attention as we examine the very heart of God.

📖 Look first at John 12:27–33. What was Jesus' condition and what was His concern, His request? Look for application points to praying God's way for your own life.

____

____

____

____

____

____

The events of these verses in John's Gospel take place shortly after Jesus raised Lazarus from the dead and made a triumphal entry into Jerusalem. Scores of visitors were in the city in conjunction with the approaching Feast of the Passover. Some of these visitors asked the disciples if they could see Jesus. As Phillip and Andrew approached Jesus on behalf of these visitors, Jesus exclaimed that He had become troubled in soul. The word *"troubled"* is a translation of *tarássō,* which means to be stirred or agitated. It was used of water boiling. As the Passover was swiftly approaching and the crowds were growing, Christ knew that His moment on the cross was also approaching, and all that Jesus knew about His mission caused Him to be troubled. Jesus could have prayed, *"Father, save me from this hour,"* but He did not. Instead, He prayed, *"Father, glorify Thy name,"* or "reveal the fullness of who You are." Jesus was praying in essence, "make people aware of who You really are, of Your will and Your ways so that they honor You." At that moment the Father spoke in a thundering voice from heaven, *"I have both glorified it, and will glorify it again."* Through the Crucifixion and the Resurrection, the Father would fulfill all He had promised and would reveal Himself through His Son in even greater ways. Jesus knew that His Father would take care of Him and that what He was about to do would be the deathblow to evil, to the devil, and to the problem of sin. As a result of Christ's work on the cross, many would be drawn to Christ and to the eternal life He alone can give. Because He was willing to do the Father's will, we can live—and He can now live in us. He lives to show us the Father's will, and when we know and do His will, we glorify Him.

"Troubled" is a translation of the Greek word *tarássō*, which means "to stir," or "to agitate," and can also mean "to boil" (water). It was used of Jesus being troubled in spirit over the weeping of many after Lazarus had died (John 11:33), of His being troubled in soul while facing the Crucifixion (John 12:27), and at the Last Supper as He contemplated the betrayal of Judas (John 13:21). *Tarássō*, was also used of the disciples being troubled in heart in John 14:1 and 14:27. Jesus overcame His troubled heart. He now gives us His peace to counter our own troubled hearts.

The applications to our praying are evident. While we do not face what Jesus faced, we do have times when we are agitated, disturbed, our circumstances and our souls boiling within. We may want to pray, "Father, remove this situation from me or remove me from it." Instead, we should pray, "Father, do what You desire, what will glorify Your name, what will reveal You more clearly."

Jesus promised His disciples that they would know a new day in their prayer lives as they learned to ask in His name.

In John 12:27–33, we see Jesus agonizing over His impending betrayal and public execution. Christ's vexation of spirit did not end on this day, however. In fact, He continued to carry that burden for the next several days. Then the day before the Crucifixion, after Jesus met with His disciples in the "Upper Room," we see again the expression of His heart, but it is not all agony. After washing the disciples feet, dismissing Judas into the darkness, and celebrating the first Lord's Supper with His own, Jesus began to tell them of the wonderful plans He had for them—some immediate and some eternal. At the same time, He spoke to them of the sorrow they would face. He promised them they would know a new day in their prayer lives as they learned to ask in His name. Then, walking with His disciples toward the Garden of Gethsemane, still near the Temple, He stopped and lifted His eyes to heaven and began to pray. We read His prayer in John 17:1–26.

📖 Read John 17 and complete all exercises pertaining to this chapter of the Bible.

What marks Jesus' prayer in John 17:1–5? What is at the heart of what He prayed in those opening verses?

____

____

____

____

____

____

In Jesus' prayer, He first focused on His relationship to His Father and expressed His longing that He would be glorified in all He did so that the Father would also be glorified. Jesus was always focused on His Father and doing His Father's will. He desired and prayed that all those the Father gave Him would know eternal life by knowing the Father and the Son, Jesus Christ. He also prayed that He would be glorified along with the Father with the glory He had even before the world existed, returning to that fullness of glory with His Father. Pleasing and glorifying His Father, as always, was at the heart of what JesWhat did Jesus pray for His disciples in John 17:6–19?

____

____

____

One of the major concerns over which Jesus prayed was their walk in the world after He left them. Jesus gave His disciples the Word the Father had given Him, and they received those words, knowing they were absolute truth and full of life. Jesus made it clear in John 7:63 that the words He spoke *"are spirit and life,"* and Peter declared, *"You have words of eternal life."* Jesus prayed that the Father would protect the disciples and make them one through their relationship to the Father (*"keep them in Thy name"*) and that they would be guarded from the world system and from the evil one (Satan). Jesus desired that His followers know His joy as they walked in truth on a daily basis experiencing the sanctifying, purifying work of the Word of God. Then, walking in that joyous relationship with the Father and the Son, He prayed that as they were sent into the world, they would be marked by the truth He spoke to them and by the oneness He desired for them.

Jesus not only prayed for those disciples present with Him that night, He also prayed for all those who would believe in Him through their word, through their testimonies, preaching, teaching, and writing. What did Jesus pray for and promise you and me, according to John 17:20–23?

____

____

____

____

What can all believers know with confidence according to John 17:24–26?

____

____

____

____

Jesus prayed that those who believe in Him based on the word of the first disciples would all be one. He desired for each one to know and experience the eternal life that He alone could give. That includes you and me and all who have believed the message of salvation through Jesus Christ alone. He promised to indwell believers, making them one with Himself and with one another, sharing that common life and love of the Son. Jesus then prayed that all His followers be with Him forever beholding His glory. He desired intensely that we experience the fullness of His glory as well as the fullness of His presence and His love forever.

After Jesus prayed what some have called His "High Priestly Prayer" in John 17, Jesus crossed over the Kidron Valley and entered into the Garden of Gethsemane on the west side of the Mount of Olives. Here we view His agony as never before seen.

Read Matthew 26:36–38. What do you discover about Jesus in these verses?

____

____

____

Jesus came to Gethsemane to pray. Here, He truly faced the struggles of being a man. This was no insignificant exercise on the way to the cross. This was a battle— a grieving, distressing, agonizing battle—a battle that brought Him to the edge of death even there in the Garden. Jesus wanted His disciples there with Him to keep watch and to pray with Him. What a picture of His humility and His anguish.

Put Yourself in Their Shoes

"NOT MY WILL, BUT YOURS, BE DONE

That has been the place to which God has brought many of His children. Abraham suggested to God that Eliezer or Ishmael could be counted as his heir, but God's will was for Abraham and Sarah to have a son named Isaac (Genesis 15:2–4; 17:15–21). Jacob wrestled with the Angel of the Lord until all Jacob could do was hold on and receive God's will and blessing for his life—which included a limp in his walk from that day forward. (See Genesis 32:24–32.) Paul prayed three times for a thorn in the flesh to be removed, but God's will was for the thorn to remain and for Paul to discover the strength of God for his every weakness (2 Corinthians 12:7–10). God always wants us to pray the prayer His Son prayed, *"nevertheless not my will, but Yours, be done"* (Luke 22:42 NKJV).

📖 What was His first cry in the Garden according to Mark 14:35–36?

Jesus cried out to His Father, *"Abba! Father!"* the heart cry of a child in need. Jesus knew the Father could do anything, and, if possible, the Father could remove this cup of suffering. He knew He would face an agonizing separation from His Father as He paid for the sins of the world. Jesus, as always, revealed His strongest desire to only please the Father, *"not what I will, but what Thou wilt."*

📖 According to Matthew 26:40–46, what occurred after Jesus first prayed? What do you see about Jesus' prayer life?

After spending the first period of time in prayer, Jesus came back to where His disciples were and found them asleep. He urged them to watch with Him and to pray so that they would not enter into temptation. He went away and prayed as He did at first, again ending with, *"Thy will by done."* When He found His disciples asleep a second time, He went back and prayed a third time in the same way. He returned to find them sleeping once again, but He was ready to face His betrayer (Judas Iscariot) and the ordeal that lay before Him.

📖 Even though Jesus was betrayed, arrested, and underwent the gruesome pains of crucifixion, His praying did not stop. What do you discover in Luke 23:33–34?

On the cross, Jesus looked down on those who had nailed him there, those who were gambling for His garments. Then, He prayed for them, *"Father, forgive them; for they do not know what they are doing."* Christ's compassion for mankind never ceased.

📖 What do you find in Matthew 27:45–50 and Luke 23:46

PRAYER OF SURRENDER

Someone has expressed the prayer of surrender to God's will this way, "Father, Your will—nothing more, nothing less, nothing else." That attitude was the heart of Jesus, and should be the heartfelt attitude of His followers.

Did You Know?

ANSWERED PRAYER ON THE CROSS

While Jesus hung on the cross, He not only prayed for others, He also answered prayer. One of the thieves acknowledged Jesus as the King and asked Him to remember him when He arrived in His kingdom. Jesus replied, *"Truly, I say to you, today you shall be with Me in Paradise"* (Luke 23:39–43).

After six hours on the cross, enduring the pain and the supernatural darkness that had been present from noon to three in the afternoon, Jesus cried out *"My God, My God, why have You forsaken Me?"* That was His agonizing cry of the separation He experienced bearing our sin, but it was also a cry that was looking to His Father to deliver Him. That is why He could pray with confidence, *"Father, into Thy hand I commit My spirit,"* knowing the Father had promised to resurrect Him. While on the cross He told John to take care of His mother, Mary, and He told the thief beside Him, *"this day you will be with Me in Paradise."* Perhaps these things along with all the events that accompanied the crucifixion that day caused one of the Roman leaders, a centurion in command of one hundred soldiers, to praise God declaring, *"Truly this was the Son of God"* and *"certainly this was a righteous Man"* (Matthew 27:54 and Luke 23:47 NKJV).

That Righteous Man truly was and is the Son of God who triumphed over sin and death. He lives today to live in us, to lead us in a walk with Himself and the Father by the power and presence of His Spirit. He wants us to experience the joy of that walk as He leads us in **praying God's way** and has assured us that we can experience joy by His power and work.

Did You Know?

RESURRECTION PROMISES

Though some are veiled, some psalms and several prophecies speak of the resurrection and reign of the Messiah. In I Peter 1:10–12, we read how the prophets who *"predicted the sufferings of Christ and the glories to follow"* themselves *"made careful search and inquiry"* about these matters. Two are found in Psalm 22 and Isaiah 50. After speaking of many of the sufferings of the Messiah, Psalm 22:21c declares, *"You have answered Me,"* and Isaiah 50:9 adds, *"Surely the Lord God will help Me"* (NKJV). Jesus knew these truths and was confident His Father would raise Him from the dead.

For Me to Pray God's Way

Jesus Prayed

DAY FIVE

We have seen much about the prayer life of Jesus. Most remarkably, we have seen one who is the God-Man, the perfect Son of God, sinless, guileless, holy in every way, yet humbly and prayerfully dependent on His Father for every step of His earthly walk. He spent time in prayer as no one else has. He cried out to His Father as no one else has. He understands human need and divine provision as no one else has and today continues to intercede for us as no one else can. There is much we can learn from Him.

First, consider this truth—If Jesus spent time in prayer, then certainly we need to spend time in prayer and not make excuses for neglecting to pray. Below is an interesting article that I believe will prove to be helpful to you. Read this article and consider its meaning.

> Ours is a harder task than that which our fathers faced. Their conveniences and appliances were fewer, but they were not caught and often submerged in the rush of affairs as we are. We have many labor-saving and time-saving devices, but somehow we find it difficult to save time enough . . . for private meditation and prayer. . . . While we make our homes more beautiful externally than our fathers' with their limited means were ever able to do, can we make them also the abode of virtue, honor and love. . . ?

Does that sound like your life, your schedule, or your dilemma? Note this astounding fact: the paragraph quoted above appeared in a weekly Christian paper, the *Christian Observer* in the March 22, **1905** edition (page 7) as a reprint from another paper, the *Congregationalist*. Read it again. Have times changed? Perhaps. Have people changed? No! We make time **for what we think** is important.

If there is anything Jesus' lifestyle should teach us, it is that we were never meant to "go it alone"—He prayed to His Father all life long. He even urged His disciples to join Him in prayer at His hour of greatest need. We cannot nor should we even try to live the Christian life on our own power. We were made to be dependent. We came equipped with needs, needs that only our Father can meet and He has chosen humble, dependent, God-exalting prayer as one of the primary ways to meet those needs.

If Jesus spent time in prayer, then certainly we need to spend time in prayer and not make excuses for neglecting to pray.

We have seen . . .

➢. . . We must **take time** to pray. Jesus did. **When** do you pray?

____

When we consider our daily schedues or our future schedules, our needs now or upcoming, the needs of others, or how God wants to use us in His kingdom purposes, we must **make time to pray.** We need to pray over each of these areas. Are you spending some measure of time praying over these things? If not, why not start? If you don't have a set time or place, make one, and follow a pattern. (You may want to look back at Lesson 2, Day Five.)

➢. . .When we face **major decisions**, we must devote **major time** to prayer. Jesus did. Are you facing any major decisions in your life? How will you focus prayer on that decision?

____

____

Word Study
INTERCESSION

The Greek word, *Entugchano,* which is found in Romans 8:27, 34 and Hebrews 7:25, means, "to make intercession." Its fuller meaning is "to fall in with a person or to turn to or meet with a person, to come with free access on behalf of another" or even "to interrupt someone in speaking for the purpose of making a request for another." It means to make intercession for someone or to entreat on behalf of another. Romans 8:27 refers to the intercession of the Spirit on behalf of all the saints (all the followers of Christ). Romans 8:34 encourages us with the fact that Jesus Himself intercedes for us at the right hand of God the Father. Hebrews 7:25 speaks of Christ as our High Priest, forever making intercession for us.

➢. . .When we remember that Jesus lives in us by His Spirit to orchestrate our lives and our praying, we can be encouraged to know He will guide us in prayer **if** we will surrender daily, even moment-by-moment control to Him. Are you walking in the fullness and power of the Holy Spirit? Jesus did. Consider these truths: To experience the fullness of God's Spirit . . .

- ☑ Confess any and all sin to God. (Of course, Jesus was sinless and did not have to do this.) Confession is agreeing with God about sin; in other words, don't argue about it (1 John 1:9). Agreeing about the sin also means turning from it—repenting, not holding on to any part of it. When you agree with Him, you are walking in the fear of the Lord.
- ☑ Present yourself to God to be filled and controlled by His Spirit (Romans 12:1–2). This means a heart and life yielded to Him. To surrender means to withhold nothing from Him.
- ☑ Ask Him in faith to fill you with His Spirit. He commanded us to be filled (controlled) in Ephesians 5:18, and so we know that is His will (1 John 5:14). He is not reluctant. Don't depend on feelings; depend on Him and His Word by faith. Expect Him to fill you as you obey His Word. Then walk in obedience to what He says.

Now let's think of how the Father wants us praying today. He wants us to come with confidence, with boldness, with humility, with an open heart to all He wants for us. We need to understand how openhearted He is and how open the way is to His throne.

There are three passages that can help us understand our open access to the Father. These scriptures speak volumes of the triumph of Jesus' work on the cross and through His resurrection, and they speak of the ongoing work of the Father, the Son, and the Spirit on our behalf. Look at each of these and note the ongoing work of Jesus in particular. Summarize what you find.

Romans 8:31–34 (also note 35–39)

____

____

____

____

Hebrews 7:24–25

____

____

____

____

1 John 2:1–2

____

____

____

____

We can be confident of our relationship with the Father because He is *"for us"* (Romans 8:31–34). He sent His Son to die for us, to give us His eternal life and multiplied blessings. We stand justified, not condemned. Jesus is at the right hand of God, a position of authority, power, and blessing. From that position, He intercedes for us. There He remains forever as our High Priest, not only opening the way to the Father, but keeping it open because of His sacrifice on the Cross then and because of His resurrection life now. His resurrection forever validates the adequacy of His life and death to bring us to the Father. He is now enthroned and *"always lives to make intercession for* [us]*"* (Hebrews 7:25). Jesus Christ is our advocate, defending us as if He were a benevolent trial lawyer determined to protect us against any accusations or charges. He, the Righteous One, is on our side, declaring our sins covered and paid for by His death and His blood. Such complete redemption is for anyone who comes to God the Father, trusting Him for salvation through the shed blood of His Son, Jesus Christ.

Jesus reigns as our loving Lord. He intercedes for us as our sympathetic High Priest. He defends us as our Righteous Advocate. He is for us! Therefore, the door is always open for praying God's way!

APPLY How should these truths affect your prayer life?

____

____

____

____

____

Jesus reigns as our loving Lord (Romans 8:39)—there is none Higher. He intercedes as our sympathetic High Priest (Hebrews 4:14–16; 7:24–25)—there is none more caring. He defends us as our righteous advocate (1 John 2:1–2)— there is none more righteous. We can come to the Father with confidence knowing we have open access made possible by the highest authority, encouraged by the most loving and caring High Priest, and guaranteed by the holiest judge. We do not have to make an appointment, wait for an appointment, nor fear having an appointment cancelled. We simply come and call on Him—humbly, open-hearted, dependent, surrendered, telling Him all that is on our hearts and minds, looking to Him to answer in His time, to accomplish His will His way. What a privilege we have! What a responsibility we have! What a joy we can have! Remember, He lives to lead us in **praying God's way**, so let's do that.

Jesus is for us and has opened the door for praying God's way

Take some time to talk to your Father about what is on your heart, perhaps some issues concerning your walk or your wants or His will in your life. You may want to read and meditate on a passage of Scripture to help you focus your heart in prayer.

Father, I thank You for sending Your Son, the Lord Jesus. Thank You that He always prayed Your will, and that He prayed for me! . . . that He is still interceding for me! Forgive me for my self-sufficient attitudes and actions. Thank You for providing forgiveness, cleansing, and an open door to the Father. Thank You for Your Word that guides me, teaches me, and focuses me in prayer. I praise You and thank You for being a loving Father and a compassionate Lord. Thank You for the way You give wisdom as I pray over my needs, as I face various trials, and as I pray for the needs and trials of others. I praise You that You are the Mighty and Victorious Warrior, able to win the battles I face. Thank You for placing me in Your Family, Your body of believers, and for teaching me about praying together with other believers. I praise You for praying for me, for continually interceding for me. I could never make it without You, but because of You, I am guaranteed to make it. Thank You! I pray with the Scriptures, *"Thanks be to God for His indescribable gift! . . . Thanks be to God, who gives us the victory through our Lord Jesus Christ. . .* [I give thanks to You, Father, that You] *qualified us to share in the inheritance of the saints in light. . . . Now to the King eternal, immortal, invisible, the only God, be honor and glory forever and ever. Amen."* (2 Corinthians 9:15, 1 Corinthians 15:57; Colossians 1:12; 1 Timothy 1:17)

We have journeyed through twelve lessons seeking to know what it means to live a life **praying God's way**. Think back over what God has shown you, how the Spirit has challenged you and changed you. Then, write your own prayer or make a journal entry in the space below.

____

____

____

____

____

____

____

____

The Prayer Life of Jesus

DATE	EVENTS	SCRIPTURE
Prophecy	The Father declared to His Son, *"Ask of Me, and I will surely give the nations as Thine inheritance."*	Psalm 2:8
Prophecy	Isaiah prophesied about the morning meeting between Jesus the Messiah and His Father. *"He awakens Me morning by morning."*	Isaiah 50:4
A.D. 7 ? Age 12	At the Temple, Jesus asked Mary and Joseph, *"Did you not know that I had to be in My Father's house,"* literally *"in the things of My Father,"* an indication Jesus had spent time in Scripture and in prayer with His Father.	Luke 2:49
A.D. 7–26? Age 12-30 In Nazareth	Jesus *"kept increasing in wisdom and stature, and in favor with God and men."* His relationship with His Father continued to grow as He grew in age and stature, indicating a continual prayer life.	Luke 2:51–52
All His life, to age 33	When Jesus came into the world, the prayer of His heart was to do the will of His Father, even to be the sacrifice offered once for all.	Hebrews 10:5–9; Psalm 40:6–8
A.D. 26 Age 30	When John the Baptist was baptizing Jesus at the Jordan River, Jesus was praying. *"While He was praying heaven was opened and the Holy Spirit descended upon Him in bodily form like a dove."*	Luke 3:21–22
A.D. 26	The Spirit led Jesus into the wilderness for a time (40 days) of fasting (and prayer) during which He was tempted by the devil.	Matt. 4:1–11; Mark 1:12–13; Lk. 4:1–13
Early A.D. 28 Age 31	*"In the early morning, while it was still dark"* Jesus *"arose and went out and departed to a lonely place, and was praying there"* (Near Capernaum). This matches the prophecy of Isaiah 50:4 about the Father speaking to the Son *"morning by morning."*	Mark 1:35
A.D. 26-30 Age 30-33	Luke records a summary statement on the lifestyle of Jesus during His ministry years: *"He Himself would often slip away to the wilderness and pray."*	Luke 5:16
A.D. 27-30	Jesus often came to the Mount of Olives with His disciples *"as was His custom"* to a certain place, most likely the Garden of Gethsemane, to meet with His disciples and pray.	Luke 22:39–40; John 18:1–2
Summer A.D. 28 Age 31	Jesus spent the entire night in prayer after which He chose the twelve apostles.	Luke 6:12, 13–16
Spring A.D. 29 Age 32	When Jesus received the five loaves and two fish, He looked up toward heaven, and *"blessed the food"* (14:19). John 6:11 adds, *"and having given thanks,"* Jesus began giving the food to the disciples. The disciples then distributed it to more than five thousand people (near Bethsaida).	Matthew 14:13–21; Mark 6:32–44; Luke 9:10–17; John 6:1–13
Spring A.D. 29	After feeding five thousand men (plus family members), Jesus sent His disciples across the Sea of Galilee. *"He went up to the mountain by Himself to pray; and when it was evening, He was there alone."*	Matthew 14:23; Mark 6:45–46; (John 6:14–15)
Spring, A.D. 29	In the area of Decapolis, Jesus, again revealing His compassion for the multitudes, fed over four thousand people. He took seven loaves and some fish and gave thanks and blessed them, He began giving the food to the disciples to distribute. All had enough.	Matthew 15:32–39; Mark 8:1–10
Summer A.D. 29	Near Caesarea Philippi, Jesus was praying alone—with His disciples nearby. He then stopped and asked ask them, *"Who do the multitudes say that I am?"* This was just before Peter's confession of Jesus as the Christ, the Son of the Living God.	Luke 9:18–20 (Matthew 16:13–17)
Summer A.D. 29	Jesus took Peter, James, and John *"and went up to the mountain to pray"* (Luke 9:28). This mountain was likely Mount Hermon. It was the occasion for the Transfiguration of Jesus before the eyes of those three.	Matthew 17:1; Mark 9:2; Luke 9:28
Summer A.D. 29	While Jesus was praying on the mountain, He was transfigured, and Elijah and Moses talked with Him. Then, in a cloud, the Father overshadowed Jesus and the three disciples and spoke, *"This is My Son, My Chosen One; listen to Him"* (Luke 9:35).	Matthew 17:1–8; Mark 9:2–8; Luke 9:29–36 2 Peter 1:16–17
Autumn A.D. 29	After the final day of the Feast of Tabernacles, Jesus went to the Mount of Olives (as He often did—[see Luke 22:39; John 18:1–2]) and apparently spent the night there, perhaps in prayer.	John 7:53; 8:1-2 (Luke 22:39–40) (John 18:1–2)

DATE	EVENTS	SCRIPTURE
Autumn A.D. 29	Jesus testified of time in prayer with the Father. *"The things . . . I heard from Him . . . I speak."* *"I speak . . . as the Father taught Me."*	John 5:19–20; 8:25–29; 12:49–50
Autumn A.D. 29	After the return of the Seventy from their mission, Jesus began to praise the Father for His work and His ways.	Luke 10:21–22; Matthew 11:25–27
Autumn A.D. 29	Once while Jesus was praying, *"after He had finished, one of His disciples"* requested, *"Lord, teach us to pray just as John also taught his disciples."*	Luke 11:1
Early A.D. 30	After Lazarus' death, Martha affirmed Jesus' life of prayer—*"whatever You ask of God, God will give You."*	John 11:22
Spring A.D. 30 Age 33	Some brought their children to Jesus *"so that He might lay His hands on them and pray; and the disciples rebuked them."* Jesus opened the way for the children and laid His hands on them.	Matthew 19:13–15
Days before Crucifixion	Jesus was troubled in soul and could have prayed, "Father, save Me from this hour." Instead He prayed, *"Father, glorify Thy name."*	John 12:27–33
Night before Crucifixion	Jesus assured Simon Peter that He had prayed for him that his faith would not fail when Satan tempted him and the other disciples. He encouraged him to strengthen his brothers.	Luke 22:31–32
Night before Crucifixion	Jesus promised His disciples He would *"ask the Father,"* and the Father would give them *"another Helper,"* the Holy Spirit.	John 14:16–17
Night before Crucifixion	Near the Temple and before going over the Brook Kidron and into Gethsemane, Jesus prayed His High Priestly Prayer to His Father	John 17:1–26; 18:1
Night before Crucifixion	Jesus went with His disciples to the Garden of Gethsemane to pray. He then took Peter, James, and John with Him closer to His place of prayer. Jesus said *"My soul is deeply grieved, to the point of death; remain here and keep watch with Me"* (Matthew 26:38).	Matthew 26:36–38; Mark 14:32–34
Night before Crucifixion	Jesus prayed the first time, *"Abba! Father! All things are possible for Thee; remove this cup from Me; yet not what I will, but what Thou wilt"* (Mark 14:36). An angel appeared and strengthened Him. He continued praying in great agony, and *"His sweat became like drops of blood"* (Luke 22:44).	Matthew 26:39; Mark 14:35–36; Luke 22:41–44
Night before Crucifixion	Jesus came to His disciples and found them sleeping. He called them to watch and pray with Him. Then He prayed a second time, *"My Father . . . Thy will be done"* (Matthew 26:42).	Matthew 26:40-42; Mark 14:37-39; Luke 22:45-46
Night before Crucifixion	Jesus came to His disciples and found them sleeping a second time. He prayed a third time to His Father.	Matthew 26:43–44; Mark 14:40
Night before Crucifixion	Jesus came to His disciples and found them sleeping a third time. Judas then came and betrayed Jesus into the hands of the soldiers.	Matthew 26:45–46; Mark 14:41–42
Night before Crucifixion	Jesus *"offered up both prayers and supplications"* to His Father asking to be saved *"out of death"*—to be resurrected—and He was *"heard because of His piety"* or *"godly fear"* (NKJV).	Hebrews 5:7
Night before Crucifixion	Jesus made it clear that, if He chose, He could pray to His Father and the Father would send more than twelve legions of angels (72,000 angels) to deliver Him from the soldiers.	Matthew 26:53
Day of Crucifixion	Jesus prayed from the cross, *"Father, forgive them; for they do not know what they are doing."*	Luke 23:34
Day of Crucifixion	Jesus prayed from the cross, *"MY GOD, MY GOD, WHY HAST THOU FORSAKEN ME?"*	Matthew 27:46; Mark 15:33-36
Day of Crucifixion	After declaring, *"I am thirsty,"* and *"It is finished"* (John 19:28–30), Jesus prayed from the cross, *"Father, INTO THY HANDS I COMMIT MY SPIRIT."* Then Jesus *"breathed His last."*	Luke 23:46
Yesterday, Today, and Forever	Our resurrected Lord Jesus intercedes for us at the right hand of God. Jesus Christ the Righteous One is our advocate with the Father.	Romans 8:34; 1 John 2:1
Yesterday, Today, and Forever	Jesus, our High Priest, *"is able to save forever those who draw near to God through Him, since He always lives to make intercession for them"* (Hebrews 7:25).	Hebrews 7:25; 9:24

Notes

Notes

How to Follow God

Starting the Journey

Did you know that you have been on God's heart and mind for a long, long time? Even before time existed you were on His mind. He has always wanted you to know Him in a personal, purposeful relationship. He has a purpose for your life and it is founded upon His great love for you. You can be assured it is a good purpose and it lasts forever. Our time on this earth is only the beginning. God has a grand design that goes back into eternity past and reaches into eternity future. What is that design?

The Scriptures are clear about God's design for man—God created man to live and walk in oneness with Himself. Oneness with God means being in a relationship that is totally unselfish, totally satisfying, totally secure, righteous and pure in every way. That's what we were created for. If we walked in that kind of relationship with God we would glorify Him and bring pleasure to Him. Life would be right! Man was meant to live that way—pleasing to God and glorifying Him (giving a true estimate of who God is). Adam sinned and shattered his oneness with God. Ever since, man has come short of the glory of God: man does not and cannot please God or give a true estimate of God. Life is not right until a person is right with God. That is very clear as we look at the many people who walked across the pages of Scripture, both Old and New Testaments.

Jesus Christ came as the solution for this dilemma. Jesus Christ is the glory of God—the true estimate of who God is in every way. He pleased His Father in everything He did and said, and He came to restore oneness with God. He came to give man His power and grace to walk in oneness with God, to follow Him day by day enjoying the relationship for which he was created. In the process, man could begin to present a true picture of Who God is and experience knowing Him personally. You may be asking, "How do these facts impact my life today? How does this become real to me now? How can I begin the journey of following God in this way?" To come to know God personally means you must choose to receive Jesus Christ as your personal Savior and Lord.

- First of all, you must admit that you have sinned, that you are not walking in oneness with God, not pleasing Him or glorifying Him in your life (Romans 3:23; 6:23; 8:5-8).
- It means repenting of that sin—changing your mind, turning to God and turning away from sin—and by faith receiving His forgiveness based on His death on the Cross for you (Romans 3:21-26; 1 Peter 3:18).
- It means opening your life to receive Him as your living, resurrected Lord and Savior (John 1:12). He has promised to come and indwell you by His Spirit and live in you as the Savior and Master of your life (John 14:16-21; Romans 14:7-9).
- He wants to live His life through you—conforming you to His image, bearing His fruit through you and giving you power to reign in life (John 15:1,4-8; Romans 5:17; 7:4; 8:29, 37).

You can come to Him now. In your own words, simply tell Him you want to know Him personally and you willingly repent of your sin and receive His forgiveness and His life. Tell Him you want to follow Him forever (Romans 10:9-10, 13). Welcome to the Family of God and to the greatest journey of all!!!

Walking on the Journey

How do we follow Him day by day? Remember, Christ has given those who believe in Him everything pertaining to life and godliness, so that we no longer have to be slaves to our "flesh" and its corruption (2 Peter 1:3-4). Day by day He wants to empower us to live a life of love and joy, pleasing to Him and rewarding to us. That's why Ephesians 5:18 tells us to "*be filled with the Spirit*"—keep on being controlled by the Spirit who lives in you. He knows exactly what we need each day and we can trust Him to lead us (Proverbs 3:5-6). So how can we cooperate with Him in this journey together?

To walk with Him *day by day* means ...

- reading and listening to His Word day by day (Luke 10:39, 42; Colossians 3:16; Psalm 19:7-14; 119:9).
- spending time talking to Him in prayer (Philippians 4:6-7).
- realizing that God is God and you are not, and the role that means He has in your life.

This allows Him to work through your life as you fellowship, worship, pray and learn with other believers (Acts 2:42), and serve in the good works He has prepared for us to do—telling others who Jesus is and what His Word says, teaching and encouraging others, giving to help meet needs, helping others, etc. (Ephesians 2:10).

God's goal for each of us is that we be conformed to the image of His Son, Jesus Christ (Romans 8:29). But none of us will reach that goal of perfection until we are with Him in Heaven, for then "we shall be like Him, because we shall see Him just as He is" (1 John 3:2). For now, He wants us to follow

Him faithfully, learning more each day. Every turn in the road, every trial and every blessing, is designed to bring us to a new depth of surrender to the Lord and His ways. He not only wants us to do His will, He desires that we surrender to His will His way. That takes trust—trust in His character, His plan and His goals (Proverbs 3:5-6).

As you continue this journey, and perhaps you've been following Him for a while, you must continue to listen carefully and follow closely. We never graduate from that. That sensitivity to God takes moment by moment surrender, dying to the impulses of our flesh to go our own way, saying no to the temptations of Satan to doubt God and His Word, and refusing the lures of the world to be unfaithful to the Lord who gave His life for us.

God desires that each of us come to maturity as sons and daughters: to that point where we are fully satisfied in Him and His ways, fully secure in His sovereign love, and walking in the full measure of His purity and holiness. If we are to clearly present the image of Christ for all to see, it will take daily surrender and daily seeking to follow Him wherever He leads, however He gets there (Luke 9:23-25). It's a faithful walk of trust through time into eternity. And it is worth everything. Trust Him. Listen carefully. Follow closely.

The *Following God* Bible Character Study Series

Life Principles from the Old Testament

Characters include: Adam, Noah, Job, Abraham, Lot, Jacob, Joseph, Moses, Caleb, Joshua, Gideon, and Samson
ISBN 0-89957-300-2   208 pages

Life Principles from the Kings of the Old Testament

Characters include: Saul, David, Solomon, Jereboam I, Asa, Ahab, Jehoshaphat, Hezekiah, Josiah, Zerubbabel & Ezra, Nehemiah, and "The True King in Israel."
ISBN 0-89957-301-0   256 pages

Life Principles from the Prophets of the Old Testament

Characters include: Samuel, Elijah, Elisha, Jonah, Hosea, Isaiah, Micah, Jeremiah, Habakkuk, Daniel, Haggai, and "Christ the Prophet."
ISBN 0-89957-303-7   224 pages

Leader's Guides for Following God™ books are available.
To order now, call (800) 266-4977 or (423) 894-6060.
Or order online at www.amgpublishers.com

The *Following God* Bible Character Study Series

***Life Principles from the Women of the Bible* (Book One)**

Characters include: Eve, Sarah, Miriam, Rahab, Deborah, Ruth, Hannah, Esther, The Virtuous Woman, Mary & Martha, Mary, the Mother of Jesus, and "The Bride of Christ."
ISBN 0-89957-302-9 224 pages

***Life Principles from the Women of the Bible* (Book Two)**

Characters include: Hagar, Lot's Wife, Rebekah, Leah, Rachel, Abigail, Bathsheba, Jezebel, Elizabeth, The Woman at the Well, Women of the Gospels, and "The Submissive Wife."
ISBN 0-89957-308-8 224 pages

Life Principles from the New Testament Men of Faith

Characters include: John the Baptist, Peter, John, Thomas, James, Barnabas, Paul, Paul's Companions, Timothy, and "The Son of Man."
ISBN 0-89957-304-5 208 pages

Call for more information (800) 266-4977 or (423) 894-6060.
Or order online at www.amgpublishers.com

Following God™ Discipleship Series

Living God's Will

ISBN 0-89957-309-6

How can I follow and identify the signs that lead to God's will? *Living God's Will* explores the answer to this all-important question in detail. It is Eddie Rasnake's deeply-held conviction that the road to God's will is well-marked with signposts to direct us. Each lesson in this twelve-week Bible study takes a look at a different signpost that reflects God's will. You will be challenged to recognize the signposts of God when you encounter them. But more importantly, you will be challenged to follow God's leading by following the direction of those signposts.

In the pages of this "Following God" study on finding and obeying God's will, you will find clear and practical advice for:

✓ Yielding your life to the Lord

✓ Recognizing God's will through Scripture, prayer and circumstances

✓ Seeking godly counsel

✓ Discovering how God's peace enters into the process of following His will

✓ Determining God's will in areas not specifically addressed in Scripture, such as choosing a wife/husband or career path.

Throughout your study you will also be enriched by the many interactive application sections that literally thousands have come to appreciate from the acclaimed **Following God** series.

To order, call (800) 266-4977 or (423) 894-6060
www.amgpublishers.com

Other Discipleship Series books now available.
Watch for new Following God™ titles to be released soon!